Energy and the
Rise and Fall
of Political Economy

Recent Titles in
Contributions in Economics and Economic History

The Pillage of Sustainability in Eritrea, 1600s–1990s: Rural
Communities and the Creeping Shadows of Hegemony
Niaz Murtaza

Opening the West: Federal Internal Improvements Before 1860
Laurence J. Malone

Oil and Coffee: Latin American Merchant Shipping from the Imperial Era to the 1950s
René De La Pedraja

The American Peasantry
Southern Agricultural Labor and Its Legacy, 1850–1995: A Study in Political Economy
Ronald E. Seavoy

Keynes: A Critical Life
David Felix

Treasure from the Painted Hills: A History of Calico, California, 1882–1907
Douglas Steeples

Ecology and the World-System
Walter L. Goldfrank, David Goodman, and Andrew Szasz, editors

Latin American Merchant Shipping in the Age of Global Competition
René De La Pedraja

Maritime Sector, Institutions, and Sea Power of Premodern China
Gang Deng

Charting Twentieth-Century Monetary Policy: Herbert Hoover and Benjamin Strong,
1917–1927
Silvano A. Wueschner

The Politics of Economic Restructuring and Democracy in Africa
Obioma M. Iheduru

Keynesian and Monetary Approaches to Managing Disequilibrium in Balance of Payments
Accounts
*Augustine C. Arize, Theologos Homer Bonitsis, Ioannis N. Kallianiotis, Krishna
Kasibhatla, and John Malindretos, editors*

Energy and the Rise and Fall of Political Economy

Bernard C. Beaudreau

Contributions in Economics and Economic History, Number 213

GREENWOOD PRESS
Westport, Connecticut • London

Library of Congress Cataloging-in-Publication Data

Beaudreau, Bernard C., 1955–
     Energy and the rise and fall of political economy / Bernard C.
Beaudreau.
         p.   cm.—(Contributions in economics and economic history,
     ISSN 0084–9235 ; no. 213)
     Includes bibliographical references and index.
     ISBN 0–313–31059–9 (alk. paper)
     1. Economic history.   2. Industrial revolution.   3. Industrial
productivity—History.   4. Technological innovations—Economic
aspects—History.   5. Power resources—Economic aspects—History.
6. Energy industries—History.   7. Manufacturing industries—Energy
consumption—History.   8. Human-machine systems—History.
I. Title.   II. Series.
HC54.B43   1999
333.79—dc21   99–25005

British Library Cataloguing in Publication Data is available.

Library of Congress Catalog Card Number: 99–25005
ISBN: 0–313–31059–9
ISSN: 0084–9235

First published in 1999

Greenwood Press, 88 Post Road West, Westport, CT 06881
An imprint of Greenwood Publishing Group, Inc.
www.greenwood.com

Printed in the United States of America

To the memory of Stuart Chase and Howard Scott

Contents

Tables and Figures   xi

Preface   xiii

Introduction   1

1 Analytical Framework   7

2 Steam Power and Political Economy   37

3 Electric Power and Early Twentieth-Century Political Economy   91

4 Boom and Bust: Energy-Deepening in the Post–World War II Period   133

5 Growth without Growth: The Post–Energy Crisis Period   157

Conclusions   177

Appendix 1: A Treatise on Energy and Price Theory   181

Appendix 2: A Treatise on Energy and Money   193

Bibliography   205

Index   215

Tables and Figures

TABLES

1.1 A Tool Taxonomy   12

1.2 NPA Energy Productivity Measures   19

1.3 NPA Organization Productivity Measures   20

1.4 Exchange Technologies   21

2.1 Total Coal Consumption, United Kingdom, 1755–1900   43

2.2 Total Power Consumption, Textiles, United Kingdom, 1835–1870   44

2.3 Coal and Cotton Consumption, Factory Workers, and Money Supply,
     United Kingdom, 1800–1860   51

2.4 Price Indexes, United Kingdom, 1805–1871   52

2.5 Output and Input Prices, Selected U.K. Textiles, 1815–1832   55

2.6 Wages Paid by a Very Respectable Manufacturer [William Cannon],
     1815–1832   56

2.7 Cost of Living Data, United Kingdom, 1815–1832   57

3.1 Installed Generating Capacity, United States, 1902–1970   95

3.2 The Ford Motor Company, Assembly Process Productivity   101

3.3 The Ford Motor Company, Production Data, 1903–1916   102

3.4 U.S. Manufacturing Data, 1912–1945   103

3.5 Wage and Productivity Data, U.S. Manufacturing, 1920–1929   104

3.6 Studies in the Economics of Overhead Costs—Table of Contents   120

4.1 KLEP Output Elasticities: U.S., German, and Japanese
     Manufacturing   137

4.2 Output and Input Growth Rates: U.S., German, and Japanese
     Manufacturing   138

4.3 Productivity Growth: U.S., German, and Japanese Manufacturing   140

4.4 NPA Output and Input Growth Rates: U.S., German, and Japanese
     Manufacturing   141

4.5 Value Added and Earnings per Production Worker,
     U.S. Manufacturing, 1947–1973   143

4.6 Consumer Credit, United States, 1901–1968   144

4.7 Gullickson and Harper's Estimates of Multifactor Productivity,
     1949–1983   151

5.1 Electric Power Consumption Growth Rates: U.S., German, and
     Japanese Manufacturing   160

5.2 Value Added and Production Workers, U.S. Manufacturing,
     1958–1993   165

FIGURES

2.1 Numbers Employed in the Cotton Industry, 1806–1862   42

3.1 Douglas' A+B Version of Underincome   122

5.1 U.S. Current-Cost Net Stock of Fixed Private Capital, 1959–1995   163

5.2 Stock Prices and Labor's Income Share, 1980–1993   167

Preface

Tout ce qui traîne se salit

—*French proverb*

Political economy as an intellectual endeavor is relatively recent, its history extending back to the early nineteenth century. It is generally held that its origins owe in large measure to a technological innovation, namely the introduction of complex machinery in the late eighteenth/early nineteenth century. Hand tools were replaced by power (machine) tools (Berg, 1980). In this book, it will be argued that while this is an accurate description of the origins of political economy, it is incomplete. Missing is the role of energy innovations, specifically, the steam engine in the nineteenth century and the electric motor in the twentieth century, in the birth of, and growth of political economy. With the advent of steam-powered machinery, inanimate, fossil-fuel-based energy replaced animate muscular energy as the source of power/work. Overall energy consumption increased dramatically as did output and conventionally defined labor productivity. This seemingly trivial substitution, I argue, is what underlies the increased interest by early nineteenth century moral philosophers in the issues of wealth creation.

It will be argued that by focusing on energy instead of machinery, important insights result. For example, there is the problem of growth, both output and conventionally defined productivity. It will be shown that energy in general, and energy consumption in particular are at the root of the first and second industrial revolutions. Rising labor productivity throughout the nineteenth and twentieth centuries, I show, is intimately tied to energy deepening. Another is the role of energy rents in the problem of income distribution. By substituting animate, muscular energy with inanimate fossil-fuel-based energy (i.e., fire power), the value of output increased by more than costs, resulting in what I refer to as energy rents. How would these rents be apportioned? Who would get what? Who could legitimately lay claim to these rents?

This book is the last in a series of works—three altogether—whose principal aim is to assign energy its rightful place in political economy (Beaudreau, 1996a, b, c, 1998). The current near-total absence of energy from production and distribution theory, as will be shown here, is autoregressive in time, having its roots in classical political economists' inability to disassociate steam power from machinery, which, technically speaking, amounts to being unable to distinguish power and tools. Radical (Marxian, utopian) and neoclassical political economists, like their classical forebearers, ignored energy, focusing instead on labor and capital. This oversight, as I shall attempt to show over the course of the next six chapters is largely responsible for the fall of political economy, by which it should be understood its failures in the areas of production, growth, distribution, pricing, and macroeconomics.

Unlike my previous work, which focused on the role of energy in a specific historical event namely the stock market crash of 1929 and the Great Depression, and on the theory of production and distribution, this work focuses on the development of thought in political economy from the mid-eighteenth century to the present. While this is a worthwhile and interesting endeavor in and of itself, the results, as I shall go on to argue, are relevant to the problems that plague the economics profession today. For example, I demonstrate that the failure of early classical political economists to distinguish between power and tools lies at the very root of the debate over the causes of the current productivity slowdown. As I have shown (Beaudreau, 1995a, b, c, 1998), by explicitly modeling energy as a factor input, the "productivity paradox" disappears. Further, their failure to see the distribution question as one involving the apportioning of energy rents lies at the root of the present distribution problem.

Introduction

Without energy, there would be nothing. There would be no sun, no wind, no
rivers, and no life at all. Energy is everywhere, and energy changing from one
form to another is behind everything that happens. Energy, defined as the
ability to make things happen, cannot be created. Nor can it be destroyed.
Plants and animals harness energy from nature to thelp them grow and
survive. The most intelligent of animals, human beings, have developed many
ways of using the available energy to improve their lives. Ancient people used
energy from fire, and they developed tools to use energy from their muscles
more effectively. But ancient people did not understand the role of energy in
their lives. Such an understanding of energy has really developed only over
the past few hundred years.

—Jack Challoner, *Energy*

It is generally held that the study of political economy owes, in large measure,
to the industrial revolution in general, and to the development of machinery in
particular. According to Maxine Berg, machinery and industrialization were
central to the making of political economy.

The machine was not an impersonal achievement to those living through the Industrial
Revolution; it was an issue. The machinery question in early nineteeth-century Britain
was the question of the sources of technical progress and the impact of the introduction
of the new technology of the period on the total economy and society. The question
was central to everyday relations between master and workman, but it was also of major
theoretical and ideological interest. The very technology at the basis of economy and
society was a platform of challenge and struggle.

The machinery question was, furthermore, an issue which stimulated analysis in political economy during the key years of the formation of this new theoretical discipline. Political economists took up the theoretical debate on the introduction, diffusion, and social impact of the radically new techniques of production associated with the era. Recognising that the machine formed the basis for an unprecedented economic transformation, political economists created new concepts and made growth potential and technological advances of the British economy the new focus of their analysis. (Berg, 1980, 8)

The corpus of nineteenth century classical and neoclassical theory, not to mention radical (utopian and socialist) political economy, can, as such, be attributed to the development and application of the steam engine. In short, machinery was, is, and judging from the current interest in innovation, will remain king, so to speak. The recent productivity slowdown in Western industrialized nations has rekindled interest in growth, and, consequently, machinery (R&D, innovation).

That this be the case, however, raises an important theoretical problem. According to classical mechanics, tools, by their very nature, are not productive. Tools simply transmit force or torque, which, according to classical mechanics, is the source of all work, and hence, output.

Machinery is used to change the magnitude, direction and point of application of required forces in order to make tasks easier. The output of useful work from any machine, however, can never exceed the total input of work and energy. (Betts, 1989, 172)

Work is an increasing function of force/energy. Thus, from a purely technical point of view, tools cannot account for the manifold increase in output that, as Berg points out, defines the industrial revolution. This only confirms what traditional historians (as opposed to economic historians) have maintained all along, namely that the industrial revolution was the result of a power innovation, not a tool innovation. "Fire power," as it was then referred to, was the defining change, not machinery.

This has important implications for political economy. Specifically, it implies that political economy was, in large measure, a response to an energy-based innovation, namely the development and introduction of the steam engine. Put differently, an energy shock in the form of steam power is what underlies the development of political economy.

Does this refinement warrant a reexamination of the origins of political economy? After all, in the nineteenthth century, energy-related innovations and capital (i.e., machinery) were highly collinear. The spread of the steam engine throughout U.K., European, U.S., and worldwide industry was accompanied by a concomitant increase in capital (i.e., machinery). Could one not simply redefine power as machinery and leave it at that? The answer, I argue, is no. The reasons are as follows. First, while the consumption of steam power/electrical power and capital were, in the early nineteenth century, highly collinear, they diverged substantially in the mid-to-late nineteenth century, and again in the twentieth century. The development of the high-pressure steam engine in the mid-to-late nineteenth century, and the shift from cumbersome belting, shafting and gearing to electric drive in the twentieth century increased energy consumption per unit of capital. Production processes were speeded up as a result. As shall be shown, this has important implications for productivity and its measurement. Second, there is the problem of distribution. Other than Adam Smith, most classical and neoclassical political economists agreed that the problem of income distribution ranked foremost among their concerns. If power is seen as synonymous with machinery, then productivity gains from power (i.e., energy) innovations will, erroneously, be attributed to the owners of capital. To do so would be misleading, not to mention theoretically incorrect. Third, there is the question of scientific accuracy. As I argued in Beaudreau (1998), labor and capital, the building blocks of classical, radical and neoclassical production theory, are organizational inputs, which, by their very nature, are not physically productive. Clearly, as a matter of historical fact, it is important to understand how political economists in the nineteenth and twentieth centuries saw these issues.

For these and many other reasons, it was felt that the time had come to disassociate power from machinery and, in the process, assign it to its rightful place in political economy and the history of political economy. Accordingly, this book sets out to reexamine the rise of political economy as an intellectual endeavor. It will be argued that the myriad issues raised by political economists over the past two centuries were, for the most part, energy related. Adam Smith's *An Inquiry into the Nature and Causes of the Wealth of Nations*, it will be argued, should be seen as (1) an ode to the virtues of "fire-power," as steam power was originally referred to, (2) an in-depth look at the myriad consequences of the shift from the domestic to the factory system, and (3) the first account of the inability of a private, competitive economy to make an immediate transition to higher growth paths in response to a technology shock, in this case, "fire power." Robert Owen's, David Ricardo's and Karl Marx's work on income distribution should be seen as a response to (1) the apparent failure of wages to increase commensurately with productivity, (2) the threat posed by higher corn prices, and consequently, higher wages to savings, investment, and growth, and (3) the deterioration of working conditions (real wages) in U.K. manufacturing.

That classical and neoclassical political economists chose not to see energy/force as a factor input, it is argued, had important, far-reaching consequences. First, they were unable to study—in a meaningful way—energy-based innovations. While this is of little or no consequence in periods of "stationary" levels of energy consumption (energy stasis), it is of great importance in periods of "radical" energy-based innovations such as the early twentieth century which saw electric power replace steam power, resulting in a marked increase in energy consumption per worker (machine operative).

Because electric drive was less capital-intensive than steam-power-based drive, this innovation went largely unnoticed. The shift to electric power marked the end of the highly collinear energy-capital relationship that had characterized the nineteenth century.

Throughout much of the twentieth century, productivity growth no longer tracked either labor or capital growth, resulting in the birth of growth accounting, the defining feature of which is the "residual," known commonly as the "Solow residual." In earlier work, I showed that when energy is properly integrated into production theory, the "Solow residual" disappears (Beaudreau, 1995a, b, c, 1998). The productivity slowdown, the bane of contemporary political economy, is attributed to the Organization of Petroleum Exporting Countries (OPEC)-induced energy crisis that arrested the rate of growth of energy consumption, and consequently, the rate of growth of work and output.

Paradoxically, while energy and energy-related innovations constitute the primary factor input in the first and second industrial revolutions, they are absent from contemporary political economy. Inanimate, fossil-fuel-based energy replaced animate, muscular energy as the source of power in industry throughout the nineteenth and twentieth centuries. Yet energy is nowhere to be found (Varian, 1992; Barro and Sala-i-Martin, 1995; Aghion and Howitt, 1998; Helpman, 1998). Analytically, output continues to be modeled as an increasing function of capital and labor. While moral philosophers were among the first to study the effects of energy innovations on production, trade and commerce, they failed to identify the leading cause of both the first and second industrial revolutions, namely, inanimate energy-related innovations. By contrast, physicists (natural philosophers) responded by developing a whole new field, namely thermodynamics. As I shall demonstrate in the following pages, this oversight has exacted an nonnegligible toll on political economy, and is, in large measure, responsible for the regrettable state in which production and distribution theory, and consequently, all of political economy currently finds itself.

I proceed as follows. As I have pointed out here, one of the—if not the—main shortcomings of classical, radical and neoclassical production theory was and is its failure to include energy as a value-adding factor input. Despite two energy-based industrial revolutions and an energy-crisis-provoked productivity slowdown, energy is conspicuous by its absence. To rectify this, I present an alternative approach to modeling production, developed in Beaudreau (1998), which is based, in large part, on basic physics (classical mechanics and thermodynamics). Chapter 1 presents the Newtonian model (energy–organization) of production activity, as well a discussion of exchange technologies, defined as the means whereby goods and services are traded. As I shall argue throughout the book, from the advent of the domestic system (putting-out system) in the middle ages to the development of the factory system (gathering-in system) in the early nineteenth century, the exchange technology has been intimately linked to corresponding production technology. To understand one is to understand the other. A bargaining theory of income distribution based on the notion of energy rents is also presented. Energy rents are defined as the difference between the value of energy productivity and its costs. As such, the owners of capital and labor bargain over the set of energy rents that result from energy deepening in one form or another. The resulting framework forms the basis of the in-depth reexamination of political economy found in the ensuing five chapters, each organized around a period (steam power, electric power, etcetera).

Each of these proceeds as follows: First, the model of production, exchange and distribution developed in Chapter 1 will be used to reexamine the issues of the day, so to speak. For example, the "nature and causes" of the wealth of nations in the late eighteenth century will be studied using Newtonian production analysis. Similarly, the problem of distribution that figures so prominently in William S. Jevons' work in the late nineteenth century will be studied using a bargaining theory of distribution. The results will then be used to better understand, and, indeed, critique the writings of contemporary political economists on, these very issues.

The results lead me to conclude that while energy in general and energy-related innovations in particular were instrumental in the rise of political economy, energy was and continues to be absent from economics. This oversight, I argue, is largely responsible for the unfortunate state economics finds itself in today.

1

Analytical Framework

The term process can in general be defined as a change in the properties of an object, including geometry, hardness, state, information content (form data), and so on. To produce any change in property, three essential agents must be available: (1) material, (2) energy, and (3) information.

—Leo Alting, *Manufacturing Engineering Processes*

INTRODUCTION

As pointed out in the Introduction, this book maintains that the study of political economy by moral philosophers was, in large measure, the result of an energy shock, namely the introduction of inanimate power sources in general and "fire power" in particular in late eighteenth/early nineteenth century manufacturing in Europe, specifically in Great Britain. The "domestic system," dominated by small-scale, artisanal production, gave way to the "factory system," literally and figuratively built around the new power source. Throughput rates increased as a result. Spinners and weavers were transformed into machine operatives (i.e., lower-level supervisors), overseeing the workings of high-throughput steam-powered machinery.

In order to understand how and why an energy shock led to the formal study of political economy by moral philosophers, one requires a model of economic activity in general, and production in particular, that explicitly incorporates energy (inanimate and animate) as a factor of production (value adding). Existing models, with few exceptions, are devoid of energy. As such, this chapter will be based on my work on the role of energy and organization in production processes (Beaudreau, 1998). Whereas conventional models of production focus almost exclusively on capital and labor, I focused on what I consider to be the two "universal" factor inputs, namely broadly defined energy and organization. Broadly defined energy includes both animate and inanimate forms of energy. By animate energy, it should be understood muscular (human and animal) power; by inanimate energy, it should be understood wind, fossil-fuel-based, hydraulic and nuclear power. All production processes, I argued, involve the consumption of energy of one type or another.[1] Organization was defined as the conception/design of, and the overseeing (i.e., supervision) of energy-consuming (i.e., entropic) production processes. The development of the steam engine by Papin, Savary, Newcommen and Watt in the seventeenth and eighteenth centuries is an example of the former, while its day-to-day operation is an example of the latter. In the natural world, the design of and supervision of energy-consuming processes is governed by forces which are not, at least yet, fully understood. Nonetheless, I shall refer to such processes as naturally occurring/spontaneous entropic processes. What differentiates these from man-made (i.e., anthropomorphic) entropic processes is the form of organization, broadly defined. From the Paleolithic era to the present, Homo sapiens—neanderthalensis and sapiens —have designed and redesigned man-made entropic processes (i.e. anthropic entropic processes). For example, the development of stone tools in the Paleolithic era altered the very nature of work. By reducing waste (i.e., increasing efficiency), primitive tools such as hammers and knives increased the amount of work that could be accomplished for a given quantity of muscular energy. In fact, the development and improvement of anthropomorphic entropic processes is what defines various prehistorical and historical eras (e.g., the stone age, the bronze age, the machine age).[2]

The resulting model of production has important implictions for distribution theory. Specifically, given that energy and energy alone is productive in the physical sense, existing theories of distribution in factory production (i.e., classical, Marxian, neoclassical) are misspecified. For example, the notion of marginal product of labor (and capital) is misspecified. In their place, I offer a bargaining model of distribution in which the owners of energy and organization bargain over the final product, in this case, value added, one in which only energy is physically productive. The notion of energy rents is introduced. Energy rents are, by definition, the difference between the value product of energy and its price (cost). The owners of the energy and organization inputs, it is argued, bargain over these rents.

Bridging the discussion of production and distribution is a discussion of exchange technologies. With the shift from the domestic system to the factory system in the eighteenth century came important changes to the relevant exchange technology. Specifically, producers (artisans and cottage industries) went from a nonmarket-based form of coordination to a market-based one, in which they transacted in factor markets (intermediate goods, labor and energy). In the putting-out system, all factor inputs were under one roof, so to speak; in the gathering-in system, there were not. Labor was hired; coal was purchased. The key change, however, was with the exchange technology. Now, producers, using bank credit, would purchase intermediate inputs, labor and energy in the market; and secondly, merchants, using bank credit, would purchase final goods and services. These changes, I argue, had important macroeconomic implications.

ORGANIZATION-AUGMENTED NEWTONIAN PRODUCTION PROCESSES

The Physical and Economic Definitions of Work

The cornerstone of the Newtonian approach to modeling production processes (Beaudreau, 1998) is Sir Issac Newton's second law of motion, namely $F = m\,a$, where F = force, m = mass, and a = acceleration. Put differently, $a = F/m$. That is, acceleration is simply force divided by mass. The corresponding definition of work is $W = f\,d$, where W = work, f = force, and d = distance: work equals force times distance. Thus, the greater is f, *ceteris paribus,* the greater is W. The greater is d, *ceteris paribus*, the greater is W. In short, the more force exerted and the longer the distance (or time period) over which the force in question is exerted, the more work performed. Redefining work as output permits us to write the basic axiom of Newtonian production analysis, namely that for any given, well-defined man-made entropic process, output is an increasing function of energy consumption.

Contrast this with the standard, time-invariant definition of work found in political economy, namely that work is an increasing function of capital and labor (i.e., $W = f(K,L)$). Capital and labor, it is argued, produce output (value added). Both are assumed to be productive. Just what it is that capital and labor do in production processes is unspecified. Terms such as capital productivity and labor productivity, however, connote the idea that both somehow work. Inanimate forms of energy such as oil, gas and electricity consumption are assumed to be intermediate inputs, and, hence, are not productive in the conventional sense. Put differently, they are not factors of production. In short, capital and labor are assumed to add value to energy and other raw materials. Broadly defined organization is also ignored. Production processes are assumed to exist. Management issues are, in general, ignored.

Clearly, the physical and economic definitions of work are worlds apart. For three centuries, physicists have focused on force and energy as the basis of work; economists, on the other hand, have focused on capital and labor. In physics, tools and machines (i.e., capital) modify and transmit force and energy, but are not, as such, sources of energy. In political economy, energy (inanimate energy forms) is viewed as an intermediate good, and, thus, is not productive in the traditional sense (value-adding).

A Physical Model of Production: The Newtonian Production Function

Here, I begin with an in-depth look at the purely physical aspect of production, namely the relationship between work and energy. To this end, I start by defining production as the following functional relationship between work (i.e., output) and the force (i.e., energy) expended in the process.

$$W(t) = F[E(t)]; \; F[E(t)] > 0 \qquad (1.1)$$

where: $W(t)$ = work in period t; and $E(t)$ = energy (i.e., force) in period t.

Animate and Inanimate Forms of Energy

In general, energy can be disaggregated into two categories, namely $E_a(t)$, animate (i.e., muscular) energy, and $E_i(t)$, inanimate energy [$E(t) = E_a(t) + E_i(t)$]. Examples of animate energy include human and animal force (i.e., muscular force), while examples of inanimate energy includes internal combustion, steam power, wind power, hydraulic power and electrical power.[3] Work will be modeled as an increasing function of animate and inanimate force/energy.

The Role of Tools/Machines

From the Paleolithic era (the Stone Age) on, work as defined above has invariably involved the use of tools/machines. These include axes, adzes, levers, presses, drills, screws, hammers, screwdrivers, saws, etcetera. This raises a number of questions. For example, what is the role of tools in broadly defined work? Are they a source of energy? Are they productive in the Newtonian sense? Similar questions were raised by Nobel prize laureate (Chemistry) Frederick Soddy in the 1920s. Who or what, he asked, was ultimately responsible for producing goods and services? As the following quote indicates, in Soddy's mind, there was no doubt: energy was the primary factor.

At the risk of being redundant, let me illustrate what I mean by the question "How do men live?" by asking what makes a railroad train go. In one sense or another, credit for the achievement may be claimed by the so-called "engine-driver," the guard, the signalman, the manager, the capitalist, the share-holder, or, again, by the scientific pioneers who discovered the nature of fire, by the inventors who harnessed it, by labour which built the railroad and the train. The fact remains that all of them by their collective effort could not drive the train. The real engine-driver is the coal. So, in the present state of science, the answer to the question how men live, or how anything lives, or how inanimate nature lives, in the sense in which we speak of the life of a waterfall or of any other manifestation of continued liveliness, is, with few and unimportant exceptions, "By sunshine." Switch off the sun and a world would result lifeless, not only in the sense of animate life, but also in respect of by far the greater part of the life of inanimate nature. (Soddy, 1924, 4)

In other words, because tools are not a source of energy, they are not productive in the Newtonian sense. That is, they do not "work." Nowhere is this better seen than in the physicist's definition of a "machine," which consists of an instrument used to transmit or modify applied force/energy.

Machinery is used to change the magnitude, direction and point of application of required forces in order to make tasks easier. The output of useful work from any machine, however, can never exceed the total input of work and energy. (Betts, 1989, 172)

Arthur Beiser, in *Modern Technical Physics*, provides a similar definition:

A machine is a device which transmits force or torque to accomplish a definite purpose. (Beiser, 1983, 208)

By using primitive hammers and knives, early man (i.e., Paleolithic and Neolithic man) was better able to direct and apply his force. Analytically speaking, however, while tools allowed him to minimize energy loss (i.e., wasted energy), they did not allow him to increase the total amount of work beyond the initial level of force. That is, they were not a source of additional energy.[4] Implicit here is the basic notion of thermodynamic efficiency, defined as *work out* relative to *work in*. By better transmitting muscular force, tools improved primitive man's thermodynamic efficiency. By expending the same amount of energy, more work could be done (e.g., skinning animals, cutting fire wood).

This raises the question of the relevant measure of tool/capital productivity. Specifically, how do we measure and define the productivity of tools/machines (i.e., capital)? The answer, I believe, is straightforward. Since tools/machines/capital are not a source of energy, they cannot be regarded as productive in the Newtonian sense (i.e., performing work/working). Rather, capital productivity must be measured in terms of its ability to transform force/energy into useful work, a concept known as second-law efficiency. As such, the notion of capital productivity is a qualitative one (i.e., a scalar), and not a quantative one. Increasing the amount of capital, *ceteris paribus*, will not increase output. However, increasing the quality of capital, for example by improving thermodynamic efficiency, will increase output. For example, James Watt's steam engine, by reducing the heat loss common to the Savary and Newcommen steam engines, increased the overall efficiency (i.e., exergy) of what at the time was known as "fire power." The fact, however, remains that it was not, is not, and will never be an energy source.

This allows us to rewrite Equation 1.1 as follows:

$$W(t) = \eta \, E(t) \tag{1.2}$$

where η is defined as second-law efficiency.[5]

Equation 1.2 defines the Newtonian approach to production processes. $W(t)$, output/work is an increasing function of $E(t)$, energy/force, and η, thermodynamic efficiency. Increasing η, thermodynamic efficiency, *ceteris paribus*, leads to higher output/work. Increasing energy, *ceteris paribus*, leads to higher work/output. η is assumed to be tool specific. Better, more efficient tools will have higher η's, and vice versa.

A Tool/Machine Taxonomy

According to classical mechanics, there are three basic tools/machines: the lever, the inclined plane and hydraulic press.[6] Each directs and applies force/energy. Table 1.1 lists the three basic tools/machines and some of their uses. We see, for example, that the lever is the basic tool/machine that transforms force in the case of a crane, a wheel barrow, and various pulleys. Last, there also exist what I choose to refer to as composite tools/machines, consisting of combinations of the three basic tools.

Table 1.1
A Tool Taxonomy

Basic Tool	*Composite Tool*
Lever	Scissor, Plier, Wheelbarrow
	Pulley
Hydraulic Press	Hydraulic Jack
Inclined Plane	Wedge, Jack, Screw

Source: Beaudreau (1998), 22.

A General Model of Production Processes: The Organization-Augmented Newtonian Production Function

The discussion of the role of tools in modern production processes brings us to the second universal factor input, namely, organization. Machines define the framework in which force/energy is transformed into work. In physics as in economics, it is implicitly assumed that (1) well-defined work processes exist (i.e., Equation 1.2) and (2) that they are self-regulating. That is, the setting in which force or energy is transformed into work is well-defined (i.e., exists), and secondly, is non-stochastic. Machine breakdown, broadly defined to include such things as feedstock breakdown, is ignored. In this section, I examine the broader question of organization. The discussion begins with a definition of what I shall refer to as anthropomorphic entropic processes. That is, man-made energy-using processes. This is then followed by two issues, namely (1) the design of and (2) the supervision of man-made (i.e., anthropomorphic) energy-consuming processes. Together with tools, these define broadly defined organization.

Natural and Anthropomorphic Entropic Processes

My treatment of organization begins with a discussion of entropic processes in general. Entropic processes are defined as environments in which energy is transferred from one system to another or others in the form of work. For the sake of discussion, I define two basic types of entropic processes: natural entropic processes that occur spontaneously in nature, and anthropomorphic entropic processes which, as their name implies, are conceived of and overseen by man (i.e., managed, supervised).[7] For example, solar radiation, the wind, the tides, river currents etcetera are examples of natural entropic processes based on solar energy. The production of food, tools, shelter and culture, however, are examples of anthropomorphic entropic processes. What distinguishes these is the nature of the relevant set of instructions. In the former case, it has evolved randomly (or so it appears) over the course of the last 15 billion years, while in the latter, it has evolved consciously over the course of the last 2,000 years. In the case of anthropomorphic entropic processes, Homo sapiens design and supervise (i.e., oversees) the work process. Take, for example, the simple wind mill, which converts the result of a temperature gradient (i.e., the wind) into work. The human body, however, is an example of a natural entropic process whose blueprint is the work of millions of years of evolution/mutation (i.e., the human genome), and whose supervision is auto-regulated.

Clearly, tools are the defining element in anthropomorphic entropic processes. They are to production processes what the human body is the process of life. They transmit and/or modify force/energy. Given the presence of friction, it follows that the better are the tools (i.e., the less friction), the higher the efficiency, and the greater the work.

The presence of energy and tools, however, is not a sufficent condition for work to occur, as both occur spontaneously in nature. Also required is an activity that I shall refer to as the "overseeing of" or "supervising of" entropic processes." For example, take the case of a simple gasoline engine-powered water pump. With an endless supply of refined hydrocarbons, it should work continuously *ad infinitum*. Suppose, however, that, for some reason, the pump arm spontaneously dislodges itself from the drive shaft. Clearly, in this case, the energy provided by the engine will be wasted, unless of course the problem is rectified. Supervision, as this example illustrates, is an important aspect of organization. Anthropomorphic entropic processes are subject to breakdown.[8] Supervision, one could argue, minimizes the resulting energy loss. Ninteenth-century political economist Alfred Marshall described the role of supervision in "modern" manufacturing concerns in the following terms:

New machinery, when just invented, generally requires a great deal of care and attention. But the work of its attendant is always being sifted; that which is uniform and monotonous is gradually taken over by the machine, which thus becomes steadily more and more automatic and self-acting; till at last, there is nothing for the hand to do, but to supply the material at certain intervals and to take away the work when it is finished. There still remains the responsibility for seeing that the machinery is in good order and working smoothly; but even this task is often made light by the introduction of automatic movement, which brings the machine to a stop the instant something goes wrong. (Marshall, 1890, 218)

To capture the role of tools and supervision in production processes, Equation 1.2 is respecified as follows:

$$W(t) = \eta \ [S(t), \ T(t)] \ E(t); \ \eta > 0 \qquad\qquad (1.3)$$

where $S(t)$ and $T(t)$ correspond to the level of supervision at time t and tools at time t, respectively. For the time being, I simply assume that second-law efficiency is an increasing function of tools and supervision. Thus, for a given quantum of energy, the more/better tools and supervision, the greater is second-law efficiency (i.e., η), and hence, the greater is output (i.e., $W(t)$). Tools and supervision, it therefore follows, are not directly productive; rather, their contribution to production is via their effect on second-law efficiency.

Here, I stop short of explicitly modeling supervisory activity, except to point out the obvious, namely that, historically, it has been carried out by people (animate supervision), and secondly, has been organized hierarchically, with conventionally defined workers (lower-level supervisors) at the bottom, line supervisors above, and senior managers (e.g., CEOs, CFOs, and the board of directors) at the top.[9]

Leibenstein's Managerial Taxonomy

This view of the organization input (broadly defined management) as a two-dimensional activity (e.g., supervision and design) is not entirely new. In work on the role of entrepreneurs in economic development, Harvey Leibenstein identified two types of managers, namely routine and innovative. Put differently, some managers are concerned with the day-to-day functioning of the firm, while others are concerned with innovation whether it involves products or processes.

I may distinguish two broad types of entrepreneurial activity: at one pole, there is routine entrepreneurship, which is really a type of management, and for the rest of the spectrum we have Schumpeterian or "new type" entrepreneurship. (We shall refer to the latter as N-entrepreneurship.) By routine entrepreneurship we mean the activities involved in coordination and carrying on a well-established, going concern in which the parts of the production function in use (and likely alternatives to current use) are well known and which operates in well-established and clearly defined markets. By N-entrepreneurs, we mean activities necessary to create or carry on an enterprise where not all markets are well established or clearly defined and/or in which the relevant parts of the production function are not completely known. (Leibenstein, 1968, 72)

The former are the equivalents of the supervisors referred to above, while the latter are the equivalent of the "designers/conceivers," those who conceive of or improve upon existing entropic processes or products. Put differently, progress requires dynamic innovative managers; otherwise, it will be condemned to manage the existing set of antropomorphic entropic processes *ad infinitum*. Recall that anthropomorphic entropic processes, unlike natural entropic processes, are man-made, subject to change if and only if changed.

The General Newtonian Production Function

As I maintained in Beaudreau (1998), this simple two-factor model (energy and organization), based on the laws of motion and thermodynamics, and the principles of organization (i.e., design and supervision), describes virtually all production processes, past, present and future. Take, for example, tree harvesting. Prior to the advent of the mechanical saw, animate energy was transmitted and applied by tools such as axes and saws to fell trees. The required supervision was typically provided by the owners of animate energy (i.e., lumberjacks). With the advent of the chain saw, animate energy (i.e., the internal combustion engine) was combined with inanimate energy, with essentially the same tools and supervision (i.e., saw teeth), to accomplish the task. More recently, with the advent of the mechanical harvester, inanimate energy alone is used in conjunction with tools to accomplish the task. The requisite supervision is provided by the operator. As this case clearly demonstrates, technological change has resulted in a case in which labor goes from providing energy and organization to providing only organization.

Another example is weaving. In the Paleolithic era, fibers or reeds were woven together to produce clothing, baskets and sieves using animate energy only. With the advent of the loom (i.e., tools), human energy was better transmitted and applied, resulting in higher output. Primitive looms, it therefore follows, are examples of anthropomorphic entropic processes. The application of water, steam and electric power to the hand- and foot-operated loom led to the power loom where human energy was replaced by water, steam or electric power, transforming labor's role from that of inanimate energy source and supervisor to that of supervisor with the result that today, little to no human energy is deployed in the weaving process. In the following passage, nineteenth-century British economist Alfred Marshall describes just such a change:

We may now pass to the effects which machinery has in relieving that excessive muscular strain which a few generations ago was the common lot of more than half the working men even in such a country as England . . . in other trades, machinery has lightened man's labours. The house carpenters, for instance, make things of the same kind as those used by our forefathers, with much less toil for themselves. . . . Nothing could be more narrow or monotonous than the occupation of a weaver of plain stuffs in the old time. But now, one woman will manage four or more looms, each of which does many times as much work in the course of a day as the old hand loom did; and her work is much less monotonous and calls for much more judgment than his did. (Marshall, 1890, 218)

The operative word here is "manage." Analytically speaking, factory workers in the nineteenth century no longer worked; instead, they managed. [10] Simon Newcomb, the nineteenth-century physicist and part-time economist, described the far-reaching change in labor's role in production brought about by steam-powered machinery as follows:

We may readily apply the principle here illustrated to the actual historical facts. The introduction of machinery during the last hundred years has to a certain extent changed the directions of man's occupations. Instead of making things with their own hands, as they formally had to do, they are now managing machines or assisting in various ways in working them. The pin-makers are no longer at work; a few of them are feeding pin-making machines, but the majority of them have learned other employments. A large class of carpenters no longer push the plane; a portion of them feed the planing machines, and the remainder are fully occupied in executing work that increased refinement which demand has encouraged. The same thing may be traced all through the channels of industry. (Newcomb, 1886, 390)

This was a recurrent theme in the nineteenth century, extending beyond political economy into such fields as engineering and mechanics. For example, James Martineau, a professional engineer, in a lecture to the Liverpool Mechanics Institute, spoke of machinery "rapidly supplanting human labour and rendering mere muscular force . . . worthless. That natural machine, the human body, is depreciated in the market. But if the body has lost its value, the mind must get into business without delay" (Tylecote, 1957, 262).

The depreciation of human "power" continued in the early twentieth century with the introduction of electric power. More flexible than steam power, it resulted in the mechanization of sectors of the economy that had resisted earlier mechanization. Consider, for example, the following excerpt describing the effects of electric-powered materials handling equipment on the nature of work in the mining industry, taken from David Nye's work on the electrification of America:

Thus for some, electrification meant unemployment as a few skilled jobs replaced unskilled labor. At Green Ridge Colliery, for example, a station engineer, motorman, and helper could run an electric locomotive that replaced six mule drivers, four boy helpers, and seveteen mules. At New York and Scranton Coal, three men and a locomotive replaced seven boys and fourteen mules. Down in the mines other electrical machines replaced hand labor, increasing productivity but reducing the need for artisanal skill. Such innovations were contributory factors in the United Mine Workers strikes of 1900, 1902, and 1912. A similar kind of labor replacement disturbed the steel workers, as General Electric designed a set of electrical motors and controls for rolling mills. The corporation proudly announced, "One man surrounded by a dozen or more operating levers controls every motion of steel from the ingot furnace to the completed rail. . . . Every motor replaced a man, but the work is done better and more quickly than formerly." In many mills, "a motor [was] installed on a charging and drawing machine, arranged so as to automatically grip and withdraw the hot bloom from the furnace, and release it when clear of the furnace door. The motorman has simply to start and stop the motor." (Nye, 1990, 206)

Substitutes or Complements

The resulting two-factor (energy and organization) model of production processes provides a rich framework in which to study production-related questions. For example, it provides a theoretical basis for studying the role of conventionally defined energy, capital, labor and organization in production. To what extent are energy and organization substitutable? Can managers be substituted for energy, and can labor be substituted for capital? Further, it provides the necessary framework to study technological change and its effects on the various factor inputs over time. For example, has second-law efficiency increased or decreased over time?

Another relevant question, especially in light of the energy crisis in the 1970s and 1980s, is whether tools (i.e., capital) and broadly-defined energy are substitutes or complements? Most political economists felt that they were substitutes (Solow, 1974). Newtonian production analysis provides valuable insights into this yet-to-be-resolved issue. The answer is a qualified no. Theoretically, for a given value of η, an increase in capital (i.e., tools) cannot make up for a loss of energy. Referring to Equation 1.3, we see that the only way in which more capital could compensate for less energy is if the result were higher second-law efficiency. That is, only if the additional capital increases η will output increase. As pointed out earlier, because machines and tools are not a source of energy, but rather, apply and transmit energy, it follows that, *ceteris paribus*, quantities of capital and energy cannot possibly be substitutes, but rather, are complementary inputs. Tools and machines cannot create energy. More tools for a given level of energy will not result in more work.

This leaves the possibility of second-law efficiency-increasing investment. In this case, the level of second-law efficiency is increasing in broadly defined capital, measured by the value of tools and machines. That is, the more capital, the higher is η. Were this to hold empirically, then capital and energy would be substitutes in the sense that more capital, by providing for higher η values, reduces the amount of energy required to perform a fixed, given amount of work. The point is that capital and energy can only be substitutes if and only if the former is heterogeneous in nature. More efficient capital can, at least theoretically, compensate for less energy; otherwise, they are complementary (Ayres and Nair, 1984).

Newtonian Production Analysis (NPA) Productivity Measures

The Generalized Newtonian Production Function provides important insights into both the definition, the construction and the use of productivity measures. Typically, productivity is measured as the ratio of output (value added) to one or many inputs. For example, in the past, political economists have defined and measured labor and capital productivity. Labor productivity is the ratio of output (value added) to labor input; capital productivity is the ratio of output (value added) to capital input. As pointed out earlier, implicit in these notions is the fact that both capital and labor are productive. This raises an important question. Does the fact that an input is physically present necessarily imply that it is productive? Take, for example, the case of managers. Are managers productive? If so, then how should their productivity be measured? After all, managers are a *sine quo non* of production. The point is that productivity measures differ both with regard to their content and, of course, with regard to their meaning. Those that refer to energy and force ought to be viewed as physically productive, while those that refer to organization ought to be viewed as organizationally productive. The fact that labor productivity increases does not imply that labor is responsible for the increase. As argued earlier, the only physically consistent measure of productivity is the ratio of output to total energy.

NPA Energy-Related Productivity Measures

Three energy-related productivity measures follow. Referring to Table 1.2, the first is the ratio of output to animate energy (i.e., $W(t)/E_a(t)$), commonly known as labor productivity. For this ratio to be relevant (i.e., in terms of thermodynamics), it must be the case that labor is a source of energy. Otherwise, labor productivity as conventionally defined is devoid of any meaning. As I shall argue later, labor in modern production processes is more appropriately viewed as a form of lower-level organization (i.e., supervisor).

The second productivity measure is the ratio of output to inanimate energy (i.e., $W(t)/E_i(t)$), $E_i(t)$ being broadly defined to include electrical, thermo-mechanical, and all other inanimate forms of energy. By virtue of Equation 1.2., this measure explicitly defines η, thermodynamic efficiency. The third productivity measure is the ratio of output to tools and machines (i.e., $W(t)/T(t)$), commonly referred to as capital productivity. Ideally, the capital data used in constructing this productivity measure should include only the relevant tools and machines. That is, they should be net of all energy-related capital (e.g., steam boilers, tranmissions, transformers, capacitators etcetera) and net of what we shall refer to as supervisory capital (e.g., control devices, computers etcetera). Including energy-related capital would result in double counting. Lastly, the third law of thermodynamics provides us with a fourth measure of productivity, namely the ratio of output to total energy (i.e., $E(t)$). This measures the relationship between output and the broadly defined energy input. Clearly, energy-conversion tables (i.e., labor-BTU, electric power-BTU) are required to render this measure operational. However, for production processes requiring no animate energy (i.e., $E_a(t)$), this ratio is equivalent to the output-inanimate energy ratio.

Table 1.2
NPA Energy Productivity Measures

$W(t)/E_a(t)$	Ratio of Work to Animate Energy
$W(t)/E_i(t)$	Ratio of Work to Inanimate Energy
$W(t)/E(t)$	Ratio of Work to Total Energy

Source: Beaudreau (1998), 29.

NPA Organization Productivity Measures

As pointed out above, continued energy-deepening throughout the nineteenth and twentieth centuries altered fundamentally the supervisory input (i.e., $S(t)$). In the preindustrial revolution period, the supervisory input (i.e., $S(t)$) and the source of energy (i.e., $E(t)$) were one, namely the worker. Weavers, stonecutters, shoemakers and artisans in general provided both energy and organization. In time, as inanimate energy replaced animate energy, the organizational aspect of production changed. A new class of production-related personnel came into being, namely managers. Together with workers who had been relieved of the physical demands of work, managers supervised production processes. With this was born the fully functional organization hierarchy, with workers (lower-level supervisors) at the base, and senior managers (upper-level supervisors) at the apex. To capture the developments in supervision technology, we define two subclasses of supervisors: $S_l(t)$, lower-level supervisors (i.e., workers) and $S_u(t)$, upper-level supervisors, where $S(t)=S_l(t)+S_u(t)$. The former find themselves at the base of the organizational hierarchy, while the latter find themselves at the apex. Table 1.3 defines the resulting three supervision-related productivity measures, namely the ratio of work to total supervisors, the ratio of work to lower-level supervisors, and lastly, the ratio of work to upper-level supervisors.

Table 1.3
NPA Organization Productivity Measures

$W(t)/S(t)$	Ratio of Work to Supervisors
$W(t)/S_l(t)$	Ratio of Work to Lower-Level Supervisors
$W(t)/S_u(t)$	Ratio of Work to Upper-Level Supervisors
$W(t)/T(t)$	Ratio of Work to Tools and Machines

Source: Beaudreau (1998), 30.

NPA and Empirical Work

Newtonian production analysis has important implications for empirical work. From Charles Cobb's and Paul Douglas' first attempt at estimating output elasticities and, hence, marginal revenue products, to the current practice of estimating flexible-form production functions, the underlying assumption has been that capital and labor are physically productive. Clearly, as argued here, this assumption is unsubstantiated. Paleolithic production processes notwithstanding, capital and labor are organizational variables. Capital and labor output elasticities are, as such, devoid of any meaning. Only energy is productive in the traditional sense. Such a view was borne out by my earlier empirical work on the KLEP (capital, labor, electric power) production function, where, using data from U.S., German and Japanese manufacturing, I found high output elasticities for electric power, and low output elasticities for capital and labor (Beaudreau, 1995a, b, c, 1996a, 1998).

This raises the problem of estimating production functions. Specifically, how should energy and organization be treated? Should labor and capital, for example, be included along with energy? Should they be nested in estimates of η, second-law efficiency, the idea being that they affect productivity indirectly? I will return to this later.

EXCHANGE TECHNOLOGIES AND THE PROBLEM OF UNDERINCOME

The shift from the "domestic system" to the "factory system," described earlier, did more than just increase throughput rates and conventionally defined productivity: it altered, in a nonnegligible way, the underlying exchange technology. Under the domestic system, the organization of production was carried out within the family (cottage industry). More specifically, the head of the family (producer) coordinated the energy and organization required to add value to the feedstocks (linen, wool, cotton) provided by merchants. Payments for services rendered were made once the finished goods was delivered to the merchant(s). The functional distribution of such payments was determined internally (i.e., within the family unit). Merchants, who provided the feedstocks (i.e. raw materials) and contracted to purchase the output at fixed price(s), paid the owners of capital and labor for their value added. As such, the demand for trade credit (i.e., money) was equal to the value of output.[11]

This changed with the arrival of factories. Specifically, energy and organization were now traded in a market-like setting. The in-house coordination which characterized the domestic system was replaced by market coordination.[12] Producers (capital owners or their managers) now transacted in the market for intermediate goods and factor inputs (energy and organization), using trade credit obtained from banks. Collectively, producers would now determine the level of wage income.

Table 1.4
Exchange Technologies

Nonintermediated
—Barter
—Money-Based

Intermediated
—Merchant
—Producer-Merchant

Out of this came the exchange technology that is with us today, one based on two sets of market coordination agents, namely producers and merchants. The former coordinate production activity, purchasing feedstocks and variable factor inputs, and selling output to merchants; the latter coordinate distribution activity, purchasing output from producers and selling it to individual economic agents (consumers and investors). Among the problems that arise in this system is that of overall market coordination (producers and merchants). For example, producers will coordinate production activity once merchants have placed their orders. Likewise, merchants will coordinate market activity once producers have made their hiring decisions. The problem, however, lies in coordinating joint activity, and hence avoiding indeterminacies. For example, such an economy might get stuck at a suboptimal level of output as producers hesitate to increase output given merchants' demands, and merchants hesitate to increase orders given the aggregate level of wage income determined by producers. This section examines "exchange technologies" defined as the institutional arrangements under which intermediate inputs, factors, goods and services are traded. Included are the different forms of money (e.g., barter, fiat money, credit money etcetera) as well as the various exchange/trading arrangements that have evolved over time, shown in Table 1.4. These include nonintermediated forms of exchange (barter and monetary exchange) and intermediated forms of exchange (merchant and producer-merchant). Intermediated forms of exchange, as opposed to nonintermediated forms of exchange, involve a third party in the form of either a producer, or a merchant. Distinguishing exchange technologies from standard monetary theory is, among other things, the emphasis placed on the institutional aspects of trade and exchange. Monetary theory, with a few exceptions, is devoid of institutions—other than the standard, Walrasian-style market nomenclature (Patinkin, 1965). Specifically, trade is modeled in standard Arrow–Debreu terms, and money is added as the $n+1$th good. According to David Laidler:

In the economics of Keynes, as in classical economics, money was a means of exchange; and textbook macroeconomics even now refers to "transactions" and "precautionary" motives for holding money, which are said to derive directly from that role. However, when monetary economists adopted Walrasian general equilibrium, in its IS–LM guise, as their basic vision of economic activity, they adopted a mode which could not generate such motives internally. . . . The monetarist counter-revolution was an attempt to change perceptions about empirical phenomena, not to create a new theoretical structure. It therefore did nothing to interrupt the process, already close to completion in the 1950's, of integrating monetary theory with Walrasian value theory. The more this process was pushed, the more did the representative model of a monetary economy come to resemble one of a barter economy in which there happened to exist a particular asset called "money" whose "real" (i.e., "utility-yielding") quantity varied in inverse proportion to its price in terms of goods. (Laidler, 1990, 2)

There are, of course, a number of exceptions, including Knut Wicksell's "cumulative process," Freidrich Hayek's "producer goods–consumer goods model of monetary exchange," and Robert Clower's "cash-in-advance constraint" (Wicksell, 1936 [1898], Hayek, 1935, Clower, 1967). All deal with the "mechanics" of exchange, the first being a stylized description of the workings of bank credit in an industrial economy, the second being an attempt to model the monetary transmission mechanism in an industrial setting (upstream and downstream producers), and the third being response to the absence of an exchange motive in early neoclassical models of money (e.g., Patinkin's model of a monetary economy).

The results of this section provide an analytical framework in which to examine the problem of underincome (Beaudreau, 1996a, 1998). Underincome is defined as a situation in which potential output rises in response to technological changes (mostly energy-deepening based) but where money income fails to rise commensurately, owing to (1) the nature of the game played by the producers which comprise the economy, and (2) the relevant exchange technology. Producers are assumed to play a Nash game in wages.

Given that (1) all other firms hold wages constant and (2) profits are a residual form of factor payment (paid out of producer sales revenues paid out by merchants), it follows that producers choose not to increase wages, and merchants choose not to increase orders of goods (owing to the limited market opportunities). Wage income and profit income fail to increase as a result.

Exchange Technologies

Throughout history, exchange technologies have been many and varied, ranging from simple, double-coincidence-of-wants-based bilateral barter to electronic banking-mediated exchange. This section examines exchange technologies, paying particular attention to the relationship between the organization and hence coordination of production and the organization and coordination of exchange.[13] Swedish economist Knut Wicksell was among the first to examine such a relationship. Exchange, he argued, was intimately related to production. In his cumulative process, the period of production defines exchange, first between entrepreneurs, workers and capitalists, and then between capitalists and workers, and entrepreneurs.

We may assume further that production begins everywhere at the same moment of time, at the beginning of the economic year, which need not, of course, coincide with the calendar year; and we may assume that the final product, the consumption goods, are not completed or available for exchange until the end of the year. This would correspond in some ways to the situation of former times, when in many districts the exchange of commodities was concentrated on one, or a few, great annual markets.

The total quantity of consumption goods is then the same thing as the quantity of liquid real capital in its free form; or rather it is the same thing as the quantity of this capital, inclusive of the amount with which the owners of capital have the right annually to credit themselves as remuneration for the capital employed in the previous year and which they consume on their own account during the current year.

Our imaginary procedure is then as follows: At the beginning of the year the entrepreneurs borrow their capital from the banks, in the form of a sum of money K. This is equal to the value of the total amount of available real capital, that is to say, of the total amount of consumption goods completed during the previous years minus the interest drawn in the previous year by the capitalist. This money capital is now paid to the workers and to the landlords; and at the same time entrepreneurs allocate to themselves an amount as remuneration for their own labour, risk-taking, etc., and pay the normal competitive rents for such "rent-earning goods" (sites, buildings, machines) as may be in their possession. With the aid of this money, the whole of the available commodity capital is now bought up by the consumers and the money capital K returns once again to the banks in the shape of the deposits made by the capitalist dealers.

The goods are completed only at the end of the economic year, and it is only then that the entrepreneurs can meet their liabilities. It follows that the credit which is granted by the banks to the entrepreneurs partakes of the character of one-year loans. (Wicksell, 1936 [1898], 139)

According to Wicksell, production and exchange are not spatially and sequentially independent activities, but rather, are simultaneous, occurring at the same place and time.[14] In a book published in 1938 entitled *Financial Organization and the Economic System*, Harold Moulton pointed to the often-ignored role of money in the organization of production. Under the heading, "Money in Relation to Production," he pointed out:

When money is spoken of as a medium of exchange, one usually has in mind the exchange of consumer goods. For convenience of exposition, economic treatises have commonly been divided into four parts, devoted respectively to consumption, production, exchange, and distribution. Money is treated under exchange and its chief function is usually regarded as that of effecting the exchange of goods that have already been produced and are in the market awaiting transfer to the hands of those who are to consume them.

But if one is to appreciate fully the significance of money under a capitalistic industrial regime, it is necessary to consider the part that it plays in the productive as well as in the exchange process. Exchange of consumers' goods is not to be excluded; but the role of money in getting goods ready to be exchanged as completed products must be included.

Modern business is almost universally conducted through the use of money. With money the manufacture purchases the materials needed for the construction of his plant; with money he employs an administrative staff to manage his business; and with money he purchases the raw materials and supplies and employs the labor force required to operate his business. In a similar way producers of raw materials, transportation agencies, and wholesalers and retailers employ money in connection with every other phase of their business operations; under modern conditions even the farmer makes an extensive use of money.

In short, practically the entire production process is nowadays organized and operated through the use of money.... Because of the great importance that has always been attached to money as capital, the economist has been wise in laying emphasis upon the fact that real capital consists of tangible properties. However, this emphasis has in turn tended to minimize the significant part that money plays in a capitalistic society. Productive instruments cannot be made effective in the service of society unless liquid capital is available with which to assemble raw materials and labor power in producing organizations. (Moulton, 1938, 21)

Heeding Moulton's advice, specifically, the need to include "the role of money in getting goods ready to be exchanged as completed products," I consider a simple, two-sector (consumption goods and capital goods) economy in which exchange is mediated by two types of agents, namely producers and merchants. Producers hire energy and organization to add value to feedstocks (natural resources in the primary sector, and intermediate goods in the secondary sector). Merchants, on the other hand, purchase consumer and capital goods from producers at fixed prices, and proceed to sell them to the owners of energy and organization. Both producers and merchants rely on costless bank credit to finance their activities.

Consider the following numerical example. Suppose that total value added (consumer goods and capital goods) is $100, of which 70 percent consists of consumer goods, and 30 percent of capital goods. Suppose further that (1) energy costs are zero, (2) labor's share of income (value added) is 70 percent and (3) capital's share is 30 percent. Numerically, labor's share of consumption goods value added is $49, while capital's is $21; labor's share of capital goods value added is $21, while capital's is $9.

Trade occurs sequentially. To begin with, producers contract in factor markets, and proceed to produce output. The latter is then purchased by merchants, and sold to the owners of capital and labor. Payments are made in terms of bank credit. Unlike the putting out system (cottage industry) where energy and organization (capital and labor) are owned by the same legal entity (i.e., cottage, farm), in the gathering-in system (factory system), ownership is diffuse. Specifically, capital (equity) is owned by shareholders, while labor is owned by workers. Unlike factor payments to labor and energy, factor payments to capital are a residual form of income. Producers demanded trade credit in an amount equal to their variable costs, in this case, labor costs.

Thus, in terms of our example, the demand for trade credit on the part of consumer goods and capital goods firms is $70, split 70–30. Consumer goods firms demand $49, while capital goods firms demand $21. Once the production process had run its course, merchants would then purchase the output, using trade credit ($100). This would then be used by producers to pay off their outstanding liabilities (bank credit), and pay dividends to shareholders. Lastly, the owners of labor and capital would then purchase the consumption and capital goods. Merchants' sales receipts ($100) would then be used to pay off their outstanding bank liabilities ($100). What is particularly interesting is the fact that the overall demand for money per dollar of output is now $1.70. For every dollar of output, $1.70 of credit is required, $0.70 for producers to finance variable production costs, and $1.00 for merchants to finance its sale in product markets.

Clearly, this is a highly simplified model of exchange in an industrial economy. Producers anticipate merchants' decisions correctly, and merchants anticipate producers' decisions correctly. It being the case that payments to capital are a residual form of income, it follows that merchants' collective ability to anticipate correctly the demand for both consumption and capital goods is crucial to aggregate profits. What, for example, would happen if merchants erred on the down side? That is, the demand for trade credit on the part of merchants was less than the value of total output. In this case, profits would fall, decreasing the demand for capital goods. The demand for consumer goods, being based on wage income, would not be affected, at least not initially. Clearly, merchants' expectations, taken collectively, play a key role in determining the level of aggregate output, the level of aggregate wage income and the level of aggregate profit income.

The Problem of Underincome

Provided that merchants' expectations are, on average, correct, it is highly likely that this hypothetical economy will produce at capacity. Now, suppose that it is hit by an energy-based technological shock, specifically, potential output doubles, the result of energy-based machine speed-ups. Existing capital and labor are, as a result, twice as productive as before. The question then becomes, will income and expenditure rise as a result? As shown here, for output to be transformed into income, two things are necessary. First, wage income must increase; second, merchants, basing their decisions on the overall level of wage income, must increase their orders. The problem, however, is that there are no private incentives for individual consumption and capital goods firms to increase wage income in response to the technology shock (energy-deepening). Doubling wages in a Nash setting, as shown in Beaudreau (1996a), is a profit-decreasing proposition. In light of this, there are no private incentives on the part of merchants to increase orders of consumption and capital goods (i.e., the increased output). Doing so would be ruinous as the goods in question would sit on their store shelves.

This, in short, is the problem of underincome described in my earlier work. Firms have no private incentives to increase wages in response to energy-based technology shocks. Merchants have no private incentives to increase orders of consumption and capital goods given the failure of income, particularly wage income, to increase. Income, as such, fails to increase, as do profits. In short, the problem of income inertia arises. As pointed out in Beaudreau (1996a), were consumption and capital goods firms to act collectively and increase wages commensurately (in this case, double), then overall income and profits would also double. Merchants would double their orders from consumption goods and capital goods firms, thus consumption and capital goods firms' revenues, and consequently, doubling their profits. Sales would then double, the result of higher (double) labor and capital income.

Profits in Knut Wicksell's Cumulative Process

More than anyone before—and after—him, Swedish economist Knut Wicksell came closest to describing the exchange technology and, consequently, the demand for money in an industrial—as opposed to an agricultural—economy. As pointed out earlier, the demand for money/trade credit is determined by firms' demand for factor inputs, which he restricts to labor and land. Money makes its way into the system by way of the relevant factor markets. The demand for money is, as such, equal to the total cost of production. Producers demand credit in the amount of the total cost of production. Factors are paid in credit, which they use to purchase goods and services. Sales receipts are then used to pay off the outstanding bank liability. In the next period, the process repeats itself.

Unfortunately, Wicksell stopped short of examining what I feel is the most empirically relevant case, namely an equity–capital-based economy, where the defining feature is the delayed (residual) nature of the corresponding factor payment (i.e., profits). In modern industrial economies the world over, factor payments to capital are not made before, but rather after product markets have cleared (Knight, 1921). Put differently, the demand for money on the part of producers, per dollar of output, is considerably less than the demand for money on the part of merchants per dollar of output. As shown above, the extent to which this matters depends, in large measure, on the extent of vertical integration of production processes. The lower is the latter, the greater is the problem. Specifically, the demand for credit, and thus, the level of money income, is less than the value of total output.

Energy-Deepening, Rents and Underincome

It is my contention that while the problem of underincome is not specific to energy-related innovations—at least not theoretically—it has, over the past 200 years, been the result of such innovations. As mentioned earlier, the first industrial revolution was the result of an energy-related innovation, namely, the widespread use of "firepower" in industry. Output increased more than money costs, which, in fact, had decreased, resulting in the problem of underincome. This scenario played itself out again in the early twentieth century with the coming of the electrical age.

Put otherwise, energy-deepening has given rise to energy rents, defined as the difference between the value of the marginal product of energy and its price/cost. In the presence of underincome, these rents are virtual in nature. That production capacity is, say, 100 percent higher when money income is constant has little bearing on price and costs. Potential income, potential profits and potential wages could increase; however, there is no reason to believe that actual income, actual profits and actual wages will increase.

In the next section, the problem of distribution is analyzed using bargaining theory. Specifically, the owners of energy and organization are assumed to bargain over output.

THE PROBLEM OF INCOME DISTRIBUTION

In the previous section, it was assumed that output (value added, transformation) is distributed among the owners of energy and organization. Specifically, capital receives 30 percent, while labor received the rest. In this section, the problem of distribution is examined more closely. Conventional theories of distribution (i.e., classical, Marxian and neoclassical) are considered but rejected on the grounds that neither capital nor labor is a physically productive input. As pointed out above, in postindustrial revolution production processes, both are organizational inputs, defining the set of entropic processes that defines economic activity. As such, neither is physically productive. To begin addressing the problem of income distribution when neither capital nor labor is physically productive, I draw from Beaudreau (1998), where income distribution is modeled as a cooperative bargaining problem between the owners of energy and organization over the final product, value added.

As shown above, supply does not necessarily create money income. Historically, energy-related supply shocks, while increasing potential output, have not necessarily resulted in higher nominal or real income, a condition I refer to as underincome. In this section, I abstract from this problem, and assume a one-to-one relationship between aggregate potential output, and aggregate nominal and real money income. As such, the problem of distribution will involve apportioning real money income among the owners of energy and organization.

Traditional Theories of Income Distribution

The implications of Newtonian production analysis extend well beyond production. For one, they have important ramifications for existing theories of income distribution in general. For example, the labor theory of value, the cornerstone of classical and Marxian economics, is rejected, as is the neoclassical theory of distribution. Tools (capital) have never been productive in the physical sense.[15] From the early nineteenth century on, labor ceased to be productive in the physical sense. Far from being the only source of value, labor (i.e., lower-level supervisory input), being divested of its archaic role of energy source (i.e., animate energy), is, today, a marginal factor input. The evidence is there for everyone to see. Day in and day out, newly developed control technologies, based on the microchip, continue to render animate supervision (workers) more and more redundant (Rifkin, 1995, Greider, 1997).

The neoclassical theory of income distribution, based in large measure on the notion of marginal product and Euler's theorem, fares no better. Neither capital nor labor are physically productive; rather, both are organizational variables, defining and overseeing entropic processes. Clearly, what is needed is an alternative theory of income distribution which is consistent with the basic physics of production processes

An Alternative Theory of Income Distribution

Newtonian production analysis (NPA) provides an ideal starting point for the study of income distribution, which I define as the apportioning of the final product (value added) among the owners of energy and organization. As I have emphasized from the start, energy and organization are the cornerstones of economic activity. Without energy, organization would be of no use, and likewise, without organization, energy would be of no use. It therefore follows that the study of income distribution consists of the study of the apportionment of the final product among the owners of energy and organization.

Approaching the problem of income distribution in this way raises a number of interesting questions. For example, what determines factor payments to labor? Clearly, since labor is not (i.e., no longer) a source of energy, it stands to reason that its remuneration has to be based on its role as an organizational input (i.e., lower-level supervisors) in energy-consuming (i.e., entropic) processes. What determines factor payments to those who design (i.e., conceive of) and supervise energy-consuming processes? How are they remunerated? At issue in both these cases are the two fundamental roles of organization, and hence, their share of the spoils in a world in which value added is an increasing function of inanimate energy and tools. Clearly, if production processes were self-conceiving and self-regulating, as are energy-transforming processes in nature, then the problem of distribution would be easily resolved: factor payments would simply follow an energy standard.[16] For example, if electric power supplied 80 percent of the overall energy consumption, and production workers supplied the remaining 20 percent, then an 80–20 split between the owners of electric power and production workers would result.

A Positive Theory of Distribution

To better understand the problem of income distribution, I begin by examining such a scenario. That is, one in which Newtonian production processes exist in an *ex-ante* sense and are self regulating. Put differently, organization is a superfluous input. In such a world, there is a single input, energy. Suppose that inanimate and animate energy put out the equivalent of 1,000 kilowatt hours (kWh) of work, broken down as follows: 500 kWh of electric power, 500 kWh of labor. That is, 500 kWh of animate energy and 500 kWh of inanimate energy.

In such a case, the problem of income distribution is trivial: the owners of electric power would receive half of the total product, while the owners of animate energy (i.e., labor) would receive the other half. Factor payments would simply mirror each individual factor's energy contribution. I shall refer to this as the energy-based positive theory of distribution.

It could be argued that this is precisely what the marginalists had in mind: a theory of distribution based on physical productivity. Marshall, Jevons and Walras sought a positive theory of distribution, one based on measurable phenomena. Distribution, they argued, ought to reflect the physical contribution of each factor input.

Consider next the reverse situation, namely that in which energy in general is a free good.[17] In this case, output is apportioned among the remaining factor inputs, namely those who design entropic processes, those who finance the necessary tools and machines (i.e., capital) and those who supervise them. Clearly, the issue of distribution in this context is infinitely more complex.

Notwithstanding the problems associated with knowledge capital (e.g., opportunism, market impactedness), it is clear that the distribution of income (i.e., output) will involve a bargaining process involving both parties. Neither factor is productive in the physical sense; however, each contributes to maximizing η, second-law efficiency (see Equation 1.3). Accordingly, the designers of, the financiers of and supervisors of, energy-consuming processes, will bargain over the relevant payoff space, the result of which will be either each's outside option (i.e., the null set), or production, the distribution of which will, in large measure, be determined by each factor's relevant outside option and its relative bargaining power. Since all three are essential to production, it is imperative that a bargain be struck. Otherwise, nothing will be produced (i.e., the outside option). That is, the designer of and owner of the production process cannot produce for lack of the necessary supervisors, and, likewise, the owners of the supervisory input cannot produce for lack of a well-defined production process.

I now turn to the question of bargaining power. According to cooperative bargaining theory, the agent's share of the bargaining set is, in large measure, influenced by his/her bargaining power. The more bargaining power, the greater the share of the product (i.e., bargaining set). Clearly, in this case, the distribution of output will be a function of each agent's bargaining power. If the designers and, hence, owners of production processes have more bargaining power, then it stands to reason that they will receive a larger share of the product; however, if the owners of the supervisory input have more bargaining power, then they will receive a larger share of the product.

A Bargaining Model of Income Distribution with Energy and Organization

These two extreme-case scenarios provide the basis for the study of distribution in a world in which production requires energy and organization. For example, they make it abundantly clear that income distribution is a more complex issue than hitherto believed, one that goes beyond the simple neoclassical practice of estimating output elasticities. It is argued that bargaining in general, and bargaining between the owners of energy and the owners of organization in particular, play a fundamental role in income distribution. The next task, it therefore follows, consists of modeling distribution in the presence of energy-related inputs, and organization-related inputs.

Energy- and Organization-Related Inputs

Thus far, I have identified six factor inputs: inanimate energy, animate energy, tools and machines, lower-level supervisors, upper-level supervisors and designers. The first two are energy-related, while the latter four are organization-related. As it turns out, however, there are fewer than six factor inputs in modern production processes. For my purposes here, I will assume that there are five, inanimate energy having been rendered redundant by the first and second industrial revolutions. As pointed out above, steam-powered and electric-powered tools transformed workers into lower-level supervisors. Workers no longer exerted themselves physically. The development of control technologies in the latter half of the twentieth century has further altered the nature of factor inputs. Control devices have replaced and continue to replace lower-level supervisors (i.e., labor), with the result that if the current trend continues, animate lower-level supervisors will be replaced by inanimate lower-level supervisors in the form of control devices.

Income Distribution

In Beaudreau (1998), I argued that income distribution in a world in which energy and organization are complementary inputs is best studied using cooperative bargaining theory. Accordingly, the owners of energy and organization bargain over their respective share of the product (i.e., payoff set) Theoretically, the distribution of income is the solution to this game. Since broadly defined organization is a *sine quo non* of production, it is clear that energy's overall share of the product cannot be complete (i.e., equal to one). Put differently, a pure energy standard is ruled out by the presence of organization. The difference will be appropriated by the owners of organization (i.e., the designers of and owners of the production processes, and the owners of the supervisory input).

Bargaining without Outside Options

I begin by defining the bargaining problem. The owners of energy and organization (e.g., the owners of energy (E), tools (T), the supervisory inputs (S), and lastly, the designers/owners of the production processes themselves (D) bargain over $W = min[E/\beta_1, T/\beta_2, S/\beta_3, D/\beta_4]$, the output, in this case, manufacturing value added. The owners of upper- and lower-level supervisory inputs are combined into one group, the owners of supervisory inputs. Define s_E, s_T, s_S, and s_D, where $[0 \leq s_i \leq 1, \Sigma_{i=E,T,S,D} s_i = 1]$ as the energy, tools, supervisor, and designers factor income shares, respectively. Also assume that α_i, where $i = E, T, S$ and D, defines factor i's bargaining power $[0 \leq \alpha_i \leq 1, \Sigma_{i=E,T,S,D} \alpha_i = 1]$. Lastly, assume that factor i's utility is an increasing linear function of income. More specifically, $U_i = U_i[s_iW]$ for all $i = E, T, S, D$.

This provides a general framework in which to study income distribution. In the absence of outside options, the simple bargaining problem is given by Equation 1.4, where the s_i's are chosen to maximize the product of utilities.

$$\max_{s_i} S = \prod_{i=E,T,S,D} [s_iW]^{\alpha_i} \qquad (1.4)$$

The Nash bargaining solution corresponds to the case in which $\alpha_i = 1/4$, which yields $s_i^* = 1/4$ for all $i = E, T, S, D$.

Thus, in a world devoid of outside options and in which preferences are identical, income distribution will be largely determined by bargaining power. That is, if the economic value of energy, tools, supervisors and production processes is nil, then their share of the overall income (output) pie will be determined by each factor's bargaining power. For example, the greater is lower-level supervisors' bargaining power, the greater is their share of the pie, so to speak.

Bargaining with Outside Options

The presence of outside options alters considerably the bargaining problem. For example, suppose that the owners of electric power can sell each kilowatt hour at a price of 7 cents. It stands to reason that, at the very least, the owners' share of manufacturing output must be equal to or greater than the corresponding market value of the power. Define ξ_i such that $\xi_i > 0$ to be factor i's outside option. The bargaining problem becomes:

$$\max_{s_i} S = \prod_{i=E,T,S,D} [s_i W - \xi_i]^{\alpha_i} \tag{1.5}$$

subject to:

$$s_i W - \xi_i \geq 0 \ \forall \ i = E, T, S, \text{ and } D \tag{1.6}$$

In this case, a bargain will be struck if and only if, at the very least, the various factor inputs receive their outside options; otherwise, negotiations will break down, which in this case implies that production will not occur. It therefore follows that Equation 1.6 must hold for all $i = E, T, S$ and D.

The Determinants of Outside Options and Bargaining Power

Among the determinants of the resulting bargaining solution are (1) each factor's outside option, and (2) each factor's bargaining power. This leads us to examine the determinants of outside options and bargaining power. For outide options to have any meaning, there must exist alternative uses for energy, tools, and upper and lower-level supervisors. For example, the owners of electric power could consume their kilowatt hours instead of producing value added. The owners of tools (capital) could opt for consumption over investment. Lastly, the owners of upper- and lower-level supervisory skills could devote their time to leisure activities. In a world in which the number of firms exceeds one, the owners of these factor inputs could, theoretically, bargain with another firm. The point is that outside options are conditioned by each factor's set of alternative activities.

For all bargaining problems where the number of solutions is greater than one (i.e., one corresponding to the perfectly competitive bargaining solution, defined by a strict equality for Equation 1.6), bargaining power plays a crucial role in income distribution. For example, the more bargaining power the owners of supervisory inputs have over the owners of electric power, the greater will be their share of the product.

This raises the question of bargaining power per se. What determines bargaining power within the firm (i.e., among the owners of energy, tools, the supervisory input and the conceivers of production processes)? Unfortunately, while formal bargaining models provide much insight into the process of income distribution in the presence of rents, it provides little in the way of an exact bargaining solution.

Bargaining and Energy Rents

The bargaining approach to the problem of income distribution allows for the existence of energy rents. Energy rents are, by definition, the difference between the productivity of energy (i.e., the increase in output which results from an increase in the energy input) and the cost of energy. Formally, by defining the marginal product of energy as $\partial W/\partial E$, energy rents can be expressed as $\partial W/\partial E - s_E \, \partial W/\partial E$.[18] For energy rents to be positive, it must be the case that $(1-s_E) > 0$. Put differently, the owners of energy's share of the incremental output must be less than complete.

CONCLUSIONS

Finding mainstream production, exchange and distribution theory to be deficient in its treatment of energy in production processes, the role of institutions in exchange, and the role of rents, specifically energy rents, in income distribution, this chapter has presented an alternative analytical framework, one based on my previous work on production, exchange, and distribution. Production was modeled as an increasing function of second-law efficiency, itself a function of tools (capital) and supervision (labor) and energy consumption. The former were referred to as organization-related factor inputs, while the latter was referred to as an energy-related factor input. This was followed by a discussion of exchange technologies, with particular emphasis on intermediated forms of exchange. Particular attention was paid to the domestic system in Europe, particularly the United Kingdom, and the ensuing shift to the factory system. The chapter ended with a discussion of distribution in the presence of energy rents, the latter being defined as the diffference between the marginal revenue product of energy and its price.

The result is an integrated model of production, growth, exchange and distribution, which will provide the analytical framework for my examination of the role of energy in the rise and fall of political economy over the past two centuries. In the next chapter (Chapter 2), entitled "Steam Power and Political Economy," the problems of production, exchange and distribution in the late eighteenth/early nineteenth century, which witnessed the shift from the domestic system to the factory system, will be examined. The chapter will begin with a look, using the analytical framework developed in this chapter, at the problems of production, exchange and distribution. This will serve as a basis for a reexamination of the classical, radical and neoclassical political economists' writings on the problems of production, exchange and distribution. This format is used throughout the remaining chapters, each corresponding to a period in the history of energy consumption, namely (1) the early electrification of industry (Chapter 3), (2) energy-deepening in the form of greater electric power consumption per worker (Chapter 4), and (3) the end of energy-deepening and the beginning of what I refer to as energy stasis (Chapter 5).

NOTES

1. By the consumption of energy, it should be understood the consumption or use of the available work of a particular energy source, keeping in mind that energy cannot be created or destroyed (first law of thermodynamics). As such, energy consumption is equivalent to the notion of "energy transformation" known as entropy.

2. Those interested in the evolution of production processes through time are referred to Chapter 2 of Beaudreau (1998).

3. The view that conventionally defined labor can be broken down into a force (i.e., energy) and supervisory component is as old as thermodynamics itself. German physicist and physiologist Hermann von Helmholtz argued that the forces of nature (mechanical, electrical, chemical, etcetera) are forms of a single, universal energy or *Kraft*, that cannot be either added to or destroyed. According to Anson Rabinbach, "As Helmholtz was aware, the breakthrough in thermodynamics had enormous social implications. In his popular lectures and writings, he strikingly portrayed the movements of the planets, the forces of nature, the productive forces of machines, and, of course, human labor power as examples of the principle of conservation of energy. The cosmos was essentially a system of production whose product was the universal *Kraft*, necessary to power the engines of nature and society, a vast and protean reservoir of labor power awaiting its conversion to work" (Rabinbach, 1990, 3).

4. This has important consequences for distribution. Clearly, the owner(s) of tools/machines cannot lay claim to a portion of output on the basis of work. Instead, his/her/their claim has to be based on tools/machines' contribution to second-law efficiency. Tools/machines improve second-law efficiency, thus contributing to increase output.

5. I forego a discussion of the notion of mechanical advantage for the simple reason that while tools/machines can better distribute the overall amount of work to be done,

they do not, in any way, reduce it. In other words, because they are not a source of energy, they cannot increase the overall amount of work being performed.

6. By definition, second-law efficiency consists of the ratio of the minimum theoretical amount of energy required to perform a task, to the actual of amount of energy used in any given production process.

7. By spontaneous, it should be understood independent of Homo-sapiens.

8. One could argue that natural entropic processes are also subject to breakdown. For example, take the human body and the numerous diseases that prevent energy from being transformed into work.

9. It is clear that while not a source of energy, the supervisory input is nonetheless a *sine quo non* of virtually all production processes. Without supervisors, output becomes probabilistic (including the null set). Tools and machines are apt to break down, resulting in a loss of energy and output.

10. This explains the increasing use of child labor (i.e., child supervision) in factories in the early nineteenth century.

11. By trade credit, it should be understood bills of exchange, promissory notes, bank notes etcetera.

12. Put differently, hierarchy was replaced by markets.

13. While there exists a considerable literature on money as a factor of production, it, for the most part, is devoid of institutions. For example, in Fischer (1974), money is included in the production function, on the grounds that (1) by holding money, firms forego interest, hence it must be a factor, and (2) by holding money, firms save on labor costs.

14. This is in constrast with monetary theory where both production and exchange are spatially and sequentially independent activities. A good example of this is work on the demand for money, where money demand is increasing is the level of output, the latter being independent of the former.

15. Perhaps this explains why classical political economists chose labor as the basis of value theory.

16. This, I argue, is what neoclassical political economists had in mind—a positive, verifiable theory of income distribution.

17. One could argue that such a situation characterized most of the modern era. In the mid-1900s, developments in electric generating and transmitting technology were such that many envisioned the day in the not-too-distant future when power would be free. Slogans like "too cheap to meter" were often heard.

18. It is assumed here that the relevant production function is, in fact, differentiable.

2

Steam Power and Political Economy

It is well known that, during the last half century in particular, Great Britain, beyond any other nation, has progressively increased its powers of production, by a rapid advancement in scientific improvements and arrangements, introduced, more or less, into all the departments of productive industry throughout the empire. The amount of this new productive power cannot, for want of proper data, be very accurately estimated; but your Reporter has ascertained from facts which none will dispute, that its increase has been enormous;—that, compared with the manual labour of the whole population of Great Britain and Ireland, it is, at least, as forty to one, and may be easily made as 100 to one; and that this increase may be extended to other countries; that it is already sufficient to saturate the world with wealth and that the power of creating wealth may be made to advance perpetually in an accelerating ratio.

—Robert Owen, *Report to the County of Lanark*

INTRODUCTION

The shift from the domestic system of production to the factory system, based on new sources of power, had a profound impact on the industrial and economic landscape of the United Kingdom. For example, the ownership of factor inputs (energy and organization) was no longer concentrated (i.e., within the family unit), but was diffuse. Workers which had up until then been a source of motive power were reduced to supervisory inputs (i.e., machine operatives), overseeing the workings of steam-powered machinery. Producers no longer coordinated production activity within the confines of the family farm of cottage, but rather in a market environment. So great were these changes, I maintain, that moral philosophers and political economists would devote the next hundred years to understanding them, with mixed results.

Missing from the resulting literature, whether classical, Marxian or neoclassical, however, is any mention of energy in general, and hydraulic and steam power in particular (Berg, 1980). Production continued to be modeled in terms of capital and labor. Energy is notable for its absence. This, I argue, was not inconsequential. Energy-related innovations were changing the industrial landscape; yet, in political economy, they were nowhere to be found. This is not to say that political economy was impervious to the changing industrial landscape; rather, it was impervious to the root cause. To most political economists of the time, the introduction of new machinery was the relevant technological shock.

In this chapter, using the model of production, exchange and distribution developed in Chapter 1, I reexamine the origins and evolution of nineteenth-century political economy. As pointed out in the Introduction, the approach taken is altogether different from the conventional history of economic thought. First, I abstract from the writings of classical, radical and neoclassical moral philosophers and examine, using the analytical framework presented in Chapter 1, the transition from the domestic to the factory system. This allows me to identify the major problems and issues related to the introduction of the revolutionary form of inanimate energy that was "fire power." This is then followed by an in-depth reexamination of classical, radical and neoclassical political economy, their motives, their influences, their contributions and their shortcomings.

STEAM POWER AND THE INDUSTRIAL REVOLUTION

This section is devoted to evaluating the effects of "fire power" on production, distribution and exchange in Great Britain in the late eighteenth/early nineteenth century. Particular attention will be paid to the various problems "fire power" raised. Among these are the the problems of exchange and distribution.

The Putting-Out and Gathering-In Systems

To better understand and appreciate the impact of "fire power" on industry in the United Kingdom, it is necessary to understand production, distribution and exchange activity in the years leading up to the industrial revolution. Prior to the introduction of the Watt-Boulton steam engine, work (i.e., output) in Great Britain was, for the most part, the result of the application of muscular (human and animal) force. Draft animals, supervised by farmers, provided the necessary force to till the soil. Human, muscular force, however, was required to harvest crops. Clearly, the stronger the draft animals, the more work could be done per unit of animal feed (exergy). The heightened interest in animal breeding in the preindustrial period can, as such, be viewed as a means of increasing the relevant η, the level of thermodynamic efficiency. The same is true of the tool industry, where the emphasis was on high-grade, durable steels, capable of doing more work per unit force—in this case, muscular.

In seventeenth century Great Britain, most forms of production activity were carried out on a small scale, often by the household unit. Food was grown, wool was produced, thread was spun, cloth was woven and tools/furniture were fashioned. Among the specialized activities were steel making, and, to a lesser degree, milling and, of course, religion—salvation. Autarky was, in general, the rule. Exceptions, however, involved the production of goods, most often textiles, by households for the market. Merchants from cities would contract work (cleaning, spinning and weaving) out to households in the surrounding countryside, supplying the raw material and purchasing the finished products. This is referred to as either the "domestic system," the "putting-out system" or the "cottage industry." Peter Stearns describes this period as follows:

With all these developments, however, Western technology and production methods remained firmly anchored in the basic traditions of agricultural societies, particularly in terms of reliance on human and animal power. Agriculture had scarcely changed in method since the fourteenth century. Manufacturing, despite some important new techniques, continued to entail combining skill with hand tools and was carried out in very small shops. The most important Western response to new manufacturing opportunities involved a great expansion of rural (domestic) production, particularly in textiles but also in small metal goods. Domestic manufacturing workers used simple equipment, which they usually bought themselves, and relied on labor from the household. Many combined their efforts with farming, and in general their skill levels were modest. The system worked well because it required little capital; rural households invested a bit in a spinning wheel or a hand loom, while an urban-based capitalist purchased the necessary raw materials and, ususally, arranged for the sale of the product. Output expanded because of the sheer growth of worker numbers, not because of technical advancement; indeed, the low wages paid generated little incentive for technical change. (Stearns, 1993, 18)

What is particularly interesting is the nature of production, exchange and distribution. The household unit (producer) provided the energy, tools and supervision necessary to transform, for example, raw wool into thread, thread into finished cloth or, for that matter, finished cloth into clothing. The energy was, in general, muscular in nature; the tools were primitive by today's standard and the supervision was provided by the worker.[1] Given that the energy and organization in question were owned by the household unit, there was no distribution problem—as described earlier (i.e., outside of the household). The income received from the merchants (payments for services rendered) went to the household (producer), not to the individual factors, per se.[2]

The resulting exchange technology did not pose any problems. The overall demand for trade credit was, but for the merchant's profit, equal to the value of total output. Trade credit was provided by local and regional banks. The relevant credit instruments included bills of exchange, promissory notes etcetera. Merchants demanded trade credit in the amount of the cost of their raw materials (cotton, wool, linen), and the cost of transformation (adding value). Not surprisingly, the domestic system went largely unnoticed, not being the subject of any natural or moral philosopher in the preindustrial period. The supply of human, animate, muscular energy put an upper limit on the per-capita amount of output/work, and, hence, of the growth of output and work. One could argue that in the absence of the steam engine, growth would have been limited to growth of animate, muscular energy, which, at the time, tracked population growth.

Enter the Steam Engine

Two events in eighteenth-century Great Britain changed the industrial landscape forever. The first was Richard Arkwright's waterwheel-driven spinning jenny, while the second was the development and widespread application of the Watt-Boulton rotative-power steam engine. Analytically speaking, Arkwright's water-powered spinning jenny was of monumental importance, as it altered fundamentally the nature of work. The force required to spin cotton and wool would, from that point on, no longer be animate, but inanimate. Spinning wheels (spindles) would be powered by hydraulic power, transmitted by way of complex belting, gearing and shafting. This *de facto* lifted the energy constraint. Never again would human muscular power limit the amount of work done. According to Peter Stearns:

More impressive developments occurred in the preparatory phases in cotton, James Hargreaves invented a spinning jenny device about 1764, which mechanically drew out and twisted fibers into threads—though this advance too initially was applied to handwork, not a new power source. Carding and combing machines, to ready the fiber prior to spinning, were developed at about the same time. Then in 1769, Richard Arkwright developed the first water-powered spinning machine; it twisted and wound threads by means of flyers and bobbins operating continuously. These first machines were relevant only for the cheapest kind of thread, but other inventions by 1780 began to make possible the spinning of finer cotton yarns. These new devices also could be powered by steam engines as well as waterwheels. The basic principles of mechanized thread production have not changed to this day, though machines were to grow progessively larger, and a given worker could tend to a number of spindles. (Stearns, 1993, 23)

However, moving production out of cottages (putting-out) into factories (gathering-in) raised the problem of exchange and distribution. How would total value added be apportioned among the owners of capital (i.e., the mill), the owners of lower-level supervisory skills (i.e., men, women and children), and the owners of the hydraulic resource? Moreover, given that the producer (manager) was, in most cases, also the owner of the capital (equity capital), it follows that a nonnegligible fraction of factor payments would be residual in nature, being paid out once the output had been purchased by merchants.

It is important to point out that these epoch-defining changes predate the introduction of the steam engine in industry. A good example of this is Matthew Boulton's Soho Manufactory in Bolton where the Hockley Brook powered the machines used to manufacture buttons, watch chains, plated wares etcetera. Earlier in 1765, he had left Birmingham to avoid operating an expensive horse mill.

Hockley Brook, however, was not without problems of its own. For example, in the summer, water levels were often insufficient to power the wheels, bringing the manufactory to a halt. To overcome this problem, Boulton turned to steam power, ordering a Savery engine to pump water and, in the process, turn the water wheels. According to Richard Hills:

In light of subsequent history, one of the most important people to consider using a Savery engine was Matthew Boulton when he wished to supplement the water resources of the Hockley Brook which powered his new Soho Manufactory. He had purposely moved out of Birmingham in 1765 to avoid operating an expensive horse mill, but the growth of the Manufactory presented him, with a similar dilemma once more. So his mind turned to employing a steam engine to lift water from the tail race of the waterwheel back to the mill dam. (Hills, 1989, 40)

Realizing that steam could drive machinery directly—as opposed to via waterwheels—Boulton began work with James Watt in 1768 on what was to become the defining energy innovation of the eighteenth century, namely the Watt-Boulton rotary-drive steam engine. These developments, I argue, are key to understanding Adam Smith's *An Inquiry into the Nature and Causes of the Wealth of Nations*. It is well known that Smith knew Boulton and Watt, and had personally visited the Soho Manufactory prior to 1776.

The late eighteenth century/early nineteenth century, it therefore follows, was a transitional period, with animate, muscular energy being replaced by inanimate, hydraulic-based energy, which, in turn, was replaced by inanimate, fossil-fuel-based energy in the form of steam power. According to Katrina Honeyman:

During the period 1780–1825, cotton factories varied not only in scale but also in type. S. D. Chapman has identified what he sees as three main types. The Type A mill was a small-scale operation, often employing hand-operated jennies or mules and possibly horse capstans for driving card machines. The cost of establishing and equipping this type of mill was about £1,000–£2,000. The Type B factory was more often purpose-built and comprised three or four storeys. It came in two sizes: one designed to hold approximately 1,000 spindles and requiring up to £3,000 investment; and one at least twice as large with up to 3,000 spindles, costing from £5,000. These are often referred to as Arkwright-type mills. Type C was larger, generally steam-powered, and cost about £10,000. This category of mill was not usual until the early 19th century. (Honeyman, 1982, 57)

The substitution of inanimate power for animate, muscular power occurred over a period of roughly 100 years (1760–1860). Figure 2.1, based on data from B. R. Mitchell's *British Historical Statistics* on the numbers of workers employed in the U.K. cotton industry from 1806 to 1862, shows that by 1833, there were as many factory workers as handweavers, and that by 1862, the latter had, for all intents and purposes, disappeared from the industry. Inanimate energy had completely displaced animate energy.

Figure 2.1
Numbers Employed in the Cotton Industry, 1806–1862

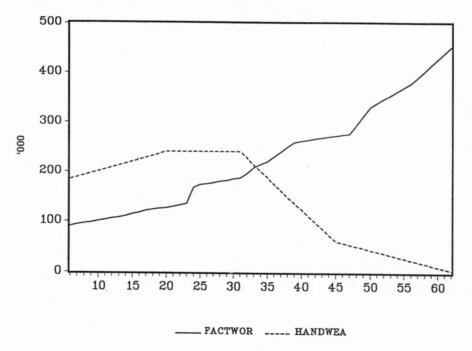

Source: Mitchell (1988), 376.

Table 2.1
Total Coal Consumption, United Kingdom, 1755–1900

Year	Coal Consumption	Rate of Growth*
1755	4,230	
1760	4,520	0.068
1765	4,950	0.095
1770	5,520	0.115
1775	6,120	0.108
1780	6,750	0.102
1785	7,550	0.118
1790	8,570	0.135
1795	9,570	0.116
1800	10,960	0.145
1805	12,960	0.182
1810	14,790	0.141
1815	16,590	0.121
1820	18,900	0.139
1825	20,900	0.105
1830	24,800	0.186
1835	29,560	0.191
1840	35,270	0.193
1845	41,706	0.182
1850	50,968	0.222
1855	64,500	0.265
1860	80,000	0.240
1865	98,200	0.227
1870	110,400	0.124
1875	133,300	0.207
1880	147,000	0.102
1885	159,400	0.084
1890	181,600	0.139
1895	189,700	0.044
1900	225,200	0.187

*5-year rate. (000)
Source: Mitchell (1988).

Industrialization being born of inanimate energy—in this case, the consumption of coal—it follows that the rate of growth of output would be an increasing function of the rate of growth of coal consumption, *ceteris paribus*. Referring to Equation 1.3 in Chapter 1, the rate of growth of output is an increasing function of the rate of growth of energy consumption [$W(t) = \eta E(t)$]. Table 2.1 reports both the level of, and rate of growth of, coal production in the United Kingdom at five-year intervals from 1755 to 1900.

From a level of 4.230 million tons in 1755, it had increased 12,049 percent to 50.968 million tons in 1850. By 1870, it had more than doubled to 110.4 million tons. At century's end, it had more than doubled again to 225.2 million tons. Referring to column 2, we see that five-year growth rates went from a low of 6.8 percent in 1755–1760, to a high of 24.031 percent in 1855–1860.

Given their broad nature, these data must be interpreted with caution. Ideally, data on industrial consumption of coal in the United Kingdom, not the overall total output of coal, would be required. Such data, unfortunately, are not available (i.e., do not exist). There do, however, exist data, collected by the factory inspectors, in accordance with the Factory Act of 1833, on the use of steam and water power in various U.K. industries from 1835 on. These data, in combination with employment data also included, provide useful information on the extent of inanimate energy-deepening in U.K. industry, especially in the textiles sector.

Table 2.2
Total Power Consumption, Textiles, United Kingdom, 1835–1870

Cotton

Year	Steam	Water	Total	$S_c(t)$	$E_c(t)/S_c(t)$
1835				219	
1838	46	12	58	259	0.2239
1850	71	11	82	331	0.2477
1856	87	9	96	379	0.2532
1861	281	12	293	452	0.6482
1867	190	12	202	401	0.5037
1870	299	8	307	450	0.6822

Wool

Year	Steam	Water	Total	$S_w(t)$	$E_w(t)/S_w(t)$
1835				55	
1838	17	10	27	87	0.3103
1850	23	10	33	154	0.2142
1856	31	9	40	167	0.2395
1861	53	11	64	173	0.3699
1867	85	12	97	262	0.3702
1870	103	12	115	239	0.4811

Miscellaneous

Year	Steam	Water	Total	$S_m(t)$	$E_m(t)/S_m(t)$
1835				33	
1838	7	4	11	42	0.2619
1850	11	3	14	68	0.2058
1856	14	4	18	80	0.2250
1861	32	4	36	94	0.3829
1867	42	5	47	135	0.3489
1870	52	5	57	146	0.3904

Source: Mitchell (1988).

Table 2.2 presents data on power employed, measured in horsepower, in the cotton, wool, and flax/jute/hemp/chinagrass factories from 1835 to 1870, as well as the corresponding employment data. The source of both series are the various returns filed by the factory inspectors and published in the *Sessional Papers of the House of Lords*. Before turning to these data, it bears reminding that workers in factories no longer exerted themselves physically as was the case in the domestic system, but, instead, supervised the spinning machines and looms (power looms). Some, however, were assigned the task(s) of managing feedstocks (inputs and outputs). As such, by dividing total horsepower say in the cotton industry by the total employment, one arrives at a crude measure of inanimate energy per lower-level supervisor $(E(t)/S(t))$. That is, the amount of energy—and hence, work—workers supervised. This ratio provides a measure of energy-deepening over time.

Take, for example, the cotton industry, which in 1838, had 46,000 horsepower of steam power, and 12,000 horsepower of water power, for a total of 58,000 horsepower of inanimate energy. Given the presence of 259,000 workers, it stands to reason that the relevant $E_c(t)/S_c(t)$ ratio stood at 0.2239. This is to say that each worker supervised the equivalent of 0.2239 of a horsepower of inanimate energy. Referring to Column 4, we see that this ratio increased monotonically in time, from 0.2239 in 1838 to 0.6822 in 1870.[3] In practical terms, this implies that supervisors (workers) in the cotton industry were overseeing three times as more inanimate power in 1870 than in 1838, a span of only 32 years. As power is synonymous with work, it follows that they were supervising three times more work in 1870 than in 1838.

This "jump" in inanimate power consumption per worker can be attributed to two factors, the first of which being the declining use of handlooms, referred to earlier (Figure 2.1). Animate energy as a power source declined steadily from 1838 and, by 1870, had virtually disappeared. The second factor is the various technological improvements in the generation of steam power. Foremost among these is the development by Richard Trevithick and Arthur Woolf of the high-pressure, noncondensing steam engine. The latter increased the "indicated" horsepower of existing and new engines far beyond their rated "nominal" horsepower.[4]

Despite the dearth of data on output growth in various British industries for the period under consideration (1800–1900), what is clear is the fact that work as defined in the Newtonian sense increased at unprecedented rates in the United Kingdom. Never before had a country, nation or people increased, in so little time, the amount of work performed. All of this, of course, was achieved by tapping into a store of energy 300 million years old, in the form of coal (Carboniferous era). Not only did the consumption of coal increase in this period, but the efficiency with which it was used also increased, increasing manifold the ability of the United Kingdom to do work.

The Importance of Speed

The manifold increase in U.K. manufacturing output in the nineteenth century resulted from, as argued here, a process of energy-deepening that characterized much of this period. The energy-deepening in question was achieved in two distinct ways, namely intensively and extensively. Starting with the latter, extensive energy-deepening refers to the increase in the number and capacity of spindles and looms in the cotton industry. With Arkwright's spinning jenny, the number of spindles in the U.K. cotton-spinning industry increased manifold. Similarly, with the advent of power looms, the weaving capacity, as measured by the size and number of looms, increased manifold.

A second source of energy-deepening was the many speed-ups that characterized the U.K. textiles industry in the nineteenth century. Existing machines, be they spinning or weaving, were speeded up, making for greater output per period of time. Characteristic of such "speed-ups" is an increase in power consumption per period in time, in keeping with the basic premises of Newtonian production analysis. Improvements in steam engines throughout the nineteenth century, along with improvements in spinning and weaving *per se*, paved the way for increases in the throughput rates per unit of capital (i.e. spindle or loom). Among these was the development and commercial use of the high-pressure steam engine by Richard Trevithick and Arthur Woolf, which increased markedly the speed of execution, and consequently, the rate of output (throughput).

References to speed-ups in the early nineteenth century are relatively few and far-between. However, the few that exist convey the essence of the power revolution that was playing itself out in Great Britain. Take, for example, William Longston's testimony on working conditions in the textiles industry before the Committee on the Factories Bill.

9397. Is the intensity of application and of labour altered, either against or in favour of the operative and of the children employed in mills and factories?—I was a great number of years out of any factory, but those who were my acquaintances during my boyhood have often conversed with me, and they very frequently say that it cannot be less than double in intensity and exertion of physical application.

9398. State why you believe that the labour of those employed has doubled since the first introduction and use of cotton machinery, or at least since you first knew it?—The reason why I believe so is from some calculations which I have been obliged to make, and by my own observation during the time I was manager of a mill in 1830 and 1831, when I had some of the same operations under my own observation.

9399. Have you any objection to put in those calculations?—Certainly not.

9400. It appears by this document that the work done is very greatly increased between the years 1810 and 1832; has the machinery been so altered as to produce that amazing difference, or does it result from accelerating the speed of the machinery?—It is from accelerating the speed generally; and another cause is, that more and more exertion is required from the individual working at the machine; these are the two causes.

9401. Those two causes, then, prove what you have been asserting, namely that double the labour and attendance is now requisite that was formerly required?—I think so.

9402. In spite of the improvements of machinery?—Yes; I believe those that are now working in the same employment as I did when I was a boy, do double the work.

9403. So that there may be a great improvement in machinery, and at the same time a great increase in actual labour to each operative?—Yes.

9404. Has that been, as far as your experience has extended, the consonant result of improvements of machinery in those mills, namely, that the labour of the hands has increased with every improvement in the machinery; rather than diminished?—Yes; the improvements in the machinery have been great, and the same physical exertion, and the same attention as was formerly applied, would certainly produce, in proportion to the altered state of machinery, a much greater quantity and better articles; but, added to that, the increased exertions make the quantities to be such as just now surprised you. (U.K. Committee on Factories Bill 1832, 430)

As is clear from his testimony, machinery speed-ups increased considerably the amount of "work" demanded of the corresponding "lower-level" supervisors. This was the direct result of the fact that not all processes were automated. Faster turning spindles and faster operating looms required more exertion on the part of the "operatives"—that is, those who supervise the machinery (machine operatives). As the data presented earlier, output per lower-level supervisor (stretcher) increased by 200 percent from 1810 to 1832. In the case of mule yarn-spinning, the number of hanks spun, for 480 spindles (*ceteris paribus*), increased by 50 percent between 1806 and 1832. According to Charles Babbage:

In turning from the smaller instruments in frequent use to the larger and more important machines, the economy resulting from the increase in velocity becomes more striking. In converting cast into wrought-iron, a mass of metal, of about a hundredweight, is heated almost to white heat, and placed under a heavy hammer moved by water or steam power. . . . But as it is important that the softened mass of red-hot iron should receive as many blows as possible before it cools, the form of the cam or projection on the axis is such, that the hammer, instead of being lifted to a small height, is thrown up with a jerk, and almost the instant after its strikes against a large beam. . . with such such velocity that by these means about double the number of strokes that can be made in a given time. (Babbage, 1835, 89)

The Role of Capital and Labor

The shift from the domestic system to the factory system altered the nature of both capital and labor. Labor, a source of energy (animate, muscular) and thus of motive drive in the domestic system, was reduced to a supervisory input, overseeing the workings of continuous-flow machinery. The men, women and children who, in the domestic system, had spun and woven cotton, wool, linen etcetera, would, from now on, supervise the workings of steam-power-driven spinning and weaving machines, and managing the various feedstocks (inputs and outputs) in factories. Alfred Marshall would describe this far-reaching change in 1890 in the following terms:

We may now pass to the effects which machinery has in relieving that excessive muscular strain which a few generations ago was the common lot of more than half the working men even in such a country as England. In other trades, machinery has lightened man's labours. The house carpenters, for instance, make things of the same kind as those used by our forefathers, with much less toil for themselves. . . . Nothing could be more narrow or monotonous than the occupation of a weaver of plain stuffs in the old time. But now, one woman will manage four or more looms, each of which does many times as much work in the course of a day as the old hand loom did; and her work is much less monotonous and calls for much more judgment than his did. (Marshall, 1890, 218)

The key word here is "manage." The woman he refers to now "manages," and, hence, no longer weaves. Moreover, as he points out, each power loom "does many times as much work in the course of a day as the old hand loom did." Conventionally defined labor productivity, it follows, increased manifold.[5] E. Baines, in the *History of the Cotton Manufacture*, published in 1835, refers to a tenfold increase in productivity for weavers.

A very good hand weaver, 25 or 30 years of age, will weave two pieces of 9-8ths shirting per week, each 24 yards long, containing 100 shoots of weft in an inch; the reed of the cloth being a 44 Bolton count, and the warp and weft hanks to 40 hanks to the lb.
In 1823, a steam-loom weaver, about 15 years of age, attending two looms, could weave seven similar pieces in a week.
In 1826, a steam-loom weaver, about 15 years of age, attending to two looms, could weave twelve similar pieces in a week; some could weave fifteen pieces.
In 1833, a steam-loom weaver, from 15–20 years of age, assisted by a girl about 12 years of age, attending to four looms, can weave eighteen similar pieces in a week; some can weave twenty pieces. (Baines, 1835, 240)

However, at this point in time, an important distinction is in order, namely, that between energy-based measures of productivity and organization-based measures of productivity. In the domestic system, workers physically exerted themselves, spinning and/or weaving, in addition to supervising the workings of their animate energy (i.e., their bodies) and the tools (rudimentary spinning wheels and hand looms). In the factory system, their job task (job definition) was reduced considerably. Specifically, it would consist, almost solely, of supervision. As such, it follows that the relevant productivity measure as found in the factory system is organization-based (see Table 1.3 on page 20).

Capital also underwent a major transformation. Specifically, the simple tools of the domestic system (spinning wheels and hand looms) were fitted with a power source (rotative power). Machinery, as a result, consisted of rudimentary tools fitted with an inanimate power source. Complex shafting, belting and gearing systems were used to transmit the torque generated by steam engines to the spindles and the looms. Capital costs per spindle or per square yard of weaving capacity increased substantially, owing to power-related costs, and to the need for more reliable spindles and looms.[6] Under the domestic system, spinning wheels and hand looms were fashioned out of wood (hardwood and softwood), harvested, in most cases, in local forests. The demands of high-throughput, continuous-flow production, however, were such that metal spindles and looms were needed, increasing, as such, the cost of capital. This, as it turns out, was true of all steam-power-driven industries.

As I shall argue later, these costs figured prominently in the works of classical political economists. The new drive technology required massive investments, both in steam engines, and in the accompanying tools, typically fashioned out of steel as opposed to wood. Consequently, the problem of saving and investment would, over the next half-century, occupy center stage in political economy.

Steam Power and the Problem of Exchange

The shift from the domestic system to the factory system, and the subsequent improvements in power-drive technology, increased vastly Great Britain's industrial capacity. More wool and cotton could be spun, more thread could be woven, more iron could be smelted, more steel could be rolled, more knives and forks could be stamped than ever before in the history of material civilization. The relevant question, however, is whether money income increased commensurately with productive capacity. Did Alfred Marshall's "managers" whose productivity increased radically earn comparable money wages?

Under the domestic system, higher money income went hand-in-hand with higher output. This owed to the relevant exchange technology. Specifically, merchants' demands were not predicated on producers' decisions in factor markets. This changed with the shift to the factory system. Now, merchants' demands would depend on producers' decisions, notably on the overall level of wage income.

Thus, the relevant question is whether the U.K. economy was beset by the problem of underincome in the nineteenth century. The answer to this question is, by no means, obvious. The reasons are numerous, including the ubiquitous problem of insufficent data. It is well-known that data for this period are sparse, and that those that exist are of questionable worth, thus limiting any serious attempt at testing for the presence of underincome. It is important to remember that, owing to the very nature of the process of energy-deepening in the nineteenth century (i.e., being a continuous phenomenon), the problem of underincome would not have been confined to a single year, or decade, but characterized much of the century. For example, the shift away from condensing engines (Newcommen, Savary, Watt), and over to high-pressure engines in the mid-1850s, increased machine speed per period of time, and, hence, increased output, thus fostering the necessary preconditions for underincome.

Theoretically, the problem of underincome refers to the inability of a private, competitive economy to generate money income (real income) at the same rate as it generates potential output (capacity). Among the main reasons are, as pointed out earlier, the failure of money income to rise commensurately at the producer level, itself the result of the absence of private incentives to increase wages, the residual nature of profits and the very nature of merchants' demand for final output (being based on the level of money income). To demonstrate the existence of the problem of underincome, one would need to show either (1) the presence of significant unused capacity, (2) the joint presence of increased productivity per worker (conventionally measured productivity) and a relatively constant nominal and real wage and (3) rising unemployment, or (1) increased output, (2) relatively constant money income and (3) falling prices. The first two conditions describe the presence of underincome in a fixed (constant) product price environment, while the latter describes it in a flexible (variable) product price environment. Both, it bears noting, result from the failure of money income to rise commensurately with the value of output. In the former, output does not rise in step with potential capacity, while in the latter, it does, resulting in generalized price deflation as the resulting value of output exceeds money income. Producers cut prices in the hope of increasing demand.

There are other possibilities such as the in-between case of excess capacity combined with price deflation. Say that capacity increases by 100 percent, but that firms choose to increase output only by 50 percent. In this case, excess capacity and price deflation will coexist.

Let us now turn to the case at hand. The evidence presented above is unequivocal: productive capacity increased manifold in the U.K. textile industry throughout the nineteenth century. The relevant empirical questions, it follows, are: (1) how did this affect actual output? and (2) how did this affect money output (nominal)? For example, did textile mills consistently produce at their new, higher capacity, or at levels that the market could absorb (fixed price), or somewhere in between? Unfortunately, the available data prevent us from answering this question, potential output data not being available.

Actual output data, however, show a marked increase in the United Kingdom's ability to transform imported raw cotton into thread and cloth. Table 2.3 shows that cotton consumption in the United Kingdom increased from 52 million pounds in 1800 to 1,084 million pounds in 1860 (just prior to the U.S. Civil War). The number of factory workers went from 100,000 in

1810 to 427,000 in 1860. The relevant question, it follows, is, did money income in the cotton industry increased commensurately? I contend that it did not owing principally to the lack of private incentives to increase wages. Remember, profits in the factory system are a residual form of payment.

Unfortunately, there are no data on the level of money income in the cotton industry for this period. Ideally, given the nature of the exchange technology, one would want data on outstanding bank credit for textile firms. Such data are not available. The only money supply data (bank credit) available are Bank of England financial data. Column 8 in Table 2.3 shows money in circulation as defined by the Bank of England, from 1833 to 1900. In the five-year interval 1850–1855, total coal consumption in the United Kingdom increased 26.5 percent, cotton consumption increased 42.6 percent, factory employment increased 12 percent, while money in circulation (Bank of England notes) increased 1.9 percent. While the former refer to a sector while the latter refers to the U.K. economy as a whole, the comparison is nevertheless suggestive. Specifically, while the value of output had increased markedly, the level of money income had not, or at least, not in proportion.

Table 2.3
Coal and Cotton Consumption, Factory Workers, and Money Supply, United Kingdom, 1800–1860

Year	Coal Cons.[1]	Growth Rate	Cotton Cons.[2]	Growth Rate	Factory Workers[3]	Growth Rate	Money Supply[4]	Growth Rate
1800	10,960	0.14	52					
1805	12,960	0.18	59	0.13				
1810	14,790	0.14	124	1.10	100			
1815	16,590	0.12	81	-0.34	114	0.14		
1820	18,900	0.13	120	0.48	126	0.10		
1825	20,900	0.15	167	0.39	173	0.37		
1830	24,800	0.18	248	0.48	185	0.06		
1835	29,560	0.19	318	0.28	220	0.18	18,207	
1840	35,270	0.19	459	0.44	262	0.19	16,839	-0.08
1845	41,706	0.18	607	0.32	273	0.04	20,674	0.18
1850	50,968	0.22	588	-0.03	331	0.21	19,448	0.06
1855	64,500	0.26	839	0.42	371	0.12	19,830	0.02
1860	80,000	0.24	1,084	0.29	427	0.15	21,252	0.06

1. (000 tons); 2. (000,000 lbs).; 3. (000); 4. (000,000).
Source: Mitchell (1988).

This result, while consistent with the predictions of the theory, must be viewed as tentative at best. Remember that there is no direct evidence that money income in the textile industry did not increase in step with potential output. Let me now turn to other evidence. As pointed out above, firms experiencing increases in productive capacity can do either of two (three) things. They can produce at capacity, and literally flood the market (?) with thread, yarn, or cloth, they can continue producing at previous levels, maintaining price, or, lastly, choose some combination thereof. The output data presented earlier, in combination with the price data presented in Column 5 of Table 2.4, indicate that firms chose to increase output, provoking price decreases throughout much of the nineteenth century. For example, the price index for cotton went from 11.73 in 1819, to 6.53 in 1835, to 3.73 in 1871. One could argue that this reflects the general conditions of oversupply that characterized the industry for most of the nineteenth century.

Table 2.4
Price Indexes, United Kingdom, 1805–1871

Year	Agriculture	Industry	Raw Cotton	Cotton
1805	175	166		
1810	190	198		
1815	164	164		
1819	160	134	9.58	11.73
1827	128	106	6.56	8.51
1835	118	106	10.25	6.53
1851	94	89	5.52	3.43
1861	117	114	8.56	3.38
1871	119	112	8.56	3.73

Source: Mitchell (1988).

Policy Debates

Understanding output, wage and price developments in the U.K. textile industry in the early nineteenth century, I maintain, is essential to understanding the various policy debates, and, as will be shown later, the bulk of the writings in political economy in the nineteenth century. Before turning to the latter, I examine, in some detail, two policy debates, notably, the creation of the National Regeneration Society in 1833, and the Repeal of the Corn Laws in 1846. Both, I shall maintain, were direct responses to the problem of underincome, as described here.

By the 1830s, it was clear that steam had conferred upon the U.K., especially its textile industry, productive powers that far exceeded its ability to consume, resulting in generalized (within manufacturing) excess supply and price and wage deflation. As nominal product prices and wages fell, so did the "standard of living" in manufacturing, owing, in large measure, to the sectorial nature of the price deflation in question. Food prices, for example, remained relatively constant throughout the nineteenth century, despite the repeal of the Corn Laws in 1846.

The ultimate irony had befallen the textile industry. More productive than ever before, working conditions and profit rates had deteriorated significantly —owing to underincome. This provoked a number of policy debates, ranging from reforming the institution of profit maximization to free trade. For example, one finds the National Regeneration Society advocating a sector-wide reduction in output. The society's ultimate goal, as outlined by John Fielden, was to improve the "condition of the productive classes."

The proposal submitted to the productive classes, recommending them to lessen their productions, in some articles one-third, in order that they may improve their condition, is so novel and unprecedented in its character, and at first appears so much opposed to accomplish its end, that I should have felt some astonishment if it had not called forth the opposition of thinking men, who are not in possession of the facts which demonstrate the necessity there is for the productive classes to adopt such a course; so far, therefore, from feeling any uneasiness at your conduct in condemning the proposal plan of eight hours' work for the present day's full day wages. (Fielden, 1972 [1833], 11)

To this end, cooperation would have to replace competition. Manufacturers would have to, as a group, reduce output, in the name of the public good. Unprecedented productivity growth in the textile industry in the presence of excessive competition, Fielden argued, had contributed to lower wages and prices.

These tables present a history of the works of those engaged in the cotton trade, for the eighteen years ending in 1832; and I have no hesitation in saying that history presents no parallel to a like increase in the taking away from the producers, for the those who do not produce. . . . When nearly three times the quantity manufactured in 1832, was paid for with less money by two millions three quarters at thirteen millions, than little more than one third of the quantity commanded in 1815, and to manufacture which increased in 1832, more than double the number of persons were employed, can you wonder, sir, at the strange anomaly of increased production being accompanied by increased and increasing distress among the manufacturers and their workmen? (Fielden, 1972 [1833], 11)

Theoretically speaking, the National Regeneration Society advocated replacing unbridled competition, the effects of which were ubiquitous, with a form of cooperation. Textile producers would agree to reduce output by 10 percent, and work hours by eight. The problem, in other words, was, paradoxically, too much output, coupled with too much competition. By reducing output, nominal product prices would rise, restoring profit margins and wages, and, in the process, increasing overall sector (labor and capital) welfare.

The second policy measure consisted of reforming, specifically, repealing, the Corn Laws. The large majority of textile manufacturers felt that by repealing the Corn Laws, U.K. imports of food would rise, and, reciprocally,

U.K. exports of textiles and other manufactures would rise. Free trade would be a win-win strategy. First, lower cereal prices would, as Ricardo argued, reduce the cost of living, and, consequently, the cost of labor. Second, and more importantly (in 1846), it would stimulate foreign demand for U.K. finished goods, and in the process lessening the link between domestic wages—and hence, overall wage income—and the demand for textiles in a producer-merchant exchange technology setting. Theoretically, it would solve the indeterminacy referred to earlier. Sales abroad would prompt merchants, regardless of domestic wage income, to increase orders, thus stimulating the manufacturing sector.

As it turned out, this was the preferred solution. The reasons are many. First, as pointed out, foreign trade alters the nature of the "exchange technology," weakening the role of domestic wage income in merchants' demand for textiles. Aggregate demand would no longer depend solely on wage income in the United Kingdom.[7] Outlets could be found for U.K. textiles, thus putting an end to years of excess supply and price deflation. Also, corn could be imported at lower prices, eliminating any upward pressure on wages.

The Problem of Income Distribution

As argued in this chapter, the shift from the domestic system to the factory system contributed greatly to increasing U.K. value added (to raw cotton, wool, linen, silk etcetera). The principal cause was, again as shown earlier, the shift from animate, muscular energy, characteristic of the domestic system, to inanimate energy in the form of steam power. Continuous-flow production processes altered the nature of work, transforming spinners and weavers into machine operatives. Productivity increased radically. This raised the question of distribution. Who would get what? How would the surplus of total value (price times potential output) over costs (wages, energy costs, raw materials) be apportioned?

To begin, I shall limit myself to the textiles industry, focusing on the distribution of textile value added (profits and real wages in kind). This will be followed by a discussion of the problem in a two-sector context, namely agriculture and manufacturing. Given that textile workers in the nineteenth century allocated a considerable part of their income to food, it stands to reason that the relevant real wage would depend greatly on the price of food. Last, I shall examine the intersectorial consequences of an increase in the relative price of food (in terms of textiles).

The first real wage, defined in the real wage "in kind," is obtained by deflating the nominal wage paid in the textile industry by the product price or product price index. The real wage, so defined, provides a measure of each factor's command over the good produced, which, in this case, consists of textile value added.

Table 2.5 presents data on product prices, raw materials, and value added for *Second Quality of 74 Calico, Common Quality of 30 Hanks Water Twist,* and *One Pound of 40 Hanks Copt Weft* for the period extending from 1815 to 1832. What is particularly noteworthy is the fact that in all three cases, the per unit product price declined monotonically. In the case of Second Quality 74 Calico, it was halved from 1815 to 1832; and in the cases of 30 Hanks Water Twist and 40 Hanks Copt Weft, it was reduced by two-thirds. In all three cases, the price of the intermediate input declined, as did the "Sum left for labour, expenses, and profits." In the case of Second Quality 74 Calico, it fell from 4s., 1-3/4d. to 1s., 9d., a decrease of 54 percent. In the cases of 30 Hanks Water Twist and 40 Hanks Copt Weft, it decreased by 66 percent.

Table 2.5
Output and Input Prices, Selected U.K. Textiles, 1815–1832

Second Quality 74s Calico Made by Power Loom

Year	Raw Material Price	Sum left for labour, expenses, and profits	Product Price
1815	7s,0d	11s,0d	18s,0d
1824	3s,0d	6s,0d	9s,0d
1831	2s,0d	3s,9d	5s,9d
1832	2s,3.5d	3s,2.5d	5s,6d

Half-Elf Velveteens-20lbs. Weight

Year	Raw Material Price	Sum left for labour, expenses, and profits	Product Price
1815	34s,8d	65s,4d	100s,0d
1824	15s,7d	36s,1d	51s,8d
1831	10s,0d	23s,4d	33s,4d
1832	11s,4d	18s,8d	30s,0d

30 Hanks Water Twist

Year	Raw Material Price	Sum left for labour, expenses and profits	Product Price
1815	1s,10d	1s,4.75d	3s,3d
1824	0s,9.75d	0s,10.75d	1s,8d
1831	0s,6.5d	0s,5.5d	1s,0d
1832	0s,7.25d	0s,5.25d	1s,0.5d

Source: Fielden (1972 [1833]), 8.

Table 2.6
Wages Paid by a Very Respectable Manufacturer [William Cannon], 1815–1832

Year	48 Reed	56Reed	70Reed
1815	11s,6d	15s,0d	21s,0d
1816	9s,0d	11s,0d	17s,0d
1817	6s,6d	8s,6d	11s,0d
1818	8s,0d	10s,0d	12s,6d
1819	7s,0d	9s,0d	11s,6d
1820	6s,6d	8s,0d	10s,6d
1821	8s,6d	10s,6d	12s,6d
1822	6s,0d	8s,6d	10s,6d
1823	6s,6d	8s,6d	10s,0d
1824	6s,6d	8s,6d	10s,0d
1825	6s,6d	8s,0d	10s,0d
1826	5s,0d	6s,6d	8s,6d
1827	4s,6d	5s,6d	8s,0d
1828	4s,6d	5s,6d	8s,0d
1829	4s,0d	5s,6d	8s,0d
1830	3s,6d	5s,0d	7s,0d
1831	3s,6d	5s,0d	7s,0d
1832	3s,6d	5s,0d	7s,0d

Source: Fielden (1972 [1833]), 30.

Clearly, throughout this period, product prices and wages decreased monotonically. As product prices fell, producers lowered wages. Table 2.6 presents nominal wages paid by "a very respectable Manufacturer [William Cannon]" from 1815 to 1832 for three different loom sizes [48, 56, 70 Reed]." We see that in all three cases, nominal wages fell by roughly 64 percent, in step with the fall in product prices. This allows us to conclude that real wages, in terms of textile value added, remained relatively constant over this period.

Thus, it is clear that the manifold increase in output (value added) did not bestow any real gains on workers (lower-level supervisors). They took home, in kind, as much in 1833 as in 1815. Further, one can only surmise that the owners of capital (machinery) appropriated the large share of the energy rents, again defined in kind.

Next, we consider developments in real wages where the relevant product price index includes food. While the price of clothing decreased monotonically in this period, the price of food remained relatively constant. Table 2.7 presents cost-of-living data in the United Kingdom as presented in Fielden (1972 [1833]). Column 1 reports the weekly cost for a family of six of "milk, bacon, potatoes, coffee, tea, and sugar." From 1815 to 1832, this cost remained relatively constant. The price of oatmeal and flour (Column 2), however, decreased by 25 percent. The weekly cost for food (Column 3) for six persons decreased by 16 percent. Clearly, the real wage in the textile industry in the intervening years fell considerably. As Column 4 indicates, the surplus weekly sum the family could earn above the cost of food had been wiped out. In 1814, this surplus stood at 66 percent of earnings (family of six); by 1833, it had been reduced to zero.

In short, the manifold increase in production and productivity in the intervening period did little to better the workers' living standard, whose real wage decreased dramatically, but did, however, advantage farmers and landowners, whose real income—wages, rents, profit—increased with the fall in the price of clothing. This, I maintain, signaled the beginning of increased sectorial tensions in the U.K. economy, and consequently, in U.K. society. Manufacturing, the crown jewel of the U.K. economy, was floundering under the weight of excess supply, while agriculture, a sector unchanged for centuries, was characterized by excess demand.

Table 2.7
Cost of Living Data, United Kingdom, 1815–1832

Year	1	2	3	4
1815	5s,0.5d	3s,11d	8s,11.5d	19s,11.5d
1816	5s,0.5d	3s,10d	8s,10.5d	12s,8.5d
1817	5s,1.5d	7s,6d	12s,7.5d	6s,3.5d
1818	5s,1.5d	5s,4.5d	10s,6d	13s,1d
1819	5s,0.5d	4s,1.5d	9s,2d	10s,7d
1820	5s,1.5d	4s,4.5d	9s,6d	8s,7d
1821	4s,11.5d	3s,7d	8s,6.5d	14s,6.25d
1822	4s,11.5d	3s,4.5d	8s,1d	9s,6d
1823	4s,11.5d	4s,4.5d	9s,4d	7s,5d
1824	4s,11.5d	4s,6d	9s,5.5d	4s,5d
1825	4s,11.5d	3s,10.5d	8s,10d	5s,0.5d
1826	3s,8.5d	3s,7.5d	7s,4d	0s,2.75d
1827	4s,11.5d	4s,3d	9s,2.5d	9s,0.5d
1828	4s,11.5d	3s,3.5d	8s,3d	2s,1.5d
1829	2s,5.5d	3s,9d	6s,2.5d	0s,0.5d
1830	4s,1.5d	4s,1.5d	9s,1d	0s,2d
1831	4s,11.5d	4s,0d	8s,11.5d	1s,7.25d
1832	4s,5d	3s,0d	7s,5d	0s,1.75d

1-Cost of milk, bacon, potatoes, coffee, tea, sugar.
2-Cost of oatmeal, 25.5lbs or 17lbs and the remainder in flour.
3-Weekly amount for food for six persons.
4-The surplus weekly sum the family could earn above cost of food.
Source: Fielden (1972 [1833]), 27.

Conclusions

The shift from the domestic to the factory system constituted a watershed in the history of material civilization (Beaudreau, 1998). Output increased markedly as high throughput, continuous-flow production techniques replaced what had, until then, been small-scale, low throughput artisanal production techniques. With the good came the bad. Among the latter were the problems of exchange and distribution. Potential output increased greatly; however, money income failed to increase in step, resulting in underincome. In hindsight, these changes were thrust upon Great Britain without any fore- or afterthought.

As it turns out, these questions were never answered, owing, in large measure, to the absence of a theory of production inclusive of energy, and the absence of a empirically consistent theory of exchange. As I shall proceed to show, production theory throughout the nineteenth century remained decidedly Paleolithic in its view of production processes. Exchange theory was, as it turns out, in even worse shape, owing in large measure to the nineteenth-century aversion to all things mercantile, of which specie (money) was the most prominent.

PRODUCTION, EXCHANGE, AND DISTRIBUTION AS SEEN BY NINETEENTH-CENTURY POLITICAL ECONOMISTS

With the benefit of hindsight, it is clear that the shift from the domestic system to the factory system ranks as one of the greatest achievements of modern civilization. Specifically, it lifted what had, since the dawning of the Neolithic era, been the main obstacle to unlimited wealth, namely the muscular, human—or animal—energy constraint.[8] Never again would the transformation of the earth's abundant natural resources be constrained by muscular energy, or, for that matter, unpredictable wind- or water-based energy. More importantly, the yoke of 2 million years of grueling, physical, often times crippling labor had been lifted. Output growth, it therefore follows, would, from this point on, track energy consumption growth, specifically the growth of "fire power" consumption. Clearly, the future looked infinitely brighter.

The problem, as it turned out, was getting there. How would Great Britain move from an economy dominated by small-scale, muscle power-driven concerns to one dominated by large-scale "fire-powered" factories. Where would it find the capital? Would its savings be sufficient? Would the "extent of its markets" permit the "division of labor" made possible by "fire power?" Such were the questions on the minds of a number of moral philosophers, politicians, businessmen and academics. In this section, it will be argued that early political economy was, in large measure, a response to these questions.

For example, I maintain that Adam Smith's *An Inquiry into the Nature and Causes of the Wealth of Nations*, was largely an attempt at identifying and analyzing the problems associated with moving to the higher growth path defined by fire power, and, that David Ricardo's *The Principles of Political Economy and Taxation*, was a politically motivated attempt at understanding the effects of higher food prices on the functional distribution of income, savings, investment and, ultimately, on economic growth in the United Kingdom.

Early political economy, as I shall argue, was overridingly normative in nature, having little in common with present-day positive political economy. Absent was any need or desire to accurately model production or distribution, let alone exchange. For Smith, Ricardo and "classical" political economists in general, there was one singular objective: moving to and staying on the new, higher growth path. The means were many, including free trade, which, by reducing the price of foodstuffs at the turn of the century, would lead to lower real wages, thus increasing profits, savings and investment. The distribution of income, as Ricardo maintained, was the key issue for in it lay the key to the future of the United Kingdom's capital stock, and, consequently, long-term growth. This section is organized chronologically and thematically. I begin with the early classical political economists. I then turn to the utopian socialists and radicals, and end with the neoclassical political economists.

The Classical Political Economists

How did early political economists perform? How did they see the changes that had been thrust upon Great Britain by the introduction of the steam engine? How did they approach this new energy form, and its myriad consequences? As I shall attempt to show here, they performed rather poorly regarding the former, and admirably regarding the latter (i.e., the consequences). Energy was, for all intents and purposes, absent from their analysis. Foremost among the causes of this oversight was the absence of a scientific tradition in moral philosophy.[9] As such, by contrast with contemporary political economy where modeling (formalizing) production processes is a goal in and of itself, classical political economists had no such interest. It sufficed to state that output was produced with labor and machinery, the former being an active factor input (source of value), and the latter being a passive one (Ricardo, 1965 [1817]).

That this was the case should not come as a surprise. After all, until then, there was no need for such a tradition. Production processes in seventeenth-century Great Britain were Neolithic in scope. The means of creating wealth had gone unchanged for thousands of years, which explains, in large part, the absence of a "science of production" per se. Put otherwise, there was simply no need. Against this bucolic setting was thrust a new power source that increased productivity, altered the nature of work, and transformed the geographical localization of production (domestic system to factory system), thus altering forever the economic landscape. Also lacking was a theory of exchange and a theory of distribution.

Adam Smith and David Ricardo

I begin with Adam Smith's *An Inquiry into the Nature and Causes of the Wealth of Nations* which, I maintain, is the first attempt at understanding the changes thrust upon British society by the "energy revolution."[10] The division of labor, according to Smith, had increased Great Britain's potential to create wealth. The problem, however, was moving to the new, higher growth path. The transition, according to Smith, was neither automatic, nor instantaneous. The division of labor, the ultimate source of wealth, was restricted by the extent of the market. As I shall argue, this is, in essence, the problem of underincome referred to above.

In Book 1, Chapter 1, entitled "Of the Causes of Improvement in the Productive Powers of Labour, and of the Order according to which its Produce is Naturally distributed among the different Ranks of the People," he begins the *Wealth of Nations* with an in-depth examination of the factors underlying the increasing "productive powers of labor."

According to Smith, the principal factor is the division of labor, broadly defined.

The greatest improvement in the productive powers of labour, and the greatest part of the skill, dexterity, and judgement with which it is anywhere directed, or applied, seem to have been the effects of the division of labour. (Smith, 1990 [1776], 3)

The division of labor, he proceeded to argue, acts upon labor productivity in three ways, namely in terms of the "increased dexterity in every particular workman," the "saving of the time which is commonly lost in passing from one species of work to another," and, lastly, to "the invention of a great number of machines which facilitate and abridge labour, and enable one man to do the work of many" (Smith, 1990 [1776], 5).

If, as I maintain, the *Wealth of Nations* is about in the "energy revolution," then why is *machinery* presented last? Why is it that energy, or power is not so much as mentioned? The reasons include (1) the state of the art of the science of heat in the late eighteenth century, (2) the state of production theory at this time, and (3) Smith's objectives. The first two are self-evident. The science of heat was still decades away, as was the very notion of "energy." The best he could do, it therefore follows, was to refer to power and machinery. Perhaps the most important reason, however, is the underlying nature of the *Wealth of Nations*. Specifically, the *Wealth of Nations* was not so much an attempt at formalizing the "science of wealth" per se, as it was an attempt to (1) convince the British public of the great potential wealth made possible by machinery and, ultimately, by the steam engine, and (2) to alert it to the factors preventing it from reaching this potential, including the notion that the "division of labor" is limited by the "extent of the market."

As argued earlier, the shift from the domestic system to the factory system altered both the underlying nature of production and the underlying nature of work. Specifically, inanimate energy replaced animate energy, reducing labor to a supervisory input (i.e., machine operatives). Labor, as such, was no longer physically productive, but, rather, was "organizationally productive." Theoretically speaking, machinery did not increase labor productivity, labor being no longer physically productive.[11]

Contrast this with Smith's view of machinery and its effets on labor productivity. Throughout the *Wealth of Nations*, it is assumed that machinery increases labor productivity. Titles such as "Of the Causes of Improvement in the Productive Powers of Labour, and the Order According to Which Its Produce Is Naturally Distributed among the Different Ranks of the People," connote the notion that labor is more productive, when, in actual fact, it is no longer physically productive. I refer to this as the "laborcentricity" of classical production theory, and attribute it to the Paleolithic nature of classical production theory. Labor was assumed to be physically productive. Technological innovation was, as such, seen as being labor-productivity augmenting.

This raises an important issue, namely, fairness. Specifically, are these criticisms fair? Can I, or anyone else, be justified in criticizing Smith's work in the then embryonic "science of wealth?" The answer, in my view, is both no and yes. No for the simple reason that Smith was operating in an intellectual vacuum as far as the "science of wealth" was concerned. He had little to work with from both natural and moral philosophy. On the other hand, one could argue that these criticisms are justified on historical grounds. For example, in my view, it is useful to know that Smith's writings on production are theoretically and empirically inconsistent, if only to follow the course of subsequent developments.

In the normal course of events, David Ricardo, with the benefit of fifty years of the factory system, would have improved, refined, corrected and extended Smith's "positive" work on the nature and causes of the wealth of nations. Less emphasis would have been placed on the first two causes of the division of labor, and more on the third, namely fire-powered machinery. By 1815, the Watt-Boulton rotary steam engine was commonplace in U.K. industry, and on the Continent. Paradoxically, nowhere in *The Principles of Political Economy and Taxation*, published in 1817, does Ricardo mention either "fire power," "steam power" or "steam engine." In Chapter 20, entitled "Value and Riches, Their Distinctive Properties," he refers, albeit indirectly, to the effects of steam power on overall wealth.

Value, then, essentially differs from riches, for value depends not on abundance, but on the difficulty or facility of production. The labour of a million of men in manufactures will always produce the same value, but will not always produce the same riches. By the invention of machinery, by improvements in skill, by a better division of labour, or by the discovery of new markets, where more advantageous exchanges may be made, a million of men may produce double, or treble the amount of riches, of "necessaries, conveniences and amusements," in one state of society that they could produce in another, but they will not, on that account, add anything to value. (Ricardo, 1965 [1817], 182)

Judging by the figures presented, it is clear that the effects of fire power on output were, in his eyes, insignificant. Fire power had lifted the yoke that was the energy constraint, a constraint which dated back to the Paleolithic era. Unfortunately, both he and Smith, not to mention other classical political economists, failed to identify by name fire power as the root cause of the sweeping changes in early nineteenth-century Great Britain.

This, I maintain, had disasterous consequences, notably in the areas of classical value theory and classical distribution theory. As if oblivious to the changing role of labor in production processes, Smith and Ricardo placed it at the center of value theory.[12] Accordingly, the greater the labor content, measured in hours, the higher the price. Clearly, from a strictly technical point of view, output in factories was increasing in the consumption of water/ steam power, not in lower-level supervisors, which, as argued earlier, constitutes an organization input. It follows that, from the outset, classical political economy in general, and classical production theory in particular, were misspecified.

Another unfortunate consequence was the machinery-labor productivity nexus that runs throughout the writings of Smith, Ricardo and other classical political economists. According to Samuel Hollander, Smith viewed machinery as labor productivity increasing: "In a more precise sense, Smith recognized that certain refinements in the degree of specialization entail extensions in the period of production; for the invention of machines is portrayed as the outcome of the division of labor, and the use of machinery increases the roundaboutness of the process with the resultant increases in labour productivity" (Hollander, 1987, 76). Here, the relevant issue is the definition of productivity. As argued earlier, steam power-driven machinery had rendered human, muscular energy redundant, transforming (reducing) labor into a supervisory input. Consequently, workers were no longer productive in the physical sense, but, instead, were productive in the organizational sense (See Chapter 1). That is, their presence was vital to the continued, uninterrupted operation of the various machines.

Clearly, classical political economists failed to recognize these important changes. The raises the question, why? Why did they fail to recognize an, consequently, formalize the new power-drive technology that was steam? Why were they unable to see the parallels between animate, human, muscular energy and inanimate energy (despite the fact that the latter was measured in terms of the former, that is horsepower? The answer, in my view, is relatively simple: classical political economy had, from the start, little to do with science as we know it today. Unlike political economy today, where knowledge of production, irrespective of policy, is an end in and of itself, in the late eighteenth/early nineteenth century, it was not. Put bluntly, there was no need for it. As such, only works that addressed specific problems were deemed to be of any value (use?). The success of Smith and Ricardo as writers, I maintain, owed to the practical nature of the issues they chose to address. Foremost in Smith's mind were the obstacles to industrialization, notably the "extent of the market." Foremost in Ricardo's mind were the obstacles to ongoing industrialization and growth, notably higher corn prices and wages, and higher taxes. The latter point is conveyed by the titles of his two most cited works, *The Principles of Political Economy and Taxation,* and "Essay on the Influence of a Low Price of Corn on the Profit of Stock."

This finding is consistent with Smith biographer Samuel Hollander's views on Smith's work.

The main purpose of the *Wealth of Nations* was evidently not to provide an analytic framework for its own sake. The object of the work was ultimately to define the necessary conditions for rapid economic development in contemporary circumstances and Smith's treatment of the price mechanism must accordingly, in the final resort, be considered with this end in view. (Hollander, 1973, 307)

I now turn to the problem of exchange. As pointed out earlier, the shift from the domestic system to the factory system altered the technology of exchange. First, given the prohibitive cost of capital (tools and energy-related capital—Watt-Boulton steam engines) it led to the creation of a new social and economic class, namely, the factory owners. Until then, the ownership of tools, supervision and energy had been concentrated at the family farm/work unit level. An important consequence, as far as the problem of exchange is concerned, was the emergence of a new set of market coordination agents, namely producers. The latter would demand trade credit, intermediate inputs, labor, and energy. Output would then be purchased by merchants. More importantly, orders for consumption and capital goods would depend on aggregate factor income (wages and profits). Lastly, the owners of capital would be remunerated from the proceeds of sales to merchants. [13]

The relevant question, as far as Smith and Ricardo are concerned, is whether they were aware of these changes. Were they aware of the possibility of underincome? The answer, as it turns out, is no. While Smith devoted a nonnegligible amount of time and effort to "monetary issues," the problem of underincome was never identified. That is not to say, however, that Smith saw the transition to higher growth paths as being frictionless; as pointed out earlier, the *Wealth of Nations* was, in essence, an account of the obstacles preventing the U.K. economy from moving to a higher growth path.

There is evidence that Smith was aware of the impact of the shift from the domestic system to the factory system on the relevant exchange technology. As pointed out in Chapter 1, from a historical point of view, specialization is increasing in energy consumption. Autarky, in general, is synonymous with low levels of energy consumption per capita. Trade, on the other hand, goes hand in hand with high levels of energy consumption per capita. Money, being the medium of trade, is increasing in energy consumption. Smith, I maintain, recognized this. Chapter IV of Book I, entitled "Of the Origin and Use of Money" establishes the existence of a relationship between the division of labor and money.

When the division of labour has been once thoroughly established, it is but a very small part of a man's wants which the produce of his own labour can supply. He supplies the far greater part of them by exchanging that surplus part of the produce of his own labour, which is over and above his consumption, for such parts of the produce of other men's labour as he has occasion for.... But when the division of labour first began to take place, this power of exchanging must frequently have been very much clogged and embarrassed in its operations. (Smith, 1990 [1776], 11)

Book II shows his appreciation of the prominent role of "money" in production. Consider, for example, the following passage from Book II, Chapter 1, entitled "Of the Division of Stock," in which he describes the "two ways in which a capital may be employed so as to yield a revenue or profit to its employer."

First, it may be employed in raising, manufacturing, or purchasing goods, and selling them again with a profit. The capital employed in this manner yields no revenue or profit to its employer, while it remains in his possession, or continues in the same shape. The goods of the merchant yield him no revenue or profit till he sells them for money and the money yields him as little until it is again exchanged for goods. His capital is continually going from him in one shape, and returning to him in another, and it is only by means of such circulation, or successive exchanges, that it can yield him any profit. Such capitals, therefore, may very well be called circulating capitals. (Smith, 1990 [1776], 133)

To Smith, profits are clearly a residual form of income. This, however, is of no apparent consequence. The problem of underincome is not broached, at least not directly. It is implicitly assumed that the value of circulating capital is identically equal to the value of production.

The problem of underincome, however, is present, albeit indirectly. In Chapter III of Book I, entitled "That the Division of Labour Is Limited by the Extent of the Market," Smith argues that the division of labor—read, mechanization—is limited by the extent of the market.

As it is the power of exchanging that gives occasion to the division of labour, so the extent of this must always be limited by the extent of that power, or, in other words, by the extent of the market. When the market is very small, no person can have any encouragement to dedicate himself entirely to one employment, for want of the power to exchange all that surplus part of his own labour, which is over and above his own consumption, for such parts of the produce of other men's labour as he has occasion for. (Smith, 1990 [1776], 9)

One could argue that this is a form of underincome, one in which the extent of the market (i.e., population), and the extent of the market alone, determines the overall level of demand. Markets grow in size with population, according to Smith. The division of labor, it therefore follows, is determined by population growth. The decision to mechanize production processes is, as such, tied to market size, which, in turn, is tied to population. Per-capita income growth (via increased wages), as a determinant of the extent of the market, is not considered. Producer behavior in the labor and capital markets has no bearing on the "extent of the market" (i.e. via higher wages and profits): rather, population is its sole determinant.

Smith's insights into the nature of exchange in industry (i.e., the factory system), notably the "residual" nature of profits, did not increase the level of interest in the problems of exchange as defined here. Take, for example, his intellectual successor, David Ricardo. Nowhere in *The Principles of Political Economy and Taxation*, is the issue of exchange technology raised, let alone discussed. That this be the case is not surprising given his more immediate objectives, namely corn prices, wages, rents, income distribution, and growth. Unlike Smith, Ricardo is not concerned with the nature and causes of the wealth of nations, but rather with the effects of high food prices on profits, savings, and, ultimately, growth. One could argue that Ricardo's writings subsume Book I of the *Wealth of Nations*.

This is not to say, however, that he was unaware of the problem of exchange and the problem of underincome. As it turned out, Ricardo was, metaphorically speaking, dragged into the early nineteenthth-century debate on underconsumption, overinvestment, and what I prefer to call underincome by a handful of "radical" political economists, including Thomas Malthus and Jean-Charles Léonard Sismonde de Sismondi, both of whom, in "Smithian" fashion, analyzed the exchange process, and who, in response, questioned the ability of a private economy (e.g., the British economy at the turn of the century) to generate the necessary money income (circulating capital) to produce at full capacity, or as they put it, "realize" its full potential.

I begin with Sismonde de Sismondi, the father of dynamic period analysis in macroeconomics. Unlike Ricardo, Sismonde de Sismondi's principal interest was in the effects of the introduction of machinery (i.e., steam or fire power) on the dynamic workings of the economy. One could argue that his apparent lack of interest in Ricardian issues (e.g., corn prices, rents, wages etcetera) owed to conditions on the Continent, specifically, the absence of food shortages, making issues relating to agriculture (e.g., food prices) of less import. As I have argued elsewhere (Beaudreau, 1996a), Sismonde de Sismondi was among—if not—the first to identify the problem of underincome, and, more importantly, the first to recognize its strategic nature. The introduction of machinery increased output, and consequently, the value of output, by more than it increased money costs, he argued. Producers have no private incentive to increase wage income; consequently, aggregate wage income remains constant. As the following passage taken from *Nouveaux principes d'économie politique*, published in 1819 shows, producers have no private interest in increasing overall money income in response to the introduction of a "procédé nouveau."

Le vendeur n'a pas par lui-même aucun moyen d'étendre don débit, qui ne réagisse sur ses confrères; il leur dispute une quantité donnée de revenu qui doit emplacer son capital; et plus, il reussit à en garder pour lui même; moins il en laisse pour les autres. Il ne dépend nullement du producteur d'augmenter les revenus de la société ou du marché qu'il sert de manière qu'ils puissent s'échanger contre une augmentation de produits. . . . Entre commerçants, on regarde comme une mauvaise action de se séduire reciproquement ses pratiques; mais, la concurrence que chacun exerce contre tous ne présente point une idée aussi précise; et un commerçant n'a pas moins d'empressement à étendre son débit aux dépens de ses confrères qu'a le proportionner à l'accroissement des richesses, lorsque celles-ci lui offrent l'échange d'un nouveau revenu. Jusqu'ici, dans l'un ou l'autre cas, la découverte d'un procédé nouveau a causé une grande perte nationale, une grande diminution de revenu, et par conséquent, la consommation. (Sismonde de Sismondi, 1970 [1819], 269)

Implicit in this passage is the problem of underincome. Unlike the domestic system where money income was increasing in the value of output, in the factory system, it was not. According to Sismondi, the introduction of machinery (division of labor) does not lead producers to increase money income. Producers have no private incentives to increase what he refers to as "débit," with the result that, at the aggregate level, wage income does not rise, prompting a failure on the part of merchants to increase orders. Aggregate income, it therefore follows, is less than the value of potential output as defined by the new, higher productive capacity. This result lies at the heart of Sismonde de Sismondi's dynamic periodic analysis, where money income lags behind the value of output, resulting in underincome.

Eight years later, Thomas Robert Malthus addressed the problem of underincome without, however, referring to it by name. To him, an increase in output or productive capacity was not a sufficient condition for "the progress of wealth," as he referred to economic growth.

We have seen that the powers of production, to whatever extent they may exist, are not alone sufficient to secure the creation of a proportionate degree of wealth. Something else seems necessary in order to call these powers fully in action. This is effectual and unchecked demand for all that is produced. And what appears to contribute most to the attainment of this object, is, such a distribution of produce, and such an adaptation of this produce to the wants of those who are to consume it, as constantly to increase the exchangeable value of the whole mass.... In the same manner, the greatest stimulus to the continued production of commodities, taken altogether, is an increase in the exchangeable value of the whole mass, before a greater value of capital has been employed upon them. (Malthus, 1951 [1827], 361)

This quote, taken from Book II, Chapter 1, Section 6 of *Principles of Political Economy*, highlights Malthus' interest in exchange-related issues. By his use of the word "distribution," it should be understood the distribution of the wealth in money form, and not the functional distribution of income. Thus, to Malthus, the mere act of producing commodities was not a sufficient condition for the "Progress of Wealth." Also necessary is a commensurate increase in distribution, or, put differently, money income.

By definition, underincome implies underexpenditure, or, more specifically, underconsumption. More precisely, because money income (as determined by producers) is less than the value of output at capacity (potential GDP), it only follows that the value of expenditure would be less than the value of output at capacity. However, as pointed out above, a good knowledge of the workings of monetary exchange (producers–merchants) in the factory system was a necessary prerequisite to understanding underincome and underconsumption. Unfortunately, most—if not all—classical economists had no such knowledge. In fact, classical monetary theory was, in general, rather primitive, going scarcely beyond the notion of the "transactions" demand for money. Output automatically created income, which, in general, created expenditure. Put simply, supply creates demand.

As a result, what started as a debate over the ability of private, competitive, steam-power-driven economies to create money income commensurate with potential throughput levels, was quickly transformed into a rather sterile debate over possible gluts and underexpenditure (Sowell, 1972). Sismonde de Sismondi and Malthus openly questioned whether money income increased proprotionately with output in a mechanized economy; Jean-Baptiste Say and David Ricardo, on the other hand, assumed that output created money income, and, consequently, in aggregate, money income created demand.

That Say and Ricardo, the two protagonists, did not have a more sophisticated understanding of exchange technologies in the early nineteenth century is an interesting question. After all, Adam Smith, their spiritual father, had described, some fifty years before Sismonde de Sismondi and Malthus, the exchange technology in the factory system. Consider, for example, the following passage in which, according to Samuel Hollander (1987), Adam Smith relates employment capacity to—the aggregate demand for (productive) labour—to aggregate circulating capital.

When we compute the quantity of industry which the circulating capital of any country can employ, we must always have regard to those parts of it only, which consist in provisions, materials, and finished work: the other, which consists in money, and serves to circulate those three, must always be deducted. In order to put industry into motion, three things are requisite: materials to work upon, tools to work with, and the wages or recompence for the sake of which the work is done. Money is neither a material to work upon, nor a tool to work with; and though the wages of the workman are commonly paid to him in money, his real revenue, like that of other men, consists, not in the money, but in the money's worth; not in the metal pieces, but what can be got for them. (Smith, 1990 [1776], 279)

As this quotation unequivocally demonstrates, Smith was quite familiar with the exchange technology of the newly developed factory system. Circulating capital was needed to finance the purchase of materials, and to pay the "wages of the workman." The relevant—and, indeed, ignored—issue, however, is the interactions between producers and merchants.

This leads me to the third issue, namely the problem of income distribution. The problem of distribution is inextricably tied to the problem of underincome. As pointed out above, energy-deepening-based technological change can, at least theoretically, increase productive capacity without necessarily increasing money income, and, as such, without altering the level of and distribution of income. In this case, wages fail to increase as a result; as do profits.

The classical political economists' interest in distribution, as it turns out, had little to do with apportioning energy rents—for obvious reasons. Instead, it had everything to do with the relationship between the price of food, wages and profits in a static setting. As shown earlier, rising food prices in turn-of-the-century England (nineteenth century) had contributed to increasing wages, and, consequently, lowering profits. Lower profits, in turn, implied lower savings, lower investment and, ultimately, lower growth.

In the period between Smith's *An Inquiry into the Nature and Causes of the Wealth of Nations* and Ricardo's *Principles of Political Economy and Taxation,* an important development had taken place in Great Britain, notably the rise in the price of foodstuffs, owing, in large measure, to rapid growth, restricted imports (due to the Napoleonic blockade), and lastly, the Corn Laws. Higher food prices wreaked havoc on Great Britain, especially on manufacturing. Wages increased, thus lowering profits, and, consequently, savings, investment and, ultimately, growth. Rents to landowners increased with every increase in the price of corn, inhibiting prosperity.

This development, I argue, predicates developments in the theory of distribution from Smith to Ricardo. As its title indicates, *An Inquiry into the Nature and Causes of the Wealth of Nations* was more about wealth than it was about the distribution of wealth. According to Smith, increases in the price of corn led to higher wages; however, however wages merely led to higher prices, profits being unaffected. Whether the result of a keen sense of observation or an acute faculty of reason, Ricardo, some half-century later, rejected this view, arguing that higher corn prices increased wages, and, more importantly, reduced profits. According to Samuel Hollander:

To summarize thus far: according to Smith, a wage increase raises the costs and this the prices of manufactured products. According to Ricardo, it is solely the structure, not the level of prices, that is altered. Smith had failed to follow through consistently the relativity dimensions of pricing; for what is true of a disturbance affecting one industry alone—an increase in the wage raises costs and the price of that commodity—is not true of a disturbance affecting all industries. It was Ricardo's valid contention that Smith had fallen into error in approaching a general-equilibirum problem in terms appropriate for partial-equilibrium analysis.

Since a wage increase cannot be passed on in higher prices, as Smith maintained, its effect—apart from possibly disturbing the price structure—must be to reduce profits. The theorem on distribution we shall henceforth refer to as the "inverse wage-profit relation." (Hollander, 1987, 88)

This laid the foundations for one of Ricardo's seminal theoretical contributions, namely the "inverse wage-profit relationship," which holds that at the aggregate level, an increase in wages results, forcibly, in a decrease in profits, and viceversa. In short, income distribution was a zero-sum game. From a policy point of view, an increase in the price of corn would, by increasing wages, reduce profits and, consequently, savings, investment and ultimately growth.

The notion of energy rent per se is absent from Smith's and Ricardo's work. It is, however, present, albeit indirectly, in Ricardo's account of the effects of the introduction of machinery on profits, prices and welfare. Accordingly, the introduction of machinery gives rise to profits in the short term (i.e., the equivalence of energy rents); however, in the long run, as competitors adopted the new technology, the price would decrease to the cost of production, thus conferring a welfare gain on all of society.

Ever since I first turned my attention to questions of political economy, I have been of the opinion that such an application of machinery to any branch of production as should have the effect of saving labour was generally a general good, accompanied only with that portion of inconvenience which in most cases attends the removal of capital and labour from one employment to another. It appeared to me that, provided the landlords had the same money rents, they would be benefitted by the reduction of price of the commodities on which those rents were expended, and which reduction of price could not fail to be the consequence of the employment of machinery. The capitalist, I thought, was eventually benefited precisely in the same manner. He, indeed, who made the discovery of the machine, he who first usefully applied it, would enjoy an additional advantage by making great profits for a time; but, in proportion as the machine came into general use, the price of the commodity produced would, from the effects of competition, sink to its cost of production, when the capitalist would get the same money profits as before, and he would participate in the general advantage as a consumer, by being enabled, with the same money revenue, to command an additional quantity of comforts and enjoyments. (Ricardo, 1965 [1817], 263)

Put differently, the resulting surplus is appropriated initially by the owner of tools, but, in the long run, by society as a whole by way of lower prices. Real wages and profits rise as a result. In others words, the owners of labor and the owners of capital do not openly bargain for these rents; instead, they are distributed by the price mechanism in terms of lower product prices, which, for constant nominal wages and profits, result in higher real income and welfare. Implicit here is the assumption of Walrasian-style markets. Like farmers with a new, more productive piece of equipment, textile and clothing producers, Ricardo assumes, go on to produce at maximum rated capacity, increasing, at least in the short run, their share of the market, until such time as rivals also adopt the new technology, at which point in time, the price or prices virtually collapse(s), resulting ultimately in a welfare gain for all involved.

Summary

As I have attempted to show here, classical political economy, the product of the changes thrust upon British society by the introduction of the steam engine, failed to explicitly incorporate energy in any form in its analysis of the transformation of raw materials and intermediate inputs into finished products, thus precluding, in my view, any claim to being scientific—in the current sense of the word. Using a model of Paleolithic production processes, they set out to provide analytical constructs for what they saw as the true problem of political economy, namely demand-constrained growth in the case of Smith, and lower profits, savings, investment, the capital stock and, ultimately, the rate of growth of the U.K. economy, in the case of Ricardo.

The absence of a veritable science of wealth per se is further corroborated by the classical political economists' limited understanding, Adam Smith notwithstanding, of the exchange process, which, like their understanding of production, is preindustrial. The value of output is, by definition, equal to total money costs. The value of aggregate output, it therefore follows, is equal to the national money income. Clearly, this did not square with the facts.

The failure of classical political economy to accurately model production and exchange in early nineteenth century British—and European—manufacturing, I maintain, contributed to its downfall and subsequent usurpation by Marxian and neoclassical political economy. While a power revolution in the form of steam-powered machinery constituted the defining force behind the phenomena they sought to understand, it was, for all intents and purposes, absent from their analysis. As I shall argue below, these shortcomings (i.e., labor theory of value) in combination with the worsening problem of underincome, are what, in large measure, led to its *antithesis*, namely Marxian political economy, and, subsequently, to the classical counterrevolution, namely neoclassical political economy. If labor was the source of all value, as Smith and Ricardo maintained, then, it only followed that it be its sole claimant (i.e., in terms of distribution). One could argue that the rise of radical political economy was one of the costs of doing bad science. Paradoxically, at a time when energy-deepening was at its zenith, the status of energy as a factor input was at its nadir.

Robert Owen and Karl Marx

Judging by modern scientific standards, classical political economy as an attempt at understanding the effects of the shift from the domestic system to the factory system has to be considered less than a success. This is not altogether surprising given the absence of a well-established scientific tradition, and second, the heightened interest in policy (e.g., maximizing growth, repealing the corn laws). In fact, one could go as far as to argue that classical political economists did not need—or at least they thought—an empirically consistent model of production and exchange. It sufficed to point out that output was produced by labor and machinery, the former being paid wages and the latter profits; and workers consumed most of their earnings while the owners of capital saved most of theirs. Wages were, in large measure, determined by the price of food. Hence, higher food prices, like taxes on profits, reduced savings, investment and growth.

Value theory was a second-order consideration, as evidenced by its primitive nature. Goods, argued Smith and Ricardo, exchanged at ratios determined by the relative amount of labor in each. Just why they chose labor as the relevant standard at a time when it had been marginalized as a factor input is anyone's guess. The reason, I maintain, had little to do with logic, and everything to do with convenience.[14] The issue of value was not a first-order consideration, nor was the problem of exchange.

As a general rule, policy based on faulty analysis is, in the long run, destined to fail. This is especially true when the policy in question involves something as vital to the human condition as wages. Classical political economists in general argued that increasing profits would, in the long run, be good for all of society, as more machinery would be put in place, increasing productivity in all sectors of the economy.[15] Profits were a social "good" as they conferred benefits on all of society, including workers. The process by which increased profits would lead to higher savings, investment, growth and, ultimately, a higher standard of living, was assumed to be frictionless. While relative inequities might persist, absolute inequities would diminish as real per-capita income increased (owing to a fall in product prices).

The operative word here is "assumed." Reality painted an altogether different picture of the new industrial age. "Fire power" had revolutionized manufacturing production processes, marginalized workers, all but eliminated the various workers guilds, and, last but not least, altered the way in which goods were exchanged. First, as the data in Tables 2.5 and 2.6 show, steam-power-induced increases in output, especially in the textiles sector, did not lead to higher nominal money income, but instead, to lower prices and, ultimately, to lower wages. Combined with non-decreasing food costs, these developments contributed to a drastic decline in workers' standard of living, as demonstrated so convincingly by John Fielden. Paradoxically, more productive workers (i.e., in the conventional sense) were worse off.

These developments, set against a theory of value based on labor, are, in my view, what fomented a number of "radical" movements in the nineteenth century. In short, the industrial revolution had passed labor by. Machinery decreased the demand for labor, all the while marginalizing it as a factor input, as evidenced by the increased use of children in factories. Workers' standard of living had not increased, at least not commensurately with productivity. Moreover, the industrial system was, according to many, prone to crises of overproduction.

In this section, I examine the work of two "radicals," namely industrialist Robert Owen, and radical political economist Karl Marx, two unlikely bedfellows, one being a factory owner, the other being an intellectual. It will be argued that their work should be understood as reactions to (1) the introduction of "fire power," (2) the resulting trivialization of labor, (3) "classical political economy" per se and (4) the falling relative price of manufactures—and hence, manufacturing wages—to food. Owen, a successful businessman, had witnessed the effects of the introduction of "scientific mechanical power" first hand, having been the manager and, subsequently, the owner-manager of a number of textile mills, the most celebrated being at New Lanark, in Scotland. Consider, for example, the following passage taken from the *Report to the County of Lanark*, published in 1820:

It is well known that, during the last half century in particular, Great Britain, beyond any other nation, has progressively increased its powers of production, by a rapid advancement in scientific improvements and arrangements, introduced, more or less, into all the departments of productive industry throughout the empire. The amount of this new productive power cannot, for want of proper data, be very accurately estimated; but your Reporter has ascertained from facts which none will dispute, that its increase has been enormous;—that, compared with the manual labour of the whole population of Great Britain and Ireland, it is, at least, as *forty to one*, and may be easily made as *100 to one*; and that this increase may be extended to other countries; that it is already sufficient to saturate the world with wealth and that the power of creating wealth may be made to advance perpetually in an accelerating ratio. (Owen, 1927 [1820], 246)

That Owen, more so than either Smith or Ricardo, accurately identified and analyzed the changes thrust upon society by "fire power," can be attributed, in large measure, to his previous occupations, specifically to his work in then nascent energy sector. After having, with John Jones, manufactured and sold rovings and machinery to the spinning industry, he went to work for Peter Drinkwater, the first man to build a mill in Manchester powered by a Watt-Boulton rotary steam engine (Butt, 1971, 169).

Throughout his writings, Owen refers, often in endearing terms, to the energy-based innovation that was the introduction of steam-power-based drive in British manufacturing. Not knowing how to describe it, he refers to it both as "mechanical" and "chemical" power as the following passage bears witness:

It must be admitted that scientific or artificial aid to man increases his productive powers, his natural wants remaining the same; and in proportion as his productive powers increase he becomes less dependent on his physical strength and on the many contingencies connected with it. . . . That the direct effect of every addition to scientific, or mechanical and chemical power is to increase wealth; and it is found, accordingly, that the immediate cause of the present want of employment from the working classes is an excess of production of all kinds of wealth, by which, under the existing arrangements of commerce, all the markets of the world are overstocked. (Owen, 1927 [1820], 247)

Unlike the classical political economists, Owen was acutely aware of the consequences of "scientific power" for labor. As I pointed out in Chapter 1, it had transformed labor into a form of lower-level supervisory input, overseeing the workings of steam-powered machine. He referred to this as "mental power." In short, Owen was the first "energy economist," having been the first one to describe in considerable detail the many changes thrust upon British society by the introduction of a new energy source, namely "scientific power."

In many ways, Owen had much in common with Smith and Ricardo. Take, for example, the question of motives. Like Smith and Ricardo, he sought to promote growth based on the newly discovered source of inanimate power. Where they differed, however, is with regard to the relevant "means." Smith and Ricardo held that lower wages, by increasing profits, would increase savings and investment and, ultimately, growth. Owen saw things differently. Whereas Ricardo held that productive capacity (i.e., supply) creates a proportionate level of income, and that this income creates a proportionate level of demand, Owen disagreed, on account of his experience with "scientific power" in industry. In short, Owen had put his finger on the problem of underincome. Given that profits are a residual form of money income, an increase in output, due to "scientific power," did not result in an increase in money income and, consequently, "consumption" as expenditure was then known. In fact, argued Owen, wages had fallen, exacerbating the problem of underincome.

Owen was painfully aware that an increase in productive capacity, due to "scientific power," did not increase money income. "Prime costs," as he referred to them, did not increase with output. The move to the factory system, as pointed out earlier, had altered the underlying nature of exchange. Textile producers in Manchester and elsewhere, financed their variable costs [Prime costs] with trade credit. As I shall argue here, this flaw in the newly instituted factory system was the motivating factor underlying and running through most of his writings. "Scientific power" had increased productive capacity and productivity, yet workers and society as a whole were worse off. Consider, for example, the closing passage of his *Report to the County of Lanark*:

Your Reporter solicits no favour from any party; he belongs to none. He merely calls upon those who are the most competent to the task, honestly, as men valuing their own interests and the interests of society, to investigate, without favour or affection, a "Plan (derived from thirty years' study and practical experience) for relieveing public distress and removing discontent, by giving permanent productive employment to the poor and working classes, under arrangements which will essentially improve their character and ameliorate their condition, diminish the expenses of production and consumption, and create markets coextensive with production." (Owen, 1927 [1820], 298)

The problem of underincome runs throughout the *Report to the County of Lanark*. Consider, for example, the preamble to the "Plan."

Having taken this view of the subject, your Reporter was induced to conclude that the want of beneficial employment for the working classes, and the consequent public distress, were owing to the rapid increase of the new productive power, for the advantageous application of which, society had neglected to make the proper arrangements. Could these arrangements be formed, he entertained the most confident expectation that productive employment might again be found for all who required it; and that the national distress, of which all now so loudly complain, might be gradually converted into a much higher degree of prosperity than was attainable prior to the extraordinary accession lately made to the productive powers of society.

Cheered by such a prospect, your Reporter directed his attention to the consideration of the possibility of devising arrangements by means of which the whole population might participate in the benefits derivable from the increase of scientific productive power; and has the satisfaction to state to the meeting, that he has strong grounds to believe that such arrangements are practicable.

His opinion on this important part of the subject is founded on the following considerations:

First.—It must be admitted that scientific or artificial aid to man increases his productive powers, his natural wants remaining the same; and in proprotion as his productive powers increase he becomes less dependent on his physical strength and on the many contingenices connected with it.

Second.—That the direct effect of every addition to scientific or mechanical and chemical power is to increase wealth; and it is found, accordingly, that the immediate cause of the present want of employment for the working classes is an excess of production of all kinds of wealth, by which, under the existing arrangements of commerce, all the markets of the world are overstocked.

Third.—That, could markets be found, an incalcuable addition might yet be made to the wealth of society, as is most evident from the number of persons who seek employment, and the far greater number who, from ignorance, are inefficiently employed, but still more from the means we possess of increasing, to an unlimited extent, our scientific powers of production.

Fourth.—That the deficiency of employment for the working classes cannot proceed from a want of wealth or capital, or of the means of greatly adding to that which now exists, but from some defect in the mode of distributing this extraordinary addition of new capital throughout society, or, to speak commercially, from the want of a market, or means of exchange, co-extensive with the means of production. (Owen, 1927 [1820], 248)

To address these problems, Owen, in his report to the *Committee of Gentlemen of the Upper Ward of Lanarkshire*, proposed a "radical" reorganization of distribution, and, to a lesser extent, production, both for agriculture and industry. Briefly, the producer-merchant exchange technology, characteristic of the factory system, would be replaced by local cooperatives ; money would be replaced by labor certificates. The core change proposed by Owen is the standard of value. Specifically, he proposed replacing an "artificial" standard of value (i.e., money) by a natural one, namely human labor, which he refers to as the "combined manual and mental powers of men called into action." In actual fact, what Owen had in mind was an energy-based theory of value, based on labor's manual and mental power.

Already, however, the average physical power of men as well as of horses (equally varied in individuals), has been calculated for scientific purposes, and both now serve to measure inanimate powers. On the same principle the average of human labour or power may be ascertained; and as it forms the essence of all wealth, its value in every article of produce may also be ascertained, and its exchangeable value with all other goods fixed accordingly; the whole to be permanent for a given period. (Owen, 1927 [1820], 251)

This was the first step in Owen's plan for "distribution." Scientific power, in combination with lower nominal wages, had reduced the cost of labor (i.e., supervision) per unit output. To reverse this trend, Owen argued in favor of a labor standard of value in which the amount of labor per unit output would be determined and held fixed (i.e., for a given period). Any increase in output would, as such, automatically lead to an increase in wages, thus resolving, at least in part, the problem of underincome. Income would increase commensurately with output.

Judged on purely scientific grounds, Owen's plan, while feasible, was at odds with the facts. As pointed out above, "scientific power" had trivialized conventionally defined labor, making it "child's play," so to speak. The labor standard, as Owen referred to it, was orthogonal to the technological reality of the early nineteenth century. How, then, should Owen's plan be understood? One could argue that the labor standard had more to do with the problem of exchange than with the problem of production. By asserting, *prima facie*, that labor was the source of all value, Owen could then proceed to mount a case for higher wages, consumption, and, consequently, profits. Consider the following passage in which he describes such a system.

The genuine principle of barter was, to exchange the supposed prime cost of, or value of labour in, one article, against the prime cost of, or value of labour contained in any other article. This is the only equitable principle of exchange; but, as inventions increased and human desires multiplied, it was found to be inconvenient in practice. Barter was succeeded by commerce, the principle of which is, to produce or procure every article at the *lowest*, and to obtain for it, in exchange, the *highest* amount of labour. To effect this, an artificial standard of value was necessary; and metals were, by common consent among nations, permitted to perform the office.

This principle, in the progress of its operation, has been productive of important advantages, and of very great evils; but, like barter, it has been suited to a certain stage of society. It has stimulated invention; it has given industry and talent to the human character; and has secured the future exertion of these energies which otherwise might have remained dormant and unknown.

But it has made man ignorantly, individually selfish; placed him in opposition to his fellows; engendered fraud and deceit; blindly urged him forward to create, but deprived him of the wisdom to enjoy. In striving to take advantage of others, he has over-reached himself. The strong hand of necessity will now force him into the path which conducts to that wisdom in which he has been so long deficient. He will discover the advantages to be derived from uniting in practice the best parts of the principles of barter and commerce, and dismissing those which experience has proved to be inconvenient and injurious. (Owen, 1927 [1820], 263)

In short, to Owen, the introduction of "scientific power" had shaken the foundations of eighteenth-century British society. Potential output had increased manifold, yet welfare had failed to increase. In fact, according to Owen, things had deteriorated. A new system was needed. The "Report to the County of Lanark" should be seen as Owen's blueprint for the future, one where scientific power is put to use to better mankind's material and intellectual existence.

Let me now turn to German political economist Karl Marx, who, like Owen, was both scientist and ideologue. In Chapters 14 and 15 of *Das Capital*, published in 1867, he presented the most scientifically accurate description of production processes both before and after the industrial revolution. Consider, for example, the following passage, which describes the role of tools and power in "heterogeneous" and "serial" manufactures, the former referring to the domestic system, and the latter, to the factory system.

Mathematicians and mechanicians, and in this they are followed by a few English economists, call a tool a simple machine, and a machine a complex tool. They see no essential difference between them, and even give the name of machine to the simple mechanical powers, the lever, the inclined plane, the screw, the wedge, etc. As a matter of fact, every machine is a combination of those simple powers, no matter how they may be disguised. From the economical standpoint this explanation is worth nothing, because the historical element is wanting. Another explanation of the difference between tool and machine is that, in the case of the tool, man is the motive power, while the motive power of a machine is something different from man, is, for instance, an animal, water, wind and so on. According to this, a plough drawn by oxen, which is a contrivance common to the most different epochs, would be a machine, while Claussen's circular loom, which, worked by a single labourer, weaves 96,000 picks per minute, would be a mere tool. Nay, this very loom, though a tool when worked by hand, would, if worked by steam, be a machine. And, since the application of animal power is one of man's earliest inventions, production by machinery would have preceded production by handicrafts. When in 1735, John Wyalt brought out his spinning machine and began the industrial revolution of the eighteenth century, not a word did he say about an ass driving it instead of a man. and yet this part fell to the ass. He described it as a machine "to spin without fingers."

All fully developed machinery consists of three essentially different parts, the motor mechanism, the transmitting mechanism, and finally the tool of working machine. The motor mechanism is that which puts the whole in motion. It either generates its own motive power, like the steam engine, the caloric engine, the electro-magnetic machine, etc., or it receives its impulse from some already existing natural force, like the waterwheel from a head of water, the windmill from wind, etc. The transmitting mechanism, composed of flywheels, shafting, cogwheels, pulleys, straps, ropes, bands, pinions, and gearing of the most varied kinds, regulates the motion, changes its form where necessary, as, for instance, from linear to circular, and divides and distributes it among the working machines. These two parts of the whole mechanism are there soley for putting the working machines in motion, by means of which motion the subject of labour is siezed upon and modified as desired. The tool or working machine is that part of machinery with which the industrial revolution of the eighteenth century started. And, to this day it constantly serves as such a starting point whenever a handicraft, or a manufacture, is turned into industry carried on by machinery. (Marx, 1906 [1867], 405)

What is particularly interesting—and, to a certain extent, puzzling—is the location of these two chapters in *Das Capital* (chapters 14 and 15), notably after the bulk of his substantive analysis on exchange, surplus value, exploitation, etcetera (chapters 1–13). Also interesting—and equally puzzling— is the fact that in Chapters 1–13, labor is the source of all value. That is, labor is the only productive factor. How then are we to understand what, by all accounts, is a fundmental contradiction? Specifically, he was well aware of the fact that labor had been transformed from a source of energy and organization, to a source of organization only (machine operatives), yet in the crux of his analysis, he focuses exclusively on labor.

The answer, I believe, lies in the duality noted earlier in Robert Owen's work. Fifty years earlier, Owen understood that labor had become a minor input in the factory system, yet, when it came time to examine the problem of distribution, he put it at the center of his analysis. The reason, as argued earlier, has little to do with science, and everything to do with *ideology*. Labor, Owen felt, should receive a larger share of energy rents. Marx held similar views, which, I maintain, explains the subsidiary nature of his work on machines and power. It also delineates, quite well, the duality of Marx as both a scientist and ideologue.[16]

The next question relates to the problem of exchange and the problem of underincome. Specfically, was he aware of the problem of exchange and the problem of underincome? Despite devoting the first three (3) chapters of *Das Capital* to money and exchange, he failed to describe, in a reasonably accurate way, the producer–merchant exchange technology characteristic of industrialized economies. Absent from his analysis is any mention of the demand for money by producers and by merchants, the residual nature of profits, and the indeterminacy inherent in the producer-merchant exchange technology. In short, he assumes, like Ricardo, that the value of money is identically equal to the value of output. Consequently, the problem of underincome is ignored.

The last question relates to the problem of distribution. As I have argued (Beaudreau, 1998), *Das Capital* should be seen not so much as an attempt at understanding production, exchange and distribution, but rather, as an attempt, by a highly perspicacious individual, of positively influencing labor's bargaining power (α_s in Equation 1.4) in the relevant energy-rent bargaining problem. As the data presented above reveal, factory workers in mid-nineteenth century Great Britain suffered greatly from falling textile prices and wages. The promised riches of the power revolution, so to speak, had passed them by. They were no better off in the mid 1800s than they were in the early 1800s. Marx's theory of distribution, based on labor as the sole source of value, should, as such, be seen for what it was: an attempt at influencing the parameters of the relevant bargaining problem. If labor could reasonably (read: scientifically) claim that all value was rightfully theirs, then wages would increase, and consequently, so would labor's standard of living. As it turns out, this was also the preferred approach of Robert Owen at the turn of the century, and, interestingly enough, was not inconsistent with the labor theory of value.

The Neoclassical Political Economists

By the mid-nineteenth century, a new threat to savings, investment and growth, the staples of classical political economy, had emerged in Europe, namely radical political economy, defined broadly to include Marxian political economy, glut theory and underconsumption theory. Like Smith's "extent of the market," and Ricardo's "high food prices," numerous social, political and economic radical movements now threatened the existing order. Whereas critics like Robert Owen sought to reform the factory system, this new generation of reformers aimed at nothing less than its overthrow, and the creation of a new, social and economic order built around the worker (machine operative, lower-level supervisor).

As I shall argue here, this new threat was, in large part, self-inflicted. Specifically, the classical political economists' failure to accurately model production processes, in combination with the problem of underincome, are, in large measure, responsible for the mercurial rise of radical political economy. Robert Owen and Karl Marx's basic ideological postulate (axiom) was the labor theory of value in its simplest form. Labor was the source of all value (Smith, 1990 [1776], Ricardo, 1965 [1817]). Ergo, something was askew, they reasoned, as labor income, and consequently, workers' standard of living, had fallen drastically. Theoretically, they were right. If, as the classical political economists maintained, labor was the source of all value, then to pay it anything less than its product (marginal revenue product) was akin to theft.

As pointed out earlier, the classical political economists were, for the most part, uninterested in production, beyond the obvious. Labor and tools had, were and, undoubtedly, would continue to transform raw materials into goods. Their principal preoccupation was with distribution, putting an inordinate amount of attention on the relationship between the price of corn, wages, profits and ultimately growth. As I shall argue here, their ideological successors, the neoclassical political economists, did little to correct this. Rather than providing an empirically consistent view of production based on the newly established science of thermodynamics (i.e., energy) and on organization, they chose to (1) develop a non-substantive theory of value (utility-based) and (2) add tools to the list of productive inputs. Both borrowed extensively from thermodynamics (Mirowski, 1989).

Once again, the problem of distribution took center stage, but for altogether different reasons—reasons that, at this point, were purely defensive in nature. Higher corn prices had threatened profit growth, savings growth, investment growth and overall growth at the turn of the century. Now, falling textile prices and wages in the textile industry were threatening profit growth, savings growth, investment growth and overall growth. Consequently, socialism and communism threatened the very cornerstone of capitalism, namely the institution of private property. Consider the following passage, taken from the Preface to the first edition of William S. Jevons' *The Theory of Political Economy*, published, it bears noting, in 1871, four years after Karl Marx's *Das Capital*.

There are many portions of the economical doctrine which appear to me as scientific in form as they are consonant with facts. I would especially mention the theories of population and of rent. . . . Other generally-accepted doctines have always appeared to me purely delusive, especially, the so-called wage fund theory. This theory pretends to give a solution to the main problem of the science—to determine the wages of labour—yet on close examination, its conclusion is a mere truism, namely that the average rate of wages is found by dividing the whole amount appropriated to the payment of wages by the number of those between whom it is divided. (Jevons, 1871, 1)

Roughly a century after Adam Smith's pathbreaking contribution, the problem of value and distribution had not been resolved, at least, not to everyone's satisfaction. In hindsight, Jevons was right: classical political economy was woefully inadequate. Labor, after all, was, at that point in time, a marginal factor, supervising machinery (machine operatives).[17] The relevant question, it follows, is whether Jevons, Marshall and Walras succeeded at providing a scientific theory of value and distribution.

I maintain that they were not, owing mainly to their failure to provide an empirically correct model of production. Neoclassical political economists, by moving value theory away from "substances," widened the chasm already separating theory from reality. In fact, in lieu of a theory of value based on energy as a factor of production (i.e., à la Robert Owen), they offered a theory of value based on energy as a consumption good (Edgeworth, 1881, Mirowski, 1988) fashioned in large measure on the then-nascent science of thermodynamics.

Like their classical predecessors, Jevons, Marshall and Walras continued to model production as a Paleolithic activity, centered on labor and capital. Energy is conspicuous for its absence. Take, for example, Chapter VII of Marshall's *Principles of Economics*, entitled "The Growth of Wealth," where the emphasis, despite a historical reference to water and steam power, is on capital.

The implements if the English farmer had been rising slowly in value for a long time; but the progress was quickened in the eighteenth century. After a while the use first of water power and then of steam power caused the rapid substitution of expensive machinery for inexpensive hand tools in one department of production after another. As in earlier times the most expensive implements were ships and in some cases canals for navigation and irrigation, so now they are the means of locomotion in general;—railways and tramways, canals, docks and ships, telegraph and telephone systems and water-works; even gas-works might almost come under this head, on the ground that a great part of their plant is devoted to distributing the gas. After these come mines and iron and chemical works, ship-building years, printing-presses, and other large factories full of machinery.

On whichever side we look we find that the progress and diffusion of knowledge are constantly leading to the adoption of new processes and new machinery which economize on human effort on condition that some of the effort is spent a good while before the attainment of the ultimate ends to which it is directed. (Marshall, 1890, 184)

Conceptually, capital predicates the "growth of wealth."

The whole history of man shows that his wants expand with the growth of wealth and knowledge. And with the growth of openings for investment of capital there is a constant increase in that surplus of production over the necessaries of life, which gives the power to save. When the arts of production were rude, there was very little surplus, except when a strong ruling race kept the subject masses hard at work on the bare necessaries of life, and where the climate was so mild that those necessaries were samll and easily obtained. But ever increase in the arts of production, and in the capital accumulated to assist and support labour in future production, increased the surplus out of which more wealth could be accumulated. After a time civilization became possible in temperate and even in cold climates; the increase of material wealth was possible under conditions that did not enervate the worker, and did not therefore destroy the foundations on which it rested. Thus, from step to step wealth and knowledge have grown, and with every step the power of saving wealth and extending knowledge has increased. (Marshall, 1890, 186)

Analytically, capital, unproductive in classical political economy, was rendered productive. Borrowing from the methodology of thermodynamics, specifically from second-law analysis where efficiency is increasing in the design (quality) of the capital equipment, neoclassical writers postulated rising total productivity and declining marginal productivity for both capital and labor. Factors would, from now on, be infinitely substituable, at least in theory. Most importantly, capital was now physically productive. Heretofore, tools would be productive, in direct violation of classical mechanics where they "transmit force or torque." This, however, provided the much-needed theoretical basis for a model of labor market and capital-market behavior based on the notion of marginal productivity (i.e., the demand for labor and capital).

Why was energy ignored, especially at a time when it was the toast of the natural sciences? The reasons, I believe, are numerous. For example, there is the question of motives. Neoclassical political economy, as I have maintained here, was, from the start, defensive in nature. In fact, one could go as far as to argue that were it not for the problem of underincome, we would, to this day, all be classical political economists. A second reason, is the absence of energy-deepening in the late nineteenth century. By 1860, most of industry in Great Britain had converted to high-pressure steam (as opposed to atmospheric steam—condensing engines) as the chief power source driving continuous-flow machinery. Thus, there was nothing new on the energy front, that is, to report, by 1870. One could argue counterfactually that had further energy-deepening occurred in this period, then the chances of seeing energy in the production function would have been greater—perhaps not much, however.

Not including energy in the production function had important implications for the problem of distribution as seen by neoclassical political economists. Specifically, the notion of energy rents was ignored. Now that both capital and labor were deemed to be physically productive, the problem of distribution consisted, simply, of measuring each's physical contribution to overall output, and remunerating each accordingly. This is now known as the neoclassical theory of distribution.

From a purely counterfactual point of view, one cannot help but wonder what could have been had Jevons, Marshall and Walras probed more deeply into the inner workings of production processes. Instead of being a mere cog in a psuedoscientific model of distribution, thermodynamics, the science of energy, could have become the cornerstone of production theory, and, consequently, distribution and consumption theory. In thermodynamics, political economists would have found the key to understanding the creation and "growth" of wealth, not to mention the myriad changes that had characterized the nineteenth century. The "Energetics" movement, founded by physicists such as Hermann Von Helmholtz, was, at this time, moving in this very direction. According to sociologist Anson Rabinbach:

As Helmholtz was aware, the breakthrough in thermodynamics had enormous social implications. In his popular lectures and writings, he strikingly portrayed the movements of the planets, the forces of nature, the productive forces of machines, and, of course, human labor power as examples of the principle of the conservation of energy. The cosmos was essentially a system of production whose product was the universal *Kraft,* necessary to power the engines of nature and society, a vast and protean reservoir of labor power awaiting its conversion to work. (Rabinbach, 1990, 3)

Why the likes of Edgeworth, Jevons, Marshall, Walras and others chose to ignore this development is a topic for future research.[18]

Neoclassical Exchange Theory

This leads us to the problem of exchange as seen by neoclassical political economists. Remember that the move from the domestic to the factory system had important consequences for the relevant exchange technology. Specifically, in manufacturing, a new set of market coordination agents had come into being (producers).

As it turns out, the problem of exchange was, for the most part, ignored by neoclassical political economists. The existence of gluts was, in general, denied as evidenced by the following quote from Jevons' *The Theory of Political Economy*:

The theory of distribution of labour enables us to perceive clearly the meaning of over-production in trade. Early writers on economics were always in fear of a supposed glut, arising from the powers of production surpassing the needs of consumers, so that industry would be stopped, employment fail, and all but the rich would be starved by the superfluity of commodities. The doctrine is evidently absurd and self-contradictory. As the acquirement of suitable commodities is the whole purpose of industry and trade, the greater the supplies obtained the more perfectly industry fulfills its purpose. To bring about a universal glut would be to accomplish completely the aim of the economist, which is to maximize the products of labour. But the supplies must be suitable—that is, they must be in proportion to the needs of the population. Over-production is not possible in all branches of industry at one, but it is possible in some as compared with others. If, by miscalculation, too much labour is spent producing one commodity, say silk goods, our equations will not hold true. (Jevons, 1871, 212)

That this should be the case is not particularly surprising, especially at the end of the nineteenth century. Underincome is a dynamic problem, associated with, in general, energy-related technology shocks. It is, as such, absent in periods of *stationary* power consumption. Unlike the late 1700s, the late 1800s were not characterized by an energy shock (energy-deepening). Power drive technology, based largely on steam power, was stationary. Second, in the minds of most neoclassical economists, the glut question had been resolved by classical economists, specifically by invoking Jean-Baptiste Say's Law of Markets.

Neoclassical Distribution Theory

Given the absence of energy in neoclassical production theory, it comes as no surprise to find no mention of "energy rents." Whereas Smith and others referred to non-Ricardian rents, defined as the difference between the value of output and the cost of production, no such rents are found in the writings of neoclassical political economists.[19] For them, output, the end result of capital and labor, is appropriated solely by capital and labor. Both are seen to be productive in the physical sense, despite the fact that by the end of the 1800s, both were organizational inputs.

The essence of neoclassical distribution theory is found in Phillip Wicksteed's work on distribution. Specifically, assuming that production functions are homogeneous of degree one in their inputs, output will be exactly equal to the marginal product of labor times the number of workers, and the marginal product of capital times the amount of capital employed. At the core of the analysis is the existence of well-defined, continuous, linearly homogeneous production functions defined over capital and labor. The latter are assumed to be physically productive. Additional units of either, *ceteris paribus*, increase output.

Thus, in conclusion, it is fair to say that, other than its attempt at reforming value and distribution theory, neoclassical political economy contributed little to our understanding of the industrial revolution, and this in spite of a number of notable developments in energy-related physics. By the turn of the century, the labor theory of value had been discredited as had the wage-fund theory of income distribution. Wages and profit levels were no longer the result of bargaining; rather, they were the result of the interplay of the technology of production and the technology of satisfaction, scientific in name only.[20]

Nineteenth-Century Great Britain as Seen by Contemporary Political Economists

This chapter has been highly critical of nineteenth-century political economy, from Smith to Owen, and from Marx to Marshall. Chief among the criticisms has been the little attention—in fact, the total lack of attention—paid to energy in the literature. Output is modeled in Paleolithic terms, increasing in capital and labor. This oversight, I maintain, lies at the root of what I refer to as the "fall" of political economy. That is, energy in general, and energy innovations in particular were the cause of political economy, yet, they were nowhere to be found.

Unfortunately, the passage of time has failed to correct the problem. More than two centuries after the first industrial revolution and a century after the development of neoclassical political economy, energy remains the forgotten input. In recent work on the energy and the second industrial revolution (i.e., electrification) (Beaudreau 1995a, b, c, 1996a, 1998), I alluded to the existence, in the literature, of a dichotomy regarding energy in general and electric power in particular, namely of the historical record pointing to the important role of energy in general and electric power in particular in U.S. economic growth, and of the analytical growth theory where they are absent altogether.

The bulk of the historical evidence points to energy in general, and electric power in particular, to be an important cause of productivity and output growth, yet, on the other hand, analytical studies of the sources of growth find it to be marginally important. Thus, either the historical record is incorrect, or previous studies have underestimated the role of energy in general and electric power in particular in the process of economic growth. (Beaudreau, 1995a, 232)

Ironically, but not altogether surprisingly, a similar dichotomy also characterizes the literature on steam power and economic growth in the nineteenth century. The irony in this case stems from the absence in analytical work of what is considered by most (political economists aside) to be the root cause of the industrial revolution, namely the steam engine. A good example of this is a recent compendium on British economic growth since 1700, edited by Roderick Floud and Donald McCloskey (Floud and McCloskey, 1994) in which the contibutors make ample reference to energy, energy utilization, steam power, fire power, thermal and kinetic energy, coal consumption etcetera, but stop short of including energy as a factor of production. Joel Mokyr, for example, in "Technological Change, 1700–1830," devotes a section to "Energy Utilization," where he describes in some detail the shift from hydraulic energy to thermal energy, without relating energy and productivity. Nicholas Crafts, in "The Industrial Revolution," performs standard growth accounting on the British economy for the period 1700–1860, and finds "Solow residuals," which vary in importance from 10 percent for the period 1760–1801, to 28 percent for 1700–1760. The relevant "residual" for the period 1801–1831 is 18 percent. Needless to say, energy is not included as a factor input.

Donald McCloskey, in "1780–1860: A Survey," which, in a strange way, bears a striking resemblance to the current literature on the "Productivity Paradox" and the "Productivity Slowdown," cuts to the chase. Pointing to data that show that real income per head "nowadays" is twelve times greater than in 1780, he maintains that political economy in general, and economic historians in particular, have failed in their attempts at explaining these trends.

The conclusion, then, is that Harberger triangles—which is to say the gains from efficiency at the margin—cannot explain the factor of twelve. This is lamentable, because economics is much more confident about static arguments than about dynamic arguments. (McCloskey, 1994, 270)

While McCloskey offers a number of research avenues such as "the role of persuasive talk in the economy," I maintain, in keeping with the main thesis of this book, that the essential problem with the literature on British economic growth in the eighteenth and nineteenth centuries is with the relevant model of production, specifically, with the absence of energy in the various analytical models. Ironically, while every economic historian—bar none—agrees that thermal energy in the form of steam power is what launched the industrial revolution, energy as a factor—of production—is absent from work on nineteenth-century economic growth. A.E. Musson, in "Industrial Motive Power in the United Kingdom, 1800–70," makes a similar point:

It is generally recognized that the introduction of steam power was a crucial factor in the Industrial Revolution, closely linked with the exploitation of Britain's coal and iron resources, the development of mechanical engineering, and the growth of the factory system. A considerable amount of historical research has been carried out into the scientific-technological developments involved—into how the steam engine was developed from the crude creations of Savery and Newcommen to the comparatively sophisticated products of Watt's genius, with separate condenser, air pump, direct action, rotative motion, etc.—and how steam power began to spread into coal-mining, cotton spinning, flour milling, brewing, and various other industries in the eighteenth century. . . . In contrast to the interest in the early pioneering, there has been comparatively little effort to investigate the massive growth and spread of steam power after 1800, except in a few industries and areas. Several factors have contributed to this neglect. The "heroic" theory of historical evolution has tended to concentrate attention primarily on Newcommen and Watt, though with some interest in Trevithick and Woolf for their early development of high-pressure engines. (Musson, 1976, 415)

This raises other questions. For example, why have historians concentrated on Newcommen and Watt, ignoring Trevithick, Woolf and Parsons, the creators of the high-pressure steam engine and the steam turbine? The answer, I believe, is simple, namely the absence of energy in the theory of production from Adam Smith to Paul Romer. Historically, energy has found its way into production via the technology coefficient (i.e., the A scaler in the Cobb-Douglas production function) (Jorgenson, 1983, Bresnahan and Trajtenberg, 1992, Helpman and Trajtenberg, 1994). Since shocks occur, by definition, at points in time, and not over time (i.e., a century), it stands to reason that energy innovations have been studied as distinct, one-shot events. This way of modeling energy shocks is very much alive and well in the literature today. Take, for example, Timothy Bresnahan, Elhanan Helpman and Manuel Trajtenberg's work on "General Purpose Technologies," where energy shocks are viewed as one-shot phenomena (Bresnahan and Trajtenberg, 1992, Helpman and Trajtenberg, 1994). Specifically, "GPT (General Purpose Technologies) innovations such as the "steam engine, electricity or micro-electronics" prompt investments in complementary inputs, thereby giving rise to "recurrent cycles."

During the first phase of each cycle output and productivity grow slowly or even decline, and it is only in the second phase that growth starts in earnest. The historical record of productivity growth associated with electrification, and perhaps also of computerization lately, may offer supportive evidence for this pattern. (Helpman and Trajtenberg, 1994, 1)

As for the consequences of this "neglect," Musson points out:

This neglect, however, has had serious consequences for the historical interpretation of Britain's nineteenth-century industrial development. The overwhelming emphasis on the initial growth of steam power has tended to create a very misleading of the pace and extent of early steam-powered mechanization in British industry. (Musson, 1976, 416)

CONCLUSIONS

As ironic as it may appear, despite being "the" cause of the emergence of political economy/moral philosophy in the nineteenth century, energy is, Robert Owen, Charles Babbage, and Karl Marx's writings notwithstanding, nowhere to be found in the corpus of nineteenth-century political economy. By 1890, the year in which Marshall's *Principles of Economics* was published, power/energy/force had been all but forgotten. Seen through the eyes of a modern-day scientist, such a state of affairs is completely unacceptable. That the dominant analytical model(s) and corresponding science, by which it should be understood field of inquiry (in this case, the science of wealth), should be devoid of the initial shock defies all reason. What then are we to make of what has to rank as one of the most egregious oversights in the history of the social sciences, if not the sciences in general?

I offer two responses. First, it is important to keep things in their proper historical perspective. Nothwithstanding their claims to "being scientific," Adam Smith and David Ricardo were not "scientists" in the generally accepted definition of the word. That is, they were not scientists in the sense of Newton, Leibnitz, Laplace etcetera. This can be attributed to (1) the absence of a positive tradition in the science of wealth (2) the presence of a massive technology shock, and (3) the normative nature of their work. Prior to Smith's *Wealth of Nations*, there was, in general, little interest in the science of wealth, owing, no doubt, to the stationary nature of technology, specifically, the energy or work technology. Production processes in the late seventeenth/early eighteenth century were Neolithic in scope, not having undergone substantive change for over 9,000 years. Against this somewhat stoic background was thrust a new energy technology, capable of multiplying wealth at unimaginable rates.

As has been the case in almost branches of scientific inquiry, periods characterized by massive shocks rarely yield important insights into the underlying causes (contemporaneously). The problem is akin to the degrees of freedom problem in statistical inference. Specifically, there are too few *degrees of freedom*. However, these periods are generally good for science as they foment interest in the subject matter.

This only raises another question, namely if Smith did, in fact, get it wrong—or not completely right—then why didn't his successors, of which there were many (nineteenth-century political economists), get it right? Initial incursions into a subject matter, especially in the eighteenth century, are bound to produce limited results, given the absence of a foundation on which to build. The reason, I submit, lies with the decidedly normative (read: political) nature of political economy in the nineteenth century. As I have attempted to show in this chapter, from Smith to Ricardo, from Ricardo to Marx, and from Marx to Jevons, the nineteenth-century science of wealth was normative in scope. That broadly defined energy should be absent from the debate over distribution, from Ricardo to Marshall, is evidence of its "political" nature. Energy in the form of "fire power" is what created the wealth in the textile mills of Great Britain, yet it was ignored. Capital (tools) and labor, two organization-related inputs, jostled with each other to see who would get the larger share of the resulting energy rents.

Clearly, there was nothing scientific about classical, radical or neoclassical political economy. The stakes were clearly political. Had nineteenth century moral philosophers been more interested in the positive aspects of production, exchange and distribution, they would have, in my opinion, come up with something akin to Chapter 1. Unfortunately, this was not to be. The question then is, did or does it matter? For example, would Newtonian production analysis and the models of exchange and distribution presented in Chapter 1 have made a difference?

Personally, I am convinced that it would have. The reasons are many. First, it would permitted early classical political economists to correctly identify the shock as one having to do with a new power source—not with the resulting specialization and division of labor. Second, it would have provided a clearer picture of the changing role of labor in production processes, and, consequently, avoided the acrimonious debate between utopian and radical socialists, on the one hand, and neoclassical political economists on the other, over the role of labor and capital in production. Third, it would have clarified, from very early on, the problem of distribution as a problem of energy rent sharing.

As I shall argue in the next chapter, the failures of nineteenth-century political economists, be they classical, utopian socialistic or neoclassical, weighed heavily in the twentieth-century balance. A century of discourse had failed to come to grips with the new power-drive technology that had revolutionized material civilization. In a stationary state, this would have been inconsequential. The problem, however, is that at the beginning of the twentieth century, the world was hit by another energy shock, one more far-reaching, one even greater, namely electric drive. In the immortal words of the twentieth century Spanish-American philosopher, George Santayana, "those who choose to ignore the errors of the past are bound to repeat them." Not having understood the role of steam power in production, exchange and distribution, mainstream political economy (neoclassical and Marxian), as I shall now proceed to show, was unable to identify, let alone understand, the role of a new power drive technology on the U.S. and world economies, namely electricity. While the power drive technology had changed, the problems raised by Adam Smith and Robert Owen remained. Would the "extent of the market" limit the division of labor based on electro-magnetic motors? Would income increase commensurately with output/productive capacity? Would welfare rise as a result? Would gluts arise? Chapter 3 examines these questions.

NOTES

1. In some cases, supervision may have been organized hierarchically, especially when children were involved.

2. Little is known of the functional distribution of income within the family unit. Given that ownership of all the factors was concentrated, the distribution problem as, for all intents and purposes, inexistent.

3. In more practical terms, this implies that every factory worker had the equivalent of 0.682222 of a horse supplying motive power in lieu of human, muscular energy.

4. According to A. E. Musson:

In trying to assess the growth of industrial steam power in this period, one of the main problems is that of measuring "horsepower." Concern for economy in fuel consumption had led in the eighteenth century to production figures on the "duty" of different engines, the unit being the million ft-lb per bushel (94lb) of coal, for example, by measuring the quantity of water raised, the height through which it was lifted, and the coal consumed by a pumping engine. These figures permitted calculation of the comparative thermal efficiency of engines—greatly improved from Watt's time onwards—and also provided data for calculating From roughly 1841 onwards, increases in horsepower per worker were, in large measure, the result of improvements in the design of and capacity of steam engines. (Musson, 1976, 418)

5. Conventionally defined labor productivity is defined as the ratio of output (value added) to labor input.

6. Remember that power looms/spindles operated on a continuous-time basis.

7. One could argue that U.K. merchant interest in the repeal of the Corn Laws as manifested by the "Anti-Corn Law League" is evidence, albeit circumstantial, of the presence of underincome in Great Britain. As a number of historians have pointed out, it was primarily commercial interests (producers and merchants), not the various labor organizations, that petitioned and campaigned against the Corn Laws, the underlying idea being that by opening the U.K. market to foreign corn producers, it would be better disposed to export its surplus abroad (von Schulze-Gaevernitz, 1895; Lloyd-Jones and Lewis, 1988).

8. For more on the role of energy in the history (ancient and modern) of material civilization, see Chapter 2 of Beaudreau (1998).

9. Moral philosophers, at the time, were, in general, unaware of advances in natural philosophy. Had, for example, Adam Smith been familiar with classical mechanics, as developed by Newton, Leibnitz, and Laplace, political economy may have taken a different turn. It is my view that had Smith, and to a lesser degree the French physiocrats, adopted natural philosophy as their underlying model, then political economy would have been spared two centuries of missed opportunities, paradoxes, and, failures.

10. The *Wealth of Nations*, was not the first attempt at understanding wealth in general. As is well known, the Physiocrats had set out to study wealth from a scientific point of view as early as 1759. Given Smith's familiarity with this body of literature, it could be argued that the *Wealth of Nations* is synthetic in nature, consisting of Physiocracy augmented by water- and steam-powered machinery. In passing, it should be noted that Physiocracy is consistent with the analytical framework presented in Chapter 1. According to the Physiocrats, agriculture is the only source of "economic surplus." Another way of seeing this is in terms of energy rents. Specifically, only in agriculture were energy rents, defined as the difference between output and costs, physically possible.

11. From a strictly physical point of view, the only way in which labor can be more productive is for it, as a source of energy, to use better tools (higher second-law efficiency), or for it to exert more energy/force.

12. Smith's hunting metaphor attests to the Paleolithic nature of classical value theory.

13. According to Samuel Hollander, Richard Cantillon was among the first to document this change.

We perceive, therefore, an interest in Cantillon's work in the nature and measurement of the factors directly involved in the production process, reflecting a departure from a traditional concern with the *merchant*—in contrast with the employer (master-manufacturer or farmer)—as the recipient of "profits" or the bearer of "loss." But the "net" return to the master-manufacturer or farmer to which Cantillon refers is not formally related to their function's as capitalist-employers; for all recipients of uncertain incomes were profit-earning entrepreneurs "whether they set up with a capital to conduct their enterprise" or direct their own labour "without capital." (Hollander, 1973, 40)

14. The same question could be raised with regard to the current practice of analyzing the role of information, computers, and technology from the point of view of labor productivity. Clearly, labor in its role as a supervisory input and information, computers, and control devices, are substitutes.

15. This has since become known as the "trickle down effect."

16. This duality was not inconsequential. Take, for example, the case of communism in China, whose chief architects believed that industrialization could be achieved with labor as the principal factor input. The reforms of 1979 and the current Chinese government's obsession with energy, one could argue, have righted the wrong perpetrated by Marx's writings over a century ago.

17. One could argue that, by now, its productivity was, in fact, marginal.

18. Interestingly enough, Philip Mirowski, in *More Heat Than Light, Economics as Social Physics, Physics as Nature's Economics*, does not address this question,

preferring to focus, for the most part, on the use by neoclassical political economists of the field metaphor to describe utility and production.

19. Marshall, in Chapter 1 of Book VI, does, however, refer to an energy-based surplus: "But as it is, our growing power over nature makes her yield an even larger surplus above necessaries." (Marshall, 1890, 418)

20. For more on the shortcomings of neoclassical utility theory, see Mirowski (1989).

3

Electric Power and Early Twentieth-Century Political Economy

The speed with which electricity was adopted may be readily indicated. Electric motors accounted for less than 5 percent of total installed horsepower in American manufacturing in 1899. The growth in the first years of the twentieth century was such that by 1909 their share of manufacturing horsepower was 25 percent. Ten years later the share rose to 55 percent and by 1929 electric motors completely dominated the manufacturing sector by providing over 80 percent of total installed horsepower. The sharp rise in productivity in the American economy, in the years after World War I, doubtless owed a great deal, both directly and indirectly, to the electrification of manufacturing.

—Nathan Rosenberg, *Technology and American Economic Growth*

INTRODUCTION

The shift from the domestic to the factory system, as pointed out earlier, lifted and pushed back the energy constraint that had, for over two million years, constrained Homo sapiens'—neanderthalensis and sapiens—ability to transform the earth's abundant supply of raw materials into goods and services. The constraint, however, had not been lifted completely, owing, in large measure, to the associated power transmission technology, namely what has been been described as cumbersome belting, gearing and shafting. Further, not all production processes were amenable to mechanization (i.e., driven by steam power). Part of this owed to the size of economically viable steam engines (especially high-pressure engines, and steam turbines), limiting potential applications to relatively large concerns.

Enter a new power transmission technology, namely, electro-magnetic motors (hereafter, electric motors). Unlike steam engines, electric motors came in different sizes and more importantly, different—read, faster—speeds. The energy constraint was, once again, lifted and pushed back, in this case, further than ever before. Production processes that had, hitherto, not been mechanized were. Henry Ford's electric motor-driven assembly line is a case in point. Static material-handling processes of which the final assembly of the automobile is a case in point, (i.e., the craft system) were replaced with continuous-flow material-handling processes, driven by direct-current (DC) electric motors. Secondly, production processes which were mechanized (i.e., powered by steam) were converted to electric power, resulting in even greater speeds (throughput rates), and consequently, higher throughput and productivity. The result: the second industrial revolution. Electric power transformed industry, increasing throughput rates, and mechanizing processes that had, until then, resisted inanimate power. Hand-held, electric power tools are a case in point. Electric drills, saws and planners replaced hand drills, saws and planners.

This chapter proceeds in the same way as the last. I begin by examining the impact of electric power on Western industrialized economies, paying particular attention to the manufacturing sector. This is then followed by a look at its impact on political economy. How did the economics profession view this shock? More versatile than belting, gearing and shafting, electric drive *de facto* removed the energy constraint, setting the stage for what turned out to be 75 years of energy-deepening.

Getting to the Garden of Eden, however, was not without setbacks. As shown in Chapter 1, increasing quanta of power/energy is not a sufficient condition for growth. More specifically, a condition for output growth given the necessary productive capacity is commensurate money income growth. This raises the problem of underincome, specifically, the problem of money income growth in the presence of a producer-merchant exchange technology. As I argue in this chapter, the shift from steam drive to electric drive and the ensuing increase in productive capacity, productivity etcetera, resulted in an acute case of underincome. Productive capacity in U.S. manufacturing increased faster than money income in the 1910s, 1920s and 1930s. Drawing heavily from my earlier work (Beaudreau, 1996a), I argue that the Smoot-Hawley Tariff Bill of 1929, and the National Industrial Recovery Act of 1933 were policy measures aimed at resolving the problem of underincome in the U.S. economy in the 1920s and 1930s.

This then leads me to the examine both the reaction to this new energy technology by political economists, and, secondly, its impact on political economy. As can be easily surmised, political economists in general were unable to identify the technological shock, let alone study its consequences. There were, however, exceptions, including University of Pennsylvania economics professor Simon N. Patten, Columbia University economics professor Rexford G. Tugwell, Columbia University economics professor Thornstein Veblen, British chemist and Nobel Prize laureate, Frederick Soddy, and Columbia University engineering professors Walter Rautenstrauch and Howard Scott. Finding turn-of-the century political economy to be largely irrelevant, owing to what they perceived of as conditions of ubiquitous abundance, not scarcity, they set out to replace the "economics of scarcity" by what Stuart Chase referred to as the "economics of abundance" (Chase, 1934), based on energy. Man's ability to extract increasingly greater quanta of energy/force from his environment, they maintained, had transformed the problem of economics from one based on scarcity to one based on abundance. One could argue that political economy, being born of energy shocks (i.e., the steam engine), had never been about scarcity, but rather was, from its inception, about abundance. For example, Smith's *Wealth of Nations* can be viewed as a how-to guide to abundance, one focusing, for the most part, on the "extent of the market" and specialization. That political economy be essentially British in origin is, in my view, a testimony to this. Nineteenth-century Great Britain had reached a level of material civilization unparalleled in history, a fact not lost on Alfred Marshall. It therefore follows that had political economy been born of scarcity, then it most certainly would not have been British.

For the most part, these writers were ignored. Sitting pretty in its poorly fitting, newly cut suit (i.e., Marshallian political economy), neoclassical political economy failed to take heed. The second industrial revolution was ignored. However, its effects could not be. The ensuing breakdown of the gold standard, the Smoot-Hawley Tariff Bill of 1929, the Great Depression, the National Recovery Administration and the New Deal served to cast a long shadow of doubt on classical, radical and neoclassical political economy as relevant "sciences of wealth." Lessons not learned from the past (i.e., the nineteenth century) had returned with Santayanian vengeance to haunt the Western world.

The fall was great, but not fatal, as members of the scientific community, appalled and, in some cases, outraged by the irony of poverty in the face of such great potential, set out to reconstruct the science of wealth. The Continental Committee on Technocracy, a collection of scientists and engineers, presented a new science of wealth, founded on energy. The result was, for the most part, a refined version of Claude de Saint-Simon's nineteenth-century vision of a society governed by scientists and engineers.

I begin by examining the impact of electric drive on output, distribution and exchange using the analytical framework developed in Chapter 1. This will then be followed by a look at how these changes affected political economy in general. Whereas steam power revolutionized production processes by moving production out of "cottages" and into steam power-driven "factories," electric power revolutionized production processes in two fundamental ways. First, by replacing steam engines with electric motors, throughput rates were more easily controlled, and more importantly, increased. To the naive observer, nothing will have changed, yet, output may rise by 100 percent as the speed is doubled. Second, by making inanimate power available on a smaller scale, production processes that had, up until then, resisted the shift to steam power inanimate power succumbed. In the former case, the required capital actually decreased as cumbersome belting, gearing and shafting was replaced by electric motors.

Consequently, the introduction of electric drive went largely unnoticed in political economy, where, for the most part, technological change was associated with new, often more costly, machinery. The effects of electric power on productivity, output, employment and expenditure, however, were not ignored. Last, I examine the indirect effects of the second industrial revolution on economic theory. I maintain that the fields of industrial organization, organizational behavior, industrial relations, Keynesian political economy (macroeconomics) are by-products of the second industrial revolution, more specifically of the problem of exchange (underincome), and the problem of distribution.

Electricity Production in the Early Twentieth Century

As pointed out earlier, electric power is a misnomer, electricity not being a source of energy, but rather a transmission technology.[1] In the words of David Landes, "Electricity is not a source but a form of energy. Electrical dynamos and similar generators are essentially converters, turning water, steam, or other primary power into current, which can be stored in batteries, used directly for illumination, heat, or communication, or transformed into motion by means of motors" (Landes, 1969, 277). Early developments in electro-magnetics bear this out. When Michael Faraday discovered that an electric force exposed to to a magnet repelled the latter, the force in question had been generated by the thermal energy in his body. Throughout the ensuing period, electric power continued to be generated from nonelectric (i.e., nonatomic) sources. Only recently has Homo sapiens learned how to tap the energy contained in the atom. Atomic power, however, represents but a fraction of current world total power consumption, the bulk coming from fossil-fuel and hydraulic-based energy sources, both of which are both based on solar radiation, and, ultimately, the nuclear fusion of the sun's abundant supply of hydrogen into helium.

Table 3.1 provides data on the installed generating capacity in U.S. electric utilities and industrial generating plants from 1902 to 1970, by type (i.e., hydro, steam and internal combustion). In 1902, total installed generating capacity stood at 2,987,000 kilowatts. By 1930, it had reached 41,828,000 kilowatts, a 1,277 percent increase, which corresponds to an annual average annual increase of 42 percent. By 1960, it stood at 186,534,000 kilowatts,

Table 3.1
Installed Generating Capacity, United States, 1902–1970

Year	Total*	Utilities*	Industrial*	Steam*	Hydro*
1902	2,987	1,212	1,775	1,847	1,140
1907	6,809	2,709	4,100	4,903	1,906
1912	10,980	5,165	5,815	8,186	2,794
1917	15,494	8,994	6,500	11,608	3,886
1923	23,235	15,643	7,592	17,553	5,682
1925	30,087	21,472	8,615	22,937	7,150
1927	34,574	25,079	9,495	26,647	7,927
1929	38,708	29,839	8,869	29,783	8,925
1930	41,153	32,384	8,769	31,503	9,650
1931	42,287	33,698	8,589	32,097	10,190
1933	43,037	34,587	8,450	32,707	10,330
1935	42,828	34,436	8,392	32,429	10,399
1937	44,370	35,620	8,750	33,184	11,186
1939	49,438	38,863	10,575	35,932	12,075
1941	53,995	42,405	11,590	39,474	12,912
1943	60,539	47,951	12,588	43,840	14,991
1945	62,868	49,189	12,877	45,248	15,892
1947	65,151	52,322	12,829	47,242	15,956
1949	76,570	63,100	13,470	56,472	17,662
1950	82,850	68,919	13,931	61,495	18,674
1951	90,127	75,775	14,352	67,372	19,870
1952	97,312	82,227	15,085	72,620	21,416
1953	107,354	91,502	15,852	80,960	23,054
1954	118,878	102,592	16,286	91,250	24,238
1955	130,895	114,472	16,423	101,698	25,742
1956	137,342	120,697	16,645	107,251	26,386
1957	146,221	129,123	17,098	114,660	27,761
1958	160,651	142,597	18,054	126,625	30,089
1959	175,000	157,347	17,653	139,073	31,884
1960	186,534	168,569	17,965	149,161	33,180
1961	199,216	181,312	17,904	158,588	36,301
1962	209,576	191,747	17,829	167,015	38,162
1963	228,757	210,549	18,208	183,348	40,928
1964	240,471	222,285	18,186	193,026	42,899
1965	254,519	236,126	18,393	205,423	44,490
1966	266,816	247,843	18,973	216,309	45,691
1967	288,185	269,252	18,933	234,195	45,691
1968	310,181	291,058	19,123	252,975	51,874
1969	332,606	313,349	19,257	273,534	53,447
1970	360,327	341,090	19,237	298,803	55,751

*000 kilowatts
Source: U.S. Department of Commerce (1975), S74–S77.

which corresponds to a 345 percent increase over 1930. Broken down by type, we find that in 1902, 38 percent of total installed capacity was in the form of hydro, while the remaining 62 percent was in the form of steam (i.e., turning steam turbines). By 1960, hydro had lost considerable ground to steam. Of the 186,534,000 kilowatts of total installed capacity in 1960, 18 percent (i.e., 33,180,000 kilowatts) was in the form of hydro, while the remaining 82 percent was in the form of steam (i.e., 143,116,000 kilowatts).

As the figures in Table 3.1 indicate, most of the growth in electricity-generating capacity in the United States in the twentieth century in general and the early twentieth century in particular, was coal-fossil-fuel-based. This was also true of other industrialized nations such as the United Kingdom, Germany and France. The point is that the second industrial revolution did not witness the emergence of a new power source, but rather, the emergence of a new power-drive technology, namely electricity.

ELECTRIC DRIVE AND ITS EFFECTS ON PRODUCTION, EXCHANGE, AND DISTRIBUTION

Few were the sectors of the U.S. economy not affected by the new power transmission technology. Production processes that hitherto had been driven by belting, gearing and shafting transmitting steam and hydraulic power, were converted to electric drive, resulting in substantially higher throughput rates. Production processes that had resisted "mechanization" were mechanized. Among these one finds the mining sector, the petro-chemical sector, and the material handling sector in general. Electric motor-powered conveyor belts and pumps increased throughput rates in all of these sectors, resulting in vastly greater productivity. Analytically speaking, the introduction of electric drive ought be viewed as an extension of the first industrial revolution where, as argued earlier, inanimate power replaced animate, muscular power. Now, however, the chemical energy contained in fossil fuels would drive electro-magnetic generators, the output of which would, in turn, drive production processes.

This section examines the effects of this far-reaching change on production, exchange and distribution using the analytic framework developed in Chapter 1. As I shall argue, the shift from cumbersome belting-, shafting- and gearing-based drive to electric drive, while a watershed in the history of power drive technology (Rosenberg, 1983; Devine, 1990; Nye, 1990), went largely unnoticed in political economy. Unlike the shift from muscular to steam power which, to most, defined the industrial revolution, it failed to generate much interest among political economists. Working with models in which capital and labor were the only factors of production, the shift to a new power-drive technology was ignored, especially in light of the fact that, in many cases, electric-power drive was less capital intensive (Devine, 1990).

By allowing for increased levels of energy consumption, the shift to electric drive increased output considerably. Few were the sectors that were not affected. Productivity per lower-level supervisor (machine operatives) increased, in some cases doubling. Once again, this raised the problem of distribution. Who would appropriate the new set of energy rents? Also, it raised the problem of exchange, specifically, the problem of money income growth. More productive firms have no private incentives to increase wage income. Merchants, in turn, have no private incentives to increase orders from consumer and capital goods firms. Since profits are a residual income form, it follows that both wage and profit income fail to rise.

Electric Drive, Energy Consumption, and Productivity

According to Warren D. Devine, Jr., the shift from shafting, belting and gearing drive to electric drive stands as one of the most rapid and complete transitions in "energy use" in modern history.

Perhaps the most rapid and complete transition in energy use was the shift from steam power to electric power for driving machinery. Steam power prevailed at the turn of the century, with steam engines providing around 80 percent of the total capacity for driving machinery. By 1920, electricity had replaced steam as the major source of motive power, and by 1929—just forty-five years after their first use in a factory—electric motors provided 78 percent of all mechanical drive. (Devine, 1990, 21)

While ignored by the economics profession, this change galvanized the attention of the engineering profession, broadly defined. Process and power engineers could hardly contain their enthusiasm. Consider, for example, the following excerpt from a speech by Matthew S. Sloan, President of the New York Edison Company, to the annual dinner of trust companies in Chicago in February 1929:

Mr. Sloan compared this age which he termed the "new industrial revolution" with "the industrial revolution" in the eighteenth century, when the steamboat and locomotive came into use. As steam brought in the machine era, electricity, he said, has brought in the era of mass production which has so greatly affected the general economic situation and social conditions. Thus, electricity, he said, is responsible for our present production. With all its attendant circumstances of lowered unit costs, lowered prices, increased wages, intensifying merchandising, wider markets, higher standard of living. Electricity-motivating machinery has multiplied the working power of the nation many times, he said, and the generating stations of the country now have a capacity of 35,000,000 horsepower, of the ability to do the work of about 350,000,000 men. In 1900, the generating capacity was only 3,000,000 horsepower. (*New York Times*, February 15, 1929)

In the same year, the President's Conference on Unemployment, chaired by Herbert C. Hoover, identified the electrification of U.S. industry as the "single most important change in U.S. industry." In its report, it described this far-reaching change as follows:

Characteristic also has been the rise in the use of power—three and three-quarters times faster than the growth of population—and the extent to which power has been made readily available not alone for driving tools of increased size and capacity, but for convenient purposes in the the smallest business enterprise and on the farm and in the home. Factories no longer need to cluster about the source of power. Widespread interconnection between power plants, arising out of an increasing appreciation of the value of flexibility in power and made possible by technical advances during recent years, has created huge reservoirs of power so that abnormal conditions in one locality need not stop the wheels of industry. The increasing flexibility with which electricity can be delivered from power has enabled manufacturers and farmers to meet high labor costs by the application of power-driven specialized machines; and, power in this flexible form has penetrated into every section of the United States, including many rural areas. The survey shows that as a nation we use as much electricity as all of the rest of the world combined. Through the subdivision of power, the unskilled worker has become a skilled operator, multiplying his effectiveness with specialized automatic machinery and processes. (National Bureau of Economic Research, 1929, xi)

The shift to electric drive is easily formalized in terms of Newtonian production analysis. Specifically, electric drive, by lifting the constraints imposed by belting, shafting and gearing transmission technology, allowed for greater inanimate energy consumption per period of time ($E(t)$). Higher energy consumption per unit time period increased throughput rates throughout all sectors of United States. ($W(t)$), and for that matter, in industries the world over, increasing conventionally measured productivity. Output per lower-level supervisor (i.e., conventionally defined labor productivity) increased substantially. In sectors where water, wind or steam power had failed to penetrate, electric drive provided a flexible, made-to-scale source of power, increasing productivity. As pointed out earlier, and highlighted in these quotes, there was hardly a sector of the U.S. economy that had not been affected in one way or another by electric drive.

Consider, for example, the mining sector, which had, throughout the nineteenth century, resisted "mechanization." David E. Nye describes the application of electricity in the mining sector as follows:

Mine owners had many uses for electricity. Electric lights gave safe illumination that did not exhaust scarce oxygen supplies. Electric-alarm systems signaled danger or disaster. Electric drills were more portable than other drills: "Where electric power is used, small wires take the place of cumbersome pipes necessary for the transmission of steam or compressed air." Portable electric pumps often replaced steam engines, to keep pits free from water. An electric hoist had similar advantages over a steam-driven hoist; it was "more easily installed, and when in place takes up much less room than a steam outfit of the same hoisting capacity. It does away with the boiler, coal bins, and piping." ... The greatest single change electricity made in the mines was the elimination of the mules, which were replaced by squat, powerful electric locomotives.

With such equipment one company in Pennsylvania produced 11,000 tons of coal a month in the 1890's without using a single mule. With similar equipment New York and Scranton Coal company saved five or six cents per ton of coal extracted and the Hillside Coal and Iron Company saved almost $20,000 per year on the cost of mules and laborers." . . . At Green Ridge Colliery, for example, a station engineer, a motorman, and helper could run an electric locomotive that replaced six mule drivers, four boy helpers, and seventeen mules. (Nye, 1990, 205)

No greater testimony to/of the prominent role of electric drive in the rise of twentieth-century U.S. industry is there than the "lamentations" of laggards, the most important of which, at the turn of the century, was Great Britain. As America's industrial might increased with every additional megawatt of electric power, Great Britain, mired in the glory of steam and, more importantly, a web of regulation, could only concede defeat. Beginning in 1916, a number of committees were struck to study the problem. The first was the Coal Conservation Sub-Committee, set up in 1916 under Viscount Haldane, which, in turn, appointed a subcommittee to investigate the question of electric power supply in the United Kingdom. Its report, issued in 1918, dealt in considerable detail with "the use of electric power in industry, and recommended reorganization of the generation and main transmission on a regional basis under the central supervision of a Board of Electricity Commissioners with wide powers" (Self and Watson, 1952, 35). In the same year, the Board of Trade appointed an Electrical Trades Committee to consider the position of the "electrical trades" after the war. Sir Henry Self and Elizabeth Watson summarized its findings as follows:

Reference was made in strong terms to the crippling handicaps of the local and political considerations which had prevented Great Britain from reaping the fruits of the outstanding preeminence which it had received in original constructive research and development of electricity generation at the hands of pioneers such as Faraday, Wheatstone, Kelvin, Swan, Hopkinson, and many others. The loss of that outstanding lead, the history of industry in the intervening years, and the evidence taken during their examination of the position, led the Committee to the following conclusions:

(i) That Government should recognize the dependence of the State, both from military and industrial standpoints, upon the supply of electrical energy as a "key industry."

(ii) That the distribution of electrical energy should be regarded no longer as parochial but as a national question of urgent importance.

(iii) That the present system of electrical generation and distribution is behind the times and is a serious handicap in international competition.

(iv) That the present conditions are mainly due to faulty legislation and to divided and therefore weak executive control.

(vii) That the determination of questions concerning concentration of generating plant with the resulting economy of coal and other savings, requires immediate attention.

(ix) That only by such steps can the electrical manufacturing industry of this country be fully developed, not only for the home trade, but as a consequence of the great industry now maturing overseas; that the gain to the State from a well-planned scheme of reconstruction will be inestimable; and that the items which are capable of reasonable calculation, such as saving in fuel, reduction in factory costs, and increased output will together represent not less than 100,000,000 pounds per annum. (Self and Watson, 1952, 35)

What is particularly noteworthy is the reference made in point (ix) of the "great industry now maturing overseas." This clearly demonstrates that the Electrical Trades Committee was well aware, as early as 1916, of the threat posed by the electrification of U.S. industry. Similar conclusions were reached by the Williamson Committee, struck by the Board of Trade in 1917:

(1) That when British industry is subjected to the test of keen international competition after the war, its success will depend upon the adoption of the most efficient methods and machinery, so as to reduce manufacturing costs as much as possible.

(2) That a highly important element in reducing manufacturing costs will be the general extension of the use of electric power supplied at the lowest possible price, and it is by largely increasing the amount of power used in the industry that the average output per head. and, as a consequence, the wages of the worker can be raised.

(5) That a comprehensive system for the generation of electricity, and, where necessary, reorganizing its supply should be established as soon as possible. (Self and Watson, 1952, 37)

In 1924, David Lloyd George, then Liberal member of Parliment, struck an informal committee, the purpose of which was to address the "inter-linked questions of coal and electricity." The results of the inquiry were published in a report entitled *Coal and Power Inquiry*, which "called for compulsory powers of acquisition, coordination and regulation to enable the "Electricity Commissioners" to grant to approved bodies the right of supplying power within substantial defined areas" (Self and Watson, 1952, 52). H.H. Ballin summarized the Inquiry's findings as follows:

With our various competitors going ahead swiftly in the direction of the greater utilization of power, a policy of preventing power development in industry would leave our workers in the position of having to compete on unequal terms so that the incompetence of management would have to be made up by the toil of the workers. It ushers in a vista of endless strikes, industrial trouble and internal strain. The way out is to be found in the direction of scientific production and utilisation of power. (Lloyd George, 1924, 99)

How did the resulting energy-deepening affect conventionally defined productivity in U.S. manufacturing? That is, how did it affect $W(t)/S_I(t)$ (see Table 1.3)? As it turns out, this is a particularly difficult issue, given the available data. The data for productivity in this period are rather sparse and incomplete. This notwithstanding, I proceeded in two distinct ways. First, I considered the case of the Ford Motor Company which, in 1913, moved from static assembly to electric power-driven dynamic assembly, commonly known as mass production. Second, various NPA productivity measures developed in Chapter 1 were estimated for this period.

The choice of the Ford Motor Company (FMC) as a case study was based on its early use of electric drive (Nye, 1990; Beaudreau, 1996a). It is important to note that its founder, Henry Ford, had been chief mechanical engineer at the Detroit Edison Illuminating Company from 1886 to 1899, a period of 14 years. In earlier work (Beaudreau, 1996a), I argued that this period in Ford's life is key to an understanding of the development of high-throughput continuous-flow manufacturing at the FMC and, ultimately, in the United States. From then on, Ford was, to put it mildly, a power zealot, as evidenced by his lifelong friendship with Thomas Edison, and his attempt at securing the rights to the Muscle Shoals hydroelectric project in 1919. His single most important contribution to production technology, I argued in Beaudreau (1996a), was the application of electric drive to production and assembly processes, resulting in record increases in productivity (Nye, 1990; Beaudreau, 1996a).

Table 3.2
The Ford Motor Company, Assembly Process Productivity

Process	Phase	Assembly Time	Index
Magneto	Initial	20m,0s	100
	I	13m,10s	66
	II	7m,0s	35
	III	5m,0s	25
Transmission Cover	Initial	18m	100
	I	9m	50
Chassis Assembly	Initial	12h,28m	100
	I	6h,0m	48
	II	1h,33m	12

Source: Beaudreau (1996a), 6.

To see this, consider Table 3.2, taken from Beaudreau (1996a), which presents throughput data measured in terms of time. Prior to the introduction of electric-drive-powered assembly lines, it took, on average, 20 minutes to assemble a magneto. In the initial phase of electric drive-powered assembly lines (i.e., conveyor belts), this was reduced to 13 minutes, followed by a further reduction to 7 minutes, and utlimately, to 5 minutes. Productivity, it therefore follows, had quadrupled. Even greater productivity gains were achieved in chassis assembly where the required time went from 12 hours, 28 minutes, to 6 hours, and eventually, to 1 hour, 33 minutes.

Table 3.3
The Ford Motor Company, Production Data, 1903–1916

Year	Employees	Model Ts	Output Per Employee
1903	125		
1904	300		
1905	300		
1906	700		
1907	575		
1908	450		
1909	1,655	13,840	8.36
1910	2,773	20,727	7.47
1911	3,976	53,488	13.45
1912	6,867	82,388	11.99
1913	14,366	189,088	13.16
1914	12,880	230,788	17.91
1915	18,892	394,788	20.89
1916	132,702	585,388	17,90

Source: Beaudreau (1996a), 152.

Table 3.3 presents standard labor productivity data, defined as the number of Model Ts per worker. From a level of 8.36 in 1912, it climbed, mercurially, to 20.89 in 1915, which corresponds to a 150 percent increase. Electric drive had more than doubled productivity. In the 1926 edition of the *Encyclopaedia Britannica*, Ford described "mass production" in the following terms:

Mass production is not merely quantity production, for this may be had with none of the requisites of mass production. Nor is it merely machine production, which also may exist without any resemblance to mass production. Mass production is the focusing upon a manufacturing project of the principles of power, accuracy, economy, system, continuity, and speed. (Ford, 1926, 821)

The operant words here are power and speed. Mass production, Ford style, was about speed.[3] In little time, electric drive as applied at the Ford Motor Company spread throughout the United States, and, for that matter, the world over. According to David S. Hounshell:

The story of mass production at the Ford Motor Company was not something only historians of a later generation would delve into and try to understand. Henry Ford's contemporaries, many of whom were competitors, closely watched the doings at Highland Park, attempting to understand and emulate the revolutionary developments. Henry Ford encouraged their interest. Unlike the Singer Manufacturing Company, the Ford Company was completely open about its organizational structure, its sales, and its production methods. . . . As a consequence of Ford's openness, Ford production technology diffused rapidly throughout American manufacturing. (Hounshell, 1984, 260)

Table 3.4
U.S. Manufacturing Data, 1912–1945

Year	Electric Power Consumption*	Employees**	Ratio	Productivity NBER***
1912	9,250	8,322	1,111	29.2
1917	20,750	9,872	2,101	31.7
1920	26,913	10,702	2,514	32.0
1921	23,993	8,262	2,904	36.8
1922	27,364	9,129	2,997	41.8
1923	32,585	10,317	3,158	40.2
1924	34,967	9,675	3,614	42.8
1925	39,725	9,942	3,995	45.6
1926	46,350	10,156	4,563	46.5
1927	51,012	9,996	5,103	47.6
1928	52,699	9,942	5,300	49.7
1929	55,122	10,702	5,150	52.0
1930	53,930	9,562	5,640	52.3
1931	50,410	8,170	6,170	54.0
1932	43,504	6,931	6,276	50.5
1933	46,561	7,397	6,294	54.9
1934	50,593	8,501	5,951	57.4
1935	56,706	9,069	6,252	61.2
1936	62,949	9,827	6,405	61.6
1937	64,757	10,794	5,999	60.7
1938	58,452	9,440	6,191	59.9
1939	70,518	10,278	6,861	65.4
1940	83,276	10,985	7,580	68.7
1941	104,037	13,192	7,886	71.2
1942	122,762	15,280	8,034	72.4
1943	143,995	17,602	8,180	73.4
1944	145,015	17,328	8,368	72.5
1945	134,955	15,524	8,693	71.5

*000,000 kilowatt hours.
**000.
***NBER: National Bureau of Economic Research.
Source: U.S. Department of Commerce (1975), Series D130, S124, D802.

Consumption of electric power in U.S. manufacturing increased dramatically in the ensuing years. Referring to Table 3.4, we see that from a level of 9,250 million kilowatt hours in 1912, it had more than doubled by 1917 (i.e., 20,750 million kilowatt hours), and, doubled again by 1927. Cast in per-worker terms, in 1912, each manufacturing employee supervised 1,111 kilowatt hours of electric power. This doubled by 1917, tripled by 1923, and quadrupled by 1926.[4] Conventionally defined productivity increased in-step. Productivity indexes $[W(t)/S_l(t)]$ for this period show a marked increase. For example, the NBER index goes from a level of 29.2 in 1912. to a level of 46.5 in 1926—a 60 percent increase. Like steam power a century and a half earlier, the shift to electric drive increased throughput rates, and, consequently, conventionally defined labor productivity. It is important to point out, however, that conventionally defined labor was not more productive per se; rather, it was being called upon to supervise the more and more work done, in this case, by inanimate energy. The second industrial revolution was, as such, a continuation of the first industrial revolution. Like the first, the key ingredient was power.

The Problem of Exchange

As far as productivity is concerned, the second industrial revolution mimicked the first. Greater inanimate power consumption in the form of electricity made for higher potential output, higher conventionally defined productivity, and for higher throughput rates. As it turns out, the similarities go well beyond productivity, specifically into the areas of exchange and distribution. For example, the problem of underincome, raised by Sismonde de Sismondi and Owen in the early nineteenth century reappeared in the early twentieth century. For merchants to increase orders, wage income had to increase. For wage income to increase, producers had to increase wages paid to their employees; however, producers, taken individually, had no private incentives to increase wages.

Table 3.5
Wage and Productivity Data, U.S. Manufacturing, 1920–1929

Year	Nominal Wage	CPI	Real Wage	Productivity Index	Wage Index
1920	0.55	54.60	0.84	100.00	100.00
1921	0.51	54.50	0.93	115.31	111.27
1922	0.48	50.10	0.95	130.62	113.92
1923	0.52	51.30	1.01	125.62	120.53
1924	0.54	51.20	1.05	133.75	125.41
1925	0.54	51.90	1.04	142.50	123.72
1926	0.54	51.10	1.05	145.31	125.25
1927	0.54	50.00	1.08	148.75	128.42
1928	0.56	50.80	1.10	155.31	131.08
1929	0.56	50.60	1.10	162.50	131.59

Source: U.S. Department of Commerce (1975), Series D802, F5, D68

This raised the spectre of underincome. Throughout the 1910s and 1920s, productive capacity increased, the result of higher throughput rates. Speed-ups in manufacturing resulted in higher output with what was essentially the same capital and labor. The difference, however, was energy consumption. As shown above, energy consumption per worker doubled, tripled and quadrupled in this period. Wages failed to increase commensurately with productivity. As profits are a residual, merchants had no incentives to increase orders of consumption and capital goods. In short, the U.S. economy suffered from underincome.

Nowhere is this more apparent than in the data contained in Table 3.5, which show that despite a 60 percent increase in conventionally measured productivity, real wages in U.S. manufacturing in the 1920s remained virtually constant. Wages could not increase as profits had not increased. Profits could not increased as wages had not increased.

Henry Ford and Edward A. Filene, the latter a successful Boston businessman, were acutely aware of the problem. Like Robert Owen a century earlier, both felt that the lack of income growth in general, and wage growth in particular, seriously compromised the growth of the U.S. economy.[5] The electrification of U.S. industry, they argued, had increased productive capacity beyond imagination. Preventing the realization of the corresponding potential was money income growth. Producers, they argued, had failed to collectively increase wage income, the key to aggregate income, output and profit growth. The following quote from Ford highlights the "Ignorant Idealist's" remarkable understanding of the shortcomings of the producer-merchant exchange technology described in Chapter 1.

We've got to stop that gouging process if we want to see all of the people reasonably prosperous. There is only one rule from industrialists and that is: Make the best quality of goods possible at the lowest cost paying the highest wages possible. Nothing can be right in this country until wages are right. The life of business comes forth from the people in orders. The factories are not stopped for lack of money but for lack of orders. Money loaned at the top means nothing. Money spent at the bottom starts everything. I think that if industrial leaders had been willing to push wages up during the last thirty years the present economic ills would at least not be as great as they are. If the government can help in these matters, well and good, but the government has not a rosy record in running itself so far. (*New York Times*, June 16, 1933, 1)

Clearly, Ford, more than any of his contemporaries, understood the workings of the exchange technology in industrialized economies. To him, the "lack of orders," on the part of merchants "stopped" factories. Only by spending "money at the bottom" (at the producer level) could this trend be reversed.[6]

Edward A. Filene shared Ford's concerns regarding the problem of exchange, namely underincome. Given that merchants' orders are based on expected sales and that expected sales are based largely on wage income, it follows that profits are increasing in wages.

In the future a really big business success on the basis of mass production and mass production will be impossible except as it makes for both high wages and low prices. Low wages and high prices manifestly cut down the widespread and sustained buying power of the masses without which mass production sooner or later defeats itself. In other words, the businessman of the future must produce prosperous customers as well as saleable goods. He cannot think of his business as an adventure in getting money from masses of people who, in one way or another for which he has no responsibility, have got money from someone else. His whole business policy must look forward to creating buying power among the masses. Otherwise mass production cannot succeed. The businessman of the future must fill the pockets of the workers and consumers before he can fill his pockets. (Filene, 1924, 201)

One cannot but be struck by the similarities with Robert Owen's view on the profit motive, as reported in the previous chapter.[7]

The Policy Responses to the Problem of Exchange

In earlier work (Beaudreau, 1996a), I argued that the Smoot–Hawley Tariff Bill of 1929 and the National Industrial Recovery Act of 1933 (NIRA), should be viewed as U.S. government policy responses to the problem of exchange as it existed in the United States in the 1920s. Specifically, the Smoot–Hawley Tariff Bill of 1929, the brainchild of Republican senator Reed Smoot of Utah and Joseph R. Grundy, President of the Pennsylvania Manufacturers Association, sought to close the gap between actual and potential output by further restricting imports from abroad—that is, relative to the Fordney–Mc-Cumber Act of 1922. Citing growing imports and mass production as the cause of overproduction, Smoot recommended further increasing the already high tariff rates on manufactures and agricultural products. The National Industrial Recovery Act of 1933, on the other hand, sought to close the gap between actual and potential output by increasing wages across the board, thus heeding Ford's and Filene's—and Robert Owen's—call for greater purchasing power.

Both can be understood in terms of the exchange technology described in Chapter 1. Specifically, the Smoot–Hawley Tariff Bill of 1929 was an attempt at circumventing the relationship between wage income and merchants' orders. In a closed economy, for merchant orders to increase, wage income has to increase. However, in this case, senator Smoot and the Republican Party, including President Herbert Hoover, attempted to increase U.S. merchants' orders for U.S. goods by reducing their orders for foreign goods. In so doing, producer revenues would increase without increasing costs.

As for the National Industrial Recovery Act of 1933, it sought to increase merchant orders by increasing wage income. The gains from electrification, its proponents argued, had been appropriated by the owners of capital, resulting in a situation in which orders for consumption goods had not increased commensurately with capacity. According to Senator Robert F. Wagner:

In my opinion, the depression arose in large part from failing to coordinate production and consumption. During the years, 1922–1929, corporate earnings rose much faster than wage rates. This led to an over expansion in productive equipment, particularly machinery and plant facilities. The great mass of consumers did not receive enough to take the goods off of the market. (Senate Congressional Record, June 7, 1933)

What is important to note is the role of underincome in both policy measures. As I argued in my earlier work, regarding the Smoot–Hawley Tariff Bill of 1929, Senator Reed Smoot knew full well that imports of manufactures had not increased in the mid-1920s, and that, on the contrary, the United States was exporting more manufactures than ever before (Beaudreau, 1996a, Chapter 3). Still, he clung to the politically expedient view that overproduction was an offshore problem. Later, in a hearing before the Utah state assembly, Smoot outlined his reasoning, pointing out that the underlying problem was generalized underincome.

On his return to Utah in August 1932, in preparation for his final battle in political life, Smoot advised his people that it had been the common attitude in 1930 to attribute the depression to unwise governmental policies, with the Smoot-Hawley act specified. Lest there were some obsessed with heresy, he declared, "To hold the American tariff policy, or any other policy of our government, responsible for this gigantic deflationary move is only to display one's ignorance of its sweeping universal character." He found that "The world is paying for its ruthless destruction of life and property in the World War and for its failure to adjust purchasing power to productive capacity during the industrial revolution of the decade following the war." (Merrill, 1990, 340)

As I argued in *Mass Production, the Stock Market Crash, and the Great Depression: The Macroeconomics of Electrification*, published in 1996, the Smoot–Hawley Tariff Bill of 1929 was ultimately responsible for the stock market boom and crash, the latter corresponding in time with the demise of the bill before the Senate from October 21 to October 30, 1929. Unlike the merchants of Manchester who saw free trade (Repeal of the Corn Laws) as a means of expanding markets and, as such, venting surpluses, Senator Reed Smoot and Pennsylvania Manufacturers Association President (later Senator) Joseph R. Grundy, naively saw higher tariffs as a means of increasing domestic sales, profits and earnings, and, in so doing, increasing the operating ratios of U.S. manufacturing firms. What is important to note here, as far as this chapter is concerned, is the fact that the Smoot–Hawley Tariff Bill of 1929 (initially announced in the summer of 1928) constituted a policy response to the problem of electrification-induced underincome.

The second policy response was the National Industrial Recovery Act (NIRA) of 1933, which, like the National Regeneration Society in nineteenth century Great Britain, sought to raise real wages, lower hours and, in the end, restore prosperity to the, by then, severely depressed U.S. economy. Drafted by Democratic Senator Robert F. Wagner of New York, and based on the writings of Rexford G. Tugwell of Columbia University, the NIRA set out to increase overall wage income, the underlying idea being that technological change had, as it were, passed labor by. Technological change, its proponents argued, increased output, income and profits; wages (labor income) had not increased. The Great Depression, Wagner, Tugwell and Moulton argued, was, as such, due to the increasingly skewed functional distribution of income (i.e., in favor of profits).

In Beaudreau (1996a), using U.S. income distribution data for the period in question, I showed that this was, in fact, inaccurate: income distribution in the late 1920s had not become more skewed in favor of profits and interest. I proceeded to argue that what Tugwell and Wagner had perceived of as oversavings/overproduction/underconsumption was, in actual fact, underincome. Profits had not risen for the simple reason that wages had not increased, the former being a residual form of factor payment (paid from sales revenue from merchants). With the benefit of hindsight, the problem facing twentieth-century America, was that which had faced nineteenth-century England, namely energy-deepening-induced underincome.[8]

The Problem of Distribution

The shift to electric drive, I argue, resulted in considerable energy-based rents. The value of total output far exceeded the cost of total output, resulting in a surplus which I refer to as energy-based rents, in this case, electric-power-based rents. Who would get what? Would labor or capital appropriate the lion's share? As pointed out above, conventionally defined productivity increased 40 percent from 1918 to 1929.

Clearly, the problem of distribution amounted to a bargaining problem involving the owners of the tools and electric drive apparatus, and the owners of supervisory skills. At stake were the nonnegligble energy rents generated by the greater energy consumption.

As it turns out, the problem of distribution as described here is only of theoretical interest, owing, in large measure, to the problem of underincome and the failure of overall money (wage and profit) income to rise.

Notwithstanding the problem of underincome, the problem of distribution does, however, manifest itself in this period, not surprisingly at the Ford Motor Company. Henry Ford was acutely aware of the causes of his success. Electric power, as pointed out above, was foremost on his list. The owners of capital, he reasoned, should not appropriate all of the rents (i.e., surplus), which is what led him, in 1914, to unilaterally double wages. The five-dollar day went in effect on January 7, 1914, much to the dismay of the U.S. business community. One could argue that the decision to double wages reflected the utopian socialist in Ford, arguing for a fair distribution of electric power-based "energy rents."

This, however, did not agree with shareholders who felt that Ford's benevolence both with workers (i.e., higher wages) and with consumers (i.e., lower prices) constituted an attack on their inalienable right to property, in this case, FMC's profits. In 1917, Horace and John Dodge, two Ford Motor Company shareholders, sued Ford on the grounds that wage increases and price decreases unduly reduced profits. Surprisingly, they won. Ford appealed the decision and eventually won. From that point on, he did everything in his power to rid himself of shareholders, turning the FMC into a privately-held company.

As Ford's production techniques spread throughout U.S. manufacturing, productivity increased, doubling in many industries. The problem, however, was that inspite of significantly higher productive capacity, output, income and expenditure increased at historical rates. Something was amiss, argued Ford, and later, Boston merchant Edward A. Filene. The problem, they argued, was money income, more precisely the failure of money income to rise in step with capacity and productivity. The solution: increase wages and lower prices. Throughout the 1920s, Ford and Filene, sensing the underlying disequilibrium, pleaded, to the point of begging, their fellow businessmen to increase wages.

We've got to stop that gouging process if we want to see all of the people reasonably prosperous. There is only one rule for industrialists and that is: Make the best quality of goods possible at the lowest cost paying the highest wages possible. Nothing can be right in this country until wages are right. The life of business comes forth from the people in orders. Money loaned at the top means nothing. Money spent at the bottom starts everything. I think that if industrial leaders had been willing to push wages up and up during the last thirty years the present economic ills would at least not be as great as they are. If the government can help in these matters, well and good, but the government has not a rosy record in running itself thus far. (*New York Times*, June 16, 1933)

Under mass production, however, the profit motive not only can be attached to the common welfare, but it can not escape being so attached. Under mass production, attaching it to any other aim spells loss. There can be no profit in mass production unless the masses are also profiting thereby. The time has come, however, when the greatest total profits can be secured only through supplying the masses with the best values. So there is no war now between selfishness and unselfishness; the only war is between the traditional notion of where self-interest lies and the newly discovered thruths of profit-making. (Filene, 1931, 198)

As Ford and Filene made clear, higher wages would address two problems, namely the problem of underincome, as well as the problem of equity. America had failed to realize its new-found potential for lack of money income (nominal and real). By increasing wages (and lowering prices), overall income would rise, thus increasing merchants' orders. This, in turn, would increase firm revenues and, consequently, profits, the latter being a residual form of income. Put differently, by increasing wages, the income pie would be bigger, as would labor and capital's individual share.

ELECTRIC DRIVE, ENERGY-DEEPENING, AND EARLY TWENTIETH-CENTURY POLITICAL ECONOMY

As argued in the previous chapter, nineteenth-century political economy was the product of energy innovations, namely water power and "fire power" in the form of water-powered and steam-power-driven machinery. Classical, radical and neoclassical political economy, it therefore follows, grew out of the "machine age," dating back to the late eighteenth century. The irony, as pointed out earlier, is the absence of energy *per se* in formal models of production. Energy innovations were the defining changes; yet, energy was nowhere to be found. This, I argue, is crucial to understanding the role of electric drive and energy-deepening in early twentieth century political economy.

Theoretical models of production (e.g., Cobb-Douglas) in this period focused exclusively on capital and labor (Cobb and Douglas, 1928). As a result, if energy in general and electric power in particular were to make their way into the science of wealth, it would have to be through the back door, metaphorically speaking. In this section, I show that the shift to electric drive and the ensuing energy-deepening provoked an important chasm in political economy, one based on energy. Mainstream political economy, based largely on the work of Alfred Marshall, William S. Jevons and Leon Walras, was, for the most part, unable to identify the technology shock. I refer to this body of literature as the "economics of scarcity," scarcity being the defining problem. By constrast, in the 1920s and 1930s, there emerged a group of political economists for whom the central economic problem was not scarcity, but rather abundance. Best associated with the names of Simon N. Patten, Thornstein Veblen, Rexford Tugwell, F.G. Tyron, Stuart Chase and Edward A. Filene, to mention a few, this group argued that technology, especially developments in electric-power generation, distribution and consumption, had increased America's ability to produce, far beyond imagination. The problem, as they saw it, rested with its ability to exploit this new, higher ability. In short, America had failed to exploit this new potential. While the reasons differed among writers, they share one fundamental belief, namely that the central economic problem was no longer scarcity, but abundance. I refer to the resulting body of literature as the "economics of abundance," described by Stuart Chase in his 1935 book entitled *The Economics of Abundance* as follows:

Two men are lost on a great desert. One has a full bottle of water, the other a bottle quarter filled. As they move wearily onward, hoping for an oasis, justice demands that they pool the water supply and share it equally. Failure to do so will undoubtedly result in a fight. Now let us transport these two men to a row boat on Lake Superior. Again, they are lost, and again, one has a full bottle of water, and one a bottle quarter full. The full bottle man refuses to share and a battle ensues. Maniacs! There is plenty of fresh water over the side of the boat. The Desert is the Economy of Scarcity; the lake, the

Economy of Abundance. The choice between sharing or fighting is chronic in the former, pointless in the latter. Today, throughout Western civilization, men in boats are fighting, or preparing to fight, for fresh water. They do not know they are in boats; they think they are still on camels. The lake, as we have seen in the previous chapter, is not limitless, but nobody need go thirsty. (Chase, 1934, 51)

Scarcity versus Abundance

The prominent role of energy as the key element in the economics of abundance, as defined by Patten, Tugwell, Tyron, Rautenstrauch, Scott, and numerous others, and, secondly, the absence of energy in the corpus of classical, radical, and neoclassical political economy, raise a number of interesting questions. For example, why is it that classical (radical and neoclassical) political economy is about scarcity when "fire power," like electric power in the twentieth century, had lifted and pushed back the energy constraint (i.e., animate, muscular energy)? After all, Great Britain in the nineteenth century was the richest country in the Western world; the U.K. worker the best paid. Yet, ironically, the country in which wealth abounded, relatively speaking, yielded a science of wealth based on scarcity.

Part of the answer, I believe, lies in (1) nineteenth-century developments in U.K. agriculture, and (2) the United Kingdom's growing dependency on foreigners for its industrial feedstocks (cotton, silk). While abundance reigned in U.K. industry (manufacturing value added), scarcity reigned in early nineteenth-century U.K. agriculture. Population growth in the late eighteenth century and throughout the nineteenth century had increased the demand for food, increasing price and, consequently, putting upward pressure on real wages (Ricardo, Malthus). Higher wages, whether actual or anticipated, implied lower profits, and, ultimately, lower savings, investment and growth. The United Kingdom's ability to grow, it therefore follows, was intricately linked to its ability to feed itself. Abundance and scarcity coexisted throughout the early-to-mid nineteenth century in the United Kingdom, the latter coming to dominate political economy.

Another factor is the United Kingdom's almost complete dependence on foreign nations for its industrial feedstocks (cotton, wool, silk, linen etcetera). The faster the U.K. economy grew, the more likely was it to come up against the proverbial upward-sloping Ricardian rent curves. In short, its almost complete dependence on agriculture (for food and industrial feedstocks) provided another reason for the triumph of "scarcity" over "abundance."

As it turned out, the second industrial revolution occurred in a food-abundant country, namely the United States.[9] Unlike the United Kingdom where the supply of arable land was limited, the United States had surplus land. Further lessening the food problem in the early twentieth century was the coming of age of the internal combustion engine that replaced horses, mules and oxen as a source of motive power, thus leading to conditions of excess supply in agricultural markets (i.e., throughout the 1920s). Electric power and the internal combustion engine, it therefore follows, combined to transform the economic problem in the United States from one of scarcity to one of abundance.

The discussion in the next section will be organized around these two approaches to economics in the early twentieth century, namely, the economics of scarcity and the economics of abundance. The former is epitomized by Marshallian price theory, which, at the time, dominated political economy in the United States. As will become apparent, rarely did the "twain" meet.

Electric Drive, Energy-Deepening, and Production

The Economics of Scarcity

By definition, the economics of scarcity refers to classical and neoclassical political economy. As shown in the previous chapter, classical and neoclassical production theory focuses, for the most part, on two factor inputs, namely capital and labor. Output is increasing in capital and labor; energy is ignored altogether. It being the case that early twentieth century U.S. political economy was predominantly Marshallian in origin, it comes as no surprise to find that energy in general and electric power in particular was absent from mainstream economics. It being the case that electric power was less capital intensive than steam power, the shift to electric drive witnessed a decrease in investment, and, hence, in the measured level of capital (Devine, 1990). Hence, to the orthodox, mainstream U.S. political economist, if anything, there was reason to believe that output would decrease, not increase.

This is not to say, however, that all othodox mainstream political economists were oblivious to the power revolution. While most failed to seize the importance of electric power in industry, especially in manufacturing, there were those, who understood its importance. The problem, however, was the lack of an appropriate analytical framework. As is the case today in growth accountancy (Denison, 1962, 1985) where nontraditional factors (e.g., education, infrastructure, trade) are put in the residual, in the 1920s, electric power was considered a residual cause.

This is the case of Columbia University professor Rexford G. Tugwell and Yale University professor Irving Fisher. In a book entitled *Industry's Coming of Age*, published in 1927, Tugwell listed a number of changes to industry, including "the bringing into use of new and better power resources more suited to our technique, more flexible and less wasteful."

The electrification of industry has now progressed to the extent of between 55 and 60 per cent completion. So widespread an adoption of this new flexible means of moving things cannot have taken place without numerous secondary results in lowering costs, improvements in quality, and a heightened morale among workers. For the new power is not only cheaper to use; it is also cleaner, more silent and handier. On the whole, the electrification of industry must be set down as the greatest, single cause of the industrial revolution. (Tugwell, 1927, 182)

In *The Stock Market Crash and After*, Irving Fisher identified the electrification of U.S. industry as one of the contributing factors behind the stock market's rise in the late 1920s. Changing economic fundamentals, he maintained, were the underlying cause.

But after 1919, something happened. The implications of which are not yet sufficiently gauged. It was of enough significance to cause President Hoover's Committee on Recent Economic Changes to remark that "acceleration rather than structural change is the key to an understanding of our recent economic developments." The committee added: "But the breadth of the tempo of recent developments gives them new importance." What happened was indicated by the fact that in the United States, eight million, three hundred thousand workers produced in 1925 one quarter more than nine million wage workers turned out in 1919. The new indexes of the Federal Reserve Board measuring production record this gratifying advance which reflects an increase in the American standard of living. The indexes cover, directly and indirectly, four-fifths of the industrial productivity of the nation directly in about thirty-five industries, and collaterally, in many more. The general volume of production had increased between 1919 and 1927 by 46.5 percent, primary power by 22 percent, and primary power by wage earner by 30.9 percent (between 1919 and 1925) and productivity per wage worker by 53.5 percent between 1919 and 1927. (Fisher, 1930, 120)

What is important to note is the nature of the handful of references to electric drive and electricity, namely as orthogonal to production theory. Not having a general theory of production (i.e., such as that developed in Chapter 1), references to electric drive and electricity were often included in long, exhaustive lists of nonorthodox causes of productivity growth. For example, Fisher lists electric drive among a number of causes, including "less unstable money, new mergers, new scientific management, and the new labor policy of waste saving" (Fisher, 1930, 129).

There were also those who, owing to the nature of their position (job task), were cognizant of the power revolution. This is the case of F. G. Tyron of the Institute of Economics (Brookings Institution), who in 1927 denounced the little attention paid to power by economists, and Woodlief Thomas of the Federal Reserve Board, who attributed the "Increased Efficiency of American Industry" to the increasing use of machinery and power. According to Tyron:

Anything as important in industrial life as power deserves more attention than it has received by economists. The industrial position of a nation may be gauged by its use of power. The great advance in material standard of life in the last century was made possible by an enormous increase in the consumption of energy, and the prospect of repeating the achievement in the next century turns perhaps more than anything else on making energy cheaper and more abundant. A theory of production that will really explain how wealth is produced must analyze the contribution of this element of energy. These considerations have prompted the Institute of Economics to undertake a reconnaissance in the field of power as a factor of production. One of the first problems uncovered has been the need of a long-time index of power, comparable with the indices of employment, of the volume of production and trade, of monetary phenomena, that will trade the growth of the factor of power in our national development. (Tyron 1927, 281)

One year later in 1928, Woodlief Thomas of the Division of Research and Statistics of the Federal Reserve Board published an article in the *American Economic Review* entitled "The Economic Significance of the Increased Efficiency of American Industry," in which he attributed the "striking changes in American industry" to power-related developments:

Large-scale production is dependent upon the machine process, and the increasing use of machinery and power and labor-saving devices has accompanied the growth in size of productive units. The growing use of power in manufacturing, for example, is reflected in the increase in horsepower of installed prime movers. This does not tell the whole story, moreover, for owing to increased use of electricity, the type of power used is now more efficient—requiring less fuel and labor for its production. Out of a total installed horsepower in factories of thirty-six million in 1925, twenty-six million or 72 per cent was transmitted to machines by means of electric motors, as compared with 55 percent in 1919, 30 per cent in 1909, and only 2 per cent in 1899. Between 1899 and 1925 horsepower per person employed in factories increased by 90 per cent and horsepower per unit of product increased by 30 per cent.... Power has been substituted for labor not only through machines of production but also in the form of automatic conveying and loading devices. (Thomas, 1928, 130)

Unfortunately, Tyron and Thomas were the exceptions. Mainstream political economists were, for the most part, unaware of the profound changes thrust upon U.S. industry by the application of a new power form, electricity. This oversight, I maintain, is what prompted a number of young political economists, scientists and engineers to reject orthodoxy in favor of a new science of wealth, one born of energy and based on abundance.

The Economics of Abundance

Ironically, the study of political economy, born of energy innovations in the late eighteenth century, was unable, a century later, to identify, let alone analyze, subsequent energy innovations. Engineers and accountants, businessmen and politicians reveled in the new power source; political economists, on the other hand, were oblivious to it. This, I argue, is what prompted, in the 1920s and especially 1930s, a veritable deluge of contributions in the economics of abundance. Among the leading authors—and there were many—were Edward A. Filene, Stuart Chase, Henry Ford, John Hobson, Howard Scott, Frederick Soddy, and Thornstein Veblen. Defining the economics of abundance were (1) the role of energy in general, and electric power in particular in production processes, and consequently in early-twentieth century U.S. economic growth, (2) the purported flawed nature of the for-profit economy, distribution system and/or money supply process and (3) the call for change, whether it be in the conduct of business or government regulation. Regarding the role of energy, nearly every treatise begins by extolling the virtues of the new "power age." Consider, for example, the following excerpt from Howard Scott's *Introduction to Technocracy*, published in 1933:

A century ago these United States had a population of approximately 12,000,000 whereas to-day our census figures a total of 122,000,000—a tenfold increase in the century. One hundred years ago, in these United States, we consumed less than 75 trillion British thermal units of extraneous energy per annum, whereas in 1929, we consumed approximately 27,000 trillion British thermal units—an increase of 353 fold in the century. Our energy consumption now exceeds 150,000 kilogram calories per capita per day; whereas in the year 1800 our consumption of extraneous energy was not less than 1600 or more than 2000 kilogram calories per day. . . . The United States of our forefathers, with 12,000,000 inhabitants, performed the necessary work in almost entire dependence upon the human engine, which, as its chief means of energy conversion, was aided and abetted only by domestic animals and a few water wheels. The United States to-day has over one billion installed horsepower. In 1929, these engines of energy conversion, though operated only to partial capacity, nevertheless had an output that represented approximately 50 percent of the total work of the world. When one realizes that the technologist had succeeded to such an extent that he is to-day capable of building and operating engines of energy conversion that have nine million times the output capacity of the average single human being working an eight hour day, one begins to understand the acceleration, beginning with man as the chief engineer of energy conversion and culminating with these huge extensions of his original one-tenth of a horsepower. Then add the fact that of this 9,000,000 fold acceleration, 8,766,000 has occurred since the year 1900. (Scott, 1933, 42)

Another good example is the following excerpt taken from Chapter 1 of Stuart Chase's *Economics of Abundance*, entitled "Forty to One":

Suppose that the thirteen million people living in the United States in 1830 had awakened on the morning of January 1, 1831, with forty times the physical energy they had gone to bed with the night before. An active picture meets the mind's eye; a very active picture. A lumberman can fell forty times as many trees in a week, a housewife sweep forty times as many square feet of floor; forty barns can be built in the time hitherto required for one—and forty chests and forty chairs. Porters can transport forty times their accustomed load in a day; weavers ply their shuttles forty times as fast—if the shuttles can brook the strain; and children raise forty times their normal rumpus.

Assuming no increase in the invention of labor-saving devices—and where would be the point with such an exuberance of labor available—what might we logically expect in the way of economic changes in a culture essentially handicraft? From an economy of scarcity, with barely enough to go around, the young republic would almost immediately enter an economy of abundance. (Chase, 1934, 1)

In the same chapter, Chase defines "abundance" in terms of a series of propositions:

1. A condition where the bulk of the economic work is performed not by men, but by inanimate energy, drawn from coal, oil and water power. Such a condition was reached in the United States towards the close of the nineteenth century, circa 1880.

2. A point at which living standards per capita reach an average which is, at least potentially, twice as high as ever obtained under scarcity conditions. Reached circa 1900.

3. A point at which the curve of invention, following, as it does, a geometric increase, becomes the dominant factor in economic life—precisely as the Nile was the dominating factor in the economic life of Egypt. Circa 1870.

4. A point at which the scientific method supersedes the use and want of the craftsman in the production of most material goods. Circa 1900.

5. A point where output per man hour becomes so great that total productive labor must thereafter decline, even as output grows. A point at which labor ceases to be a measure of output—as it always has been in preceding ages. Circa 1920.

6. A point at which overproduction carries a more serious threat to the financial system than shortage. Circa 1880.

7. A point at which specialization has destroyed all practicable local self-sufficiency and made economic insecurity for all classes latent, growing, and ultimately intolerable, given no change in financial methods. Circa 1900, with the closing of the American frontier.

8. A point at which consumption becomes a greater problem than production. Circa, 1920. "Our economy," says F. L. Ackerman, "is so set up that it produces goods at a higher rate that it produces income with which to purchase them."

9. A point at which the industrial plant is, substantially, constructed, requiring relatively smaller outlays for capital goods in the future, and where pecuniary savings are not only unnecessary in their old volume, but seriously embarrassing, Circa 1925.

10. A point where, due to the presence of the technical arts, costs, prices, interest rates, debts, begin a descent with zero as their objective. Circa 1920. (Chase, 1934, 12)

Unfortunately, these ideas were never formalized. Scott, Chase, Tugwell and others failed to move beyond mere descriptions in their quest for a new theory of production. What, for example, was the role of capital? What was the role of labor? Was each productive in the physical sense? Was output a function of energy only? Unfortunately, these questions were never addressed, at least satisfactorily, having been usurped in the public's eye by the New Deal with its Keynesian-style spending policies. The economics of abundance, despite holding great promise, both scientifically and politically, was forgotten.

Indirect Effects on Economic Theory

The shift to electric drive and the ensuing energy deepening in the form of higher electricity consumption, like the shift from the domestic system to the factory system some 150 years earlier, failed to change the way political economists in general (classical, radical and neoclassical) modeled production.

Capital and labor continued to be the two sole factor inputs. Nonetheless, these developments did leave their mark on political economy, specifically in the field of industrial organization, macroeconomics and industrial relations. All three were the result, in large measure, of the introduction of high-throughput, continuous-flow production techniques. Here, I provide a brief account of the role of electric drive and the ensuing energy-deepening in the development of the field of industrial organization.

Industrial Organization

It is generally held that the study of industrial organization begins, in earnest, with Edward Chamberlin and Joan Robinson's writings on monopolistic competition in the early 1930s. Before, markets were classified either as competitive or monopolistic/duopolistic. The relevant question, from a historical point of view, is what factors prompted this upheaval in price theory? Why was perfect competition, the staple of Marshallian price theory, out, and monopolistic competition, a combination of competition and monopoly, in? The answer to this question, as I shall attempt to demonstrate, is complex, having roots in Marshallian price theory, and in the electrification of U.S., and indeed, U.K., manufacturing.

Interest in price theory in the early twentieth century was a decidedly British phenomenon. From J. H. Clapham's "On Empty Economic Boxes," which appeared in the September 1922 number of the *Economic Journal* to Piero Sraffa's "The Laws of Returns under Competitive Conditions" to Joan Robinson's "The Theory of Monopolistic Competition," what stands out is the uniquely British flavor. This only serves to beg the question why? Why was interest in price theory, specifically in the failings of Marshallian price theory, concentrated in the United Kingdom? The main reason, I argue, is the debate over the gold standard, and the apparent downward inflexibility of prices. World War I saw prices increase in the United Kingdom by roughly 200 percent, and by 100 percent in the United States. A return to the gold standard at prewar parity (i.e., $4.86 per pound) would require that prices in the United Kingdom fall substantially. From 1918 to 1922, they had not, forcing a debate over the workings of markets, and more importantly, over the relevance of Marshallian price theory. World War I price developments (i.e., increases, and decreases), as it turns out, constituted the first true test of Marshallian price theory.

Assuming that markets are organized competitively (perfect competition), a decrease in demand should, in the presence of an upward-sloping supply curve, result in a lower price. Should this not be the case, then either the model is flawed, or, at the very least, it is incomplete. For example, if firms face increasing returns or decreasing costs, then a decrease in demand is less likely to lead to lower prices given what are higher unit costs. This explains, among other things, the plethora of work on returns to scale and increasing and decreasing cost industries in the 1920s.

In hindsight, one could argue that "the chickens had come home to roost." Marshallian price theory, being politically motivated, had ignored, for the most part, the reality that was high throughput, continuous-flow production processes, synonymous with the intensive use of inanimate energy. While upward-sloping supply curves were consistent with Neolithic, artisanal production processes, they were orthogonal to the large-scale textile mills of Northern England. Marshall's desire to move away from a substance theory of value—and ultimately, the Marxist critique—one could argue, had exacted a toll. The events of the post–World War I period more than confirmed this. Specifically, they set into motion a process that culminated in the study of industrial organization as an important branch of microeconomic theory.

While the original impetus for a reexamination of price theory, specifically of the role of the organization of industry, came from the United Kingdom, the study of industrial organization is, historically speaking, a U.S. phenomenon. Notwithstanding the pioneering contributions of Joan Robinson, Piero Sraffa and Arthur Pigou, the defining contributions are American. Among these are Edward Chamberlin's work on monopolisitic competition, Edward Mason's work on industry structure and performance, Paul Sweezy's work on price rigidity and Joseph Bain's Structure–Behavior–Performance model of industrial organization. Why was this the case? Why did U.S. political economists come to dominate industrial organization, and ultimately, price theory? The answer, I maintain, is intimately tied to domestic developments, namely, the development of extremely high-throughput, continuous-flow, mass-production techniques. As pointed out earlier, the second industrial revolution was, in many regards, a continuation of the first. Specifically, industries in which production processes were driven by steam saw throughput rates increase substantially with electric drive. Industries that had, up until then, resisted the power revolution, succumbed, resulting in important productivity gains. The assembly line is a case in point.

By the 1930s, U.S. firms had, for the most part, become monolithic, being characterized by "large-scale enterprise" (Sobel, 1972). Hence, it stands to reason that the need for a theory of pricing behavior by large-scale enterprise would have been greater in the United States than in the United Kingdom. One of the first to address this issue was John Maurice Clark, son of John Bates Clark, in a book entitled *Studies in the Economics of Overhead Costs*, published in 1923. The following passage, the first paragraph of the preface, sets the tone:

This volume is a bit of research into the principles of dynamic economics. It is an experiment in a type of economic theory which is largely inductive, which comes to grips with the dynamic movements and the resistances to movement, and the organized interrelations of parts, which make our economic world a dynamic social organism, rather than a static mechanism with an endless uniformity of perpetual motion. It studies the discrepancies between supply and demand; indeed the whole subject of the book might be defined as the study of discrepancies between an ever fluctuating demand and a relatively inelastic fund of productive capacity, resulting in wastes of partial idleness and many other economic disturbances. Unused capacity is its central theme. (Clark, 1923, ix)

With the advent of extremely high-throughput, continuous-flow mass-production techniques, new capacity additions (whether to existing capacity or greenfield) were increasingly lumpy. Capacity utilization rates, it therefore follows, would have decreased as firms found themselves with significant excess capacity, at least in the short run. In time, demand growth would increase capacity utilization rates until capacity was reached, and the process would begin anew.

The problem raised by Clark is as real today as it was then. How did large-scale firms price their product in what is, essentially, a dynamic environment (demand and supply). Price theory, for the most part, is static in nature, owing, in large part, to Marshall's *Principles of Economics*. The fact of the matter, however, is that in the case of large-scale firms, costs (i.e., average and marginal) are a dynamic phenomenon, fluctuating as demand grows over time, and as capacity increases at discrete points in time.

What is particularly noteworthy of *Studies in the Economics of Overhead Costs* is its timing, namely 1923, two years after the depression of 1921, but six years before the Great Depression. The bulk of work on prices and costs in the United States dates to the 1930s, and, should as such, be seen as a response to the price inertia observed during the Great Depression. Another noteworthy feature is its scope. *Studies in the Economics of Overhead Costs* was more than a simple treatise on overhead costs; it was, for all intents and purposes, Clark's attempt at a "general theory of economics" based on high throughput, continuous-flow mass production. Table 3.6 reproduces its table of contents, consisting of twenty-four chapters. The topics range from "How and Why Large Plants Bring Economy," to "Labor as an Overhead Cost," to "Overhead Costs and the Laws of Value and Distribution." *Studies in the Economics of Overhead Costs* should, as such, be seen as an attempt, visionary at the time, to provide an empirically consistent theory of high-throughput mass production and pricing.

Electric Drive, Energy-Deepening, and The Problem of Exchange

As shown earlier, the shift to electric drive and the ensuing energy-deepening failed to increase actual rates of output, income and expenditure growth, owing, in large part, to the problem of underincome. Production capacity increased; however, aggregate income did not. Merchants chose not to increase orders for lack of new purchasing power in the economy (higher wage income). Producers chose not to increase wage income for strategic reasons, specifically the absence of private incentives to increase wages (Beaudreau, 1996a). In earlier work, I referred to the ensuing situation as one of income inertia. Neither merchant not manager had any private incentive to increase money income, despite a massive increase in productive capacity.

Table 3.6
Studies in the Economics of Overhead Costs—Table of Contents

	Title
	Title
1	The Gradual Discovery of Overhead Costs
2	The Scope of the Problem
3	The General Idea of Cost and Different Classes of Costs
4	The Laws of Return and Economy, or the Variables Governing Efficiency
5	The Laws of Return and Economy, or the variables Governing Efficiency (Continued)
6	How and Why Large Plants Bring Economy
7	Economies of Combination
8	Different Kinds of Business Rhythms
9	Different Costs for Different Purposes: An Illustrative Problem
10	What is a Unit of Business?
11	Three Methods of Allocating Costs
12	Functions and Chief Methods of Cost Accounting
13	Railroads and Costs: A Statistical Study
14	Overhead Costs and the Railroad Rate Problem
15	The Transportation System as a Whole
16	Public Utilities
17	Overhead Costs in Other Industries
18	Labor as an Overhead Cost
19	Overhead Costs and the Business Cycle
20	Discrimination in the Modern Market
21	Cut-Throat Competition and the Public Interest
22	Costs of Government as Overhead Outlays
23	Overhead Costs and the Laws of Value and Distribution
24	Conclusion

Source: Clark (1923), xi.

Monetary theory being what it was in the early part of this century, the problem of underincome went largely unnoticed. Say's Law dominated mainstream political economy (Sowell, 1972). Increases in productive capacity/productivity would, accordingly, result in higher nominal money income as wages and profits would rise. This, in turn, would result in higher levels of output, income and expenditure.

The problem, as it turns out, is with the nature of monetary theory in the early part of the century, specifically, with its decidedly Smithian nature. Other than Knut Wicksell's attempt, in *Interest and Prices* published in 1898, at modeling the institutional aspects of exchange in an industrialized (read: factory system-based) economy, interest in the "nuts and bolts" of exchange, so to speak, was virtually inexistent. This is somewhat surprising, to the point of being ironic, given the heightened interest in money and monetary theory that characterized this period. Witness, for example, Arthur C. Pigou's work on monetary theory, John M. Keynes' work on money and monetary theory, and, on the other side of the Atlantic, Irving Fisher's work on money and prices. Surprisingly, neither Marhsall, Pigou, Keynes nor Fisher referred to the the demand for credit (commercial paper) by producers for the explicit purpose of financing production. Instead, the demand for money was discussed in terms of what, for all intents and purposes, was an exchange economy. In short, little progress had been achieved.

Monetary theory in this period focused, for the most part, on the relationship between the money and prices (Pigou, 1917; Fisher, 1911). Institutional aspects of exchange were ignored, prompting Williford I. King, in an article entitled "Circulating Capital: Its Nature and Relation to the Public Welfare," which appeared in the 1920 *American Economic Review*, to remark:

Despite the fact that bank notes or deposits are used in the daily business of hundreds of millions of people, there still remain numerous misconceptions concerning the nature of these media of exchange. Furthermore, it seems safe to assert that few indeed, not only the users but also of the bankers who issue the obligations, have any clear idea of just what effects upon the public such issues produce. According to the writer's observation, textbooks in economics rarely touch upon this last and most important phase of the problem. It therefore appears to be worth while to discuss in some detail the fundamental principles connected with bank credit. Bank credit is used mainly for business purposes. Some loans from banks are obtained in order to purchase consumption goods, but loans for this purpose form so small a fraction of the total that they scarcely need consideration here. The bulk of credit loaned, not only by banks, but by other lenders as well, is nowadays borrowed for purposes of investment or the use in the undertakings for profit making. (King, 1920, 738)

It should as such come as no surprise to find no mention of, nor reference to, the problem of underincome in this period. The latter is, as shown earlier, intimately related to the problem of exchange in an industrial economy (merchants and firms), which, as I argue here, generated little interest among mainstream monetary economists, Knut Wicksell notwithstanding.

There is, however, one notable exception, namely the much-maligned Clifford H. Douglas (Major Douglas), founder of the Social Credit movement. Unlike Irving Fisher, John M. Keynes, Frank Knight and other leading monetary political economists of the day, Douglas devoted considerable time and effort to the mechanics of exchange in an industrial economy. For example, in Chapter IV of *The Monopoly of Credit*, he outlines, in albeit crude fashion, the mechanics of exchange in a world in which the production of goods involves a number of stages. Figure 3.1, taken from this chapter, is an illustration of his infamous "A+B" theory according to which there exist two types of payments, Group A and Group B. Group A payments are made to individuals as wages salaries, and dividends, while Group B payments are made to other organizations for raw materials, bank charges and other external costs.

In order to appreciate Douglas' "A+B" theory, according to which the value of income in society is equal to "A" but the value of output is equal to "A+B" thus giving rise to a form of underincome, one must first appreciate (1) the primitive state of monetary theory in the 1930s, (2) the fact that Douglas was not a political economist, but a retired major and (3) the lack of a formal "social credit" school of thought. Douglas, in my view, performed admirably given the little formal training he had in matters pertaining to exchange, money and the workings of industrialized economies.

Figure 3.1
Douglas' A+B Version of Underincome

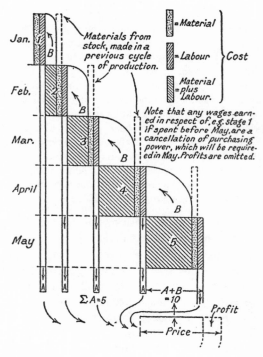

Source: Douglas (1951), 38.

To understand the much-maligned "A+B" theory, one has to understand his motives. Specifically, what were his objectives? What did he set out to do, to say, prove? The answer, I maintain, can be found in the hypothetical production and exchange example found in Chapter 4 of *The Monopoly of Credit*.

Let us imagine a capitalist to own a certain piece of land, on which is a house, and a building containing the necessary machinery for preparing, spinning, and weaving linen, and that the land is capable of growing in addtion to the flax, all the food necessary to maintain a man. Let us further imagine that the capitalist in the first place allows a man to live free of all payment in the house and to have the use of all the foodstuffs that he grows on condition that he also grows, spins and weaves a certain amount of linen for the capitalist. Let us further imagine that after a time, this arrangement is altered by the payment to the man of £1 a week for the work on the linen business, but that this £1 is taken back each week as rent for the house and payment for the foodstuffs.

Let us now imagine that from the time the flax is picked to the time the linen is delivered to the capitalist, a period of six weeks elaspses. Obviously, the cost of the linen must be £6, and this will be the price, plus profit, which the capitalist would place on it. Quite obviously only one-sixth of the purchasing power necessary to buy linen is now available, although "at some time or other," all £6 has been distributed.

Let us now imagine that half of the employee's time is devoted to making a machine which will do all the work of preparing and manufacturing linen, and that the manufacture of this machine takes twelve weeks. We may therefore say that the machine costs £6, the total value of the production of the machine and the flax being still £1 per week. At the end of the period, the machine is substituted for the man, the machine being driven, we suppose, by the burning of the food which was previously consumed by the man, and the machine being housed in the house previously occupied by the man, and being automatic. The capitalist would be justified in saying that the cost of operation of the machine is £1, per week as before, and if there is any wear, he will also be justified in allocating the cost of this wear to the cost of linen. It should be noticed, however that he will now not distribute any money at all, since it is obviously no use offering a £1 note a week to a machine. (Douglas, 1951, 40)

What Douglas is getting at is the fact that in the machine age, total money income is less than total value. Admittedly, the example he chooses is somewhat extreme; the fact remains, however, that at the core of his work is the notion of underincome, similar to the one described in Chapter 1. Further evidence of this is provided in a later paragraph where he distinguishes between "direct charges" and "indirect charges," the former referring to payments made prior to markets clearing, and the latter to those made after (i.e., residuals).

In the modern industrial system, this process can be identified easily in the form of machine charges. For instance, a modern stamping plant may require to add 600 per cent to its labour charges to cover its machine charges. This sum not being in any true sense profit. In such a case, for every £1 expended in a given period in wages, £6 making £7 in all, would be carried forward into prices. Although this is an extreme case, the constant, and in one sense desirable, tendency is for direct charges to increase as a result of the replacement of human labor by machinery. There is no difference between a plant charge of this nature and a similar sum repaid as a "B" payment. (Douglas, 1951, 42)

The "A+B" theory, it follows, is Douglas' roundabout way of describing the shortcomings of a producer-merchant exchange technology in times of technological change (mechanization). Merchants fail to place new orders for lack of income growth, which is, as shown, intimately related to the residual nature of profits. As pointed out at the start, Douglas was not a scholar; like Owen, Ricardo, and others before him, he was a self-taught student of political economy. Notwithstanding Wicksell's work on exchange technologies in industrial settings, Douglas has to, in my view, be recognized as one of the pioneers of exchange analysis.

U.S. political economist Thornstein Veblen approached the problem of exchange from a thoroughly different point of view. To his way of thinking, the "captains of industry," by restricting output, had "sabotaged" the transition to a higher equilibrium growth path in response to "mechanical industry of the new order" that was "inordinately productive" (Veblen, 1965 [1921], 8). This he attributed to profit maximization.

Without some salutary restraint in the way of sabotage on the productive use of the available industrial plant and workmen, it is altogether unlikely that prices could be maintained at a reasonably profitable figure for any appreciable time. A businesslike control of the rate and volume of output is indispensable for keeping up a profitable market, and a profitable market is the first and unremitting condition of prosperity in any community whose industry is owned and managed by business men. And the ways and means of this necessary control of the output of industry are always and necessarily something in the way of retardation, restriction, withdrawal, unemployment of plant and workmen-whereby production is kept short of productive capacity. (Veblen, 1965 [1921], 8)

To Veblen, this amounted to sabotage.

All this is matter of course, and notorious. But it is not a topic on which one prefers to dwell. Writers and speakers who dilate on the meritorious exploits of the nation's business men will not commonly allude to this voluminous running administration of sabotage, this conscientious withdrawal of efficiency, that goes into their ordinary day's work. (Veblen, 1965 [1921], 10)

One could refer to Veblen's version of underincome as "real" underincome, as price deflation *de facto* is what prevents real income from increasing. For a given level of nominal wage income, a price decrease, proportional to the rate of productivity growth, would increase real wage income, thus prompting merchants to increase orders for consumption and capital goods, thus allowing the economy to make the transition to the new higher growth path defined by the technological change, in this case energy-deepening.

Electric Drive, Energy-Deepening, and Distribution

Unlike the shift from muscular power to fire power over a century earlier, which, as shown in Chapter 2, led to the study of distribution-related issues (due to rising food prices) and, ultimately, led to the founding of political economy, the shift to electric drive generated little interest in such problems. The reasons, I believe, are many. First, there is the question of motives. As pointed out in Chapter 2, Ricardo's main objective consisted of increasing savings and investment, which, in his view, were threatened by higher real wages, the result of higher food (read: corn) prices. As it turns out, such problems were absent from the early twentieth century. The level of savings in the United States in the early part of the century was not an issue. Put differently, the U.S. economy generated sufficient savings that could be invested in electric-drive-powered tools, or, for that matter, in anything else. Second in order of importance is the fact that by the turn of the century, political economy had a "scientific" theory of distribution based on productivity. Capital and labor, Alfred Marshall, Phillip Wicksteed and John Bates Clark maintained, are remunerated according to their respective marginal productivities. Increases in the latter, according to the theory, would lead, automatically, to increases in wages and profits (dividends). In short, the market would see to it that income was distributed, and, more importantly, that it was distributed justly, according to an "objective" productivity standard.

Third, there is the question of the technology shock. As pointed out in Chapter 2, Adam Smith and David Ricardo were acutely aware of the technology shock in the form of machinery that had hit the British economy in the late eighteenth/early nineteenth century, namely machinery. This, however, was not true of the technology shock in the early twentieth century. The evidence presented above shows that but for a handful of economists, the shift to electric drive and the ensuing energy-deepening went largely unnoticed. One could attribute this to the presence of a "primacy effect," or a "novelty factor." Steam-powered drive represented a paradigm shift vis-à-vis animate, muscular drive. Electric drive, however, constituted an extension of steam-powered drive.

This is not to say, however, that distribution issues were absent from the period literature. For example, there is the problem of machinery and its effects on productivity and wages. Perviewing the *American Economic Review* from 1920 to 1935, one finds a number of articles dealing with the question of machinery and productivity (Hayes, 1923; Fisher, 1923; and Graham, 1926). With titles like "Rate of Wages and the Use of Machinery," "An Issue in Economic Theory: The Rate of Wages and the Use of Machinery," "Factors Affecting the Trend in Real Wages," and "Relation of Wage Rates and the Use of Machinery," this work provides indirect evidence of a technology shock (in this case, electrification), and the consequences for wages and, ultimately, distribution.

Unfortunately, like their nineteenth century counterparts, they were unable to identify the exact nature of the shock (electric power) and, consequently, were forced to speak in terms of generalities (e.g., machinery). Second, while the post–World War I period in the United Kingdom was the first true test of Marshallian price theory (which failed), the early part of the twentieth century in the United States was the first true test of neoclassical distribution theory. As such, in this literature machinery was seen as increasing the marginal product of labor, and, consequently, the wage.

Distribution-related issues can also be found in the underconsumption/ overinvestment literature. As pointed out earlier, most adherents of what I refer to as the economics of abundance attributed the gap between actual and potential output to the problem of income distribution. Accordingly, electric power had increased output and income, specifically profit income, leaving wage income relatively constant. A skewed functional distribution of income, Rexford Tugwell argued, is what led to the Great Depression.

But high wages are so necessary a condition for social progress that one, even, who is not a wage-earner might well argue for the strengthening of the workers' cause. For wages, more than any other income, are spent for staple goods which, in the best sense, strengthen the race by their use. These too are the goods which can be made in the most efficient ways. But quite as important, income which is distributed as wages becomes immediate purchasing power for consumer goods, and so completes that productive circuit of which we have spoken. A nation of well-paid workers, consuming most of the goods it produces, will be as near Utopia as we humans are ever likely to get. It is necessary to this result that not too much income shall go to profits; for if it does, this will either be spent for wasteful luxuries which have to be made in extravagant ways, or will, if it is not spent, be distributed by bankers to enterprises who will over expand their productive facilities, forgetting that the worker's buying power is not sufficient to create a demand for them. (Tugwell, 1933, 183)

In this case, interest in the distribution of income has less to do with the problem of distribution as defined above (i.e., functional distribution of income), and more to do with the problem of optimal consumption and savings rates. To the underconsumptionists, the distribution of income, being skewed in favor of profits and savings, contributed to crises, and, ultimately, was the root cause of business cycles per se.[10]

The Fall of the Economics of Abundance

As I have shown, the early twentieth century witnessed the emergence of an alternative science of wealth, one based on abundance and not on scarcity. For reasons described above, the for-profit economy, as Veblen referred to it, had failed to translate potential output into actual output. The U.S. economy in the 1920s and 1930s, they maintained, was, paradoxically, suffering from abundance, not scarcity.

Unfortunately, this highly promising, truly scientific line of inquiry failed to make inroads into mainstream political economy, as evidenced by its total absence today. In fact, if anything, it has become an object of scorn in the literature, as evidenced by work bearing titles like "Cranks, Heretics, and Macroeconomics in the 1930's." This raises a number of questions, one of which being, why? Why did the economics of abundance fail to make inroads into mainstream political economy? Why did a theory of production based on energy, the cornerstone of classical mechanics and thermodynamics, fail to make inroads into mainstream production theory?

The reasons, I believe, are many. In no particular order, they include (1) its emphasis on energy, which, at the time, was foreign, not to say orthogonal, to production theory, (2) its total eschewal of mainstream political economy, as best illustrated by the writings of Thornstein Veblen and the Technocrats, (3) its diagnoses of the Great Depression, (4) its policy prescriptions and, lastly, (5) the rise of Keynesian economics. Perhaps the most striking feature of the economics of abundance was the role accorded to energy. Energy was the starting point of production theory in this literature. This, as it turns out, was orthogonal to mainstream political economy, where the emphasis continued to be on capital and labor. Clearly, a veritable "Tower of Babel": the two sides speaking different languages. The second reason was the radical policy measures proposed by certain writers, notably Thornstein Veblen and the Technocrats. As pointed out above, Veblen targeted most of his criticism at the "for-profit economy," the cornerstone of mainstream political economy. While a virtue in classical and neoclassical political economy, it (i.e., profit motive) was a vice in the economics of abundance, preventing the U.S. economy from reaching its new, higher potential. Clearly, the debate, like most of nineteenth century political economy, had gone beyond the realm of science, into the realm of politics. In a true science, Veblen and the Technocrats' hypotheses, however unsettling, would have been tested scientifically. For example, did firms, as Veblen maintained, resist lowering prices? In hindsight, the data for this period (Table 3.4) reveal that, in fact, prices were rigid, or "sticky downward."

The third reason was its diagnosis of the Great Depression. The Great Depression, Technocrats argued, resulted from the U.S. economy's inability to translate potential abundance into actual abundance. This, in turn, owed to either downward price rigidity and/or deficient demand, the latter owing to insufficient income. Clearly, such views were heretical, to say the least (Say's Law). The fourth reason, and perhaps the most important, was its policy prescriptions. Veblen and the Technocrats, like Claude Henri de Saint-Simon in the early nineteenth century, called for a radical reorganization of industry, the end of finance capitalism, and the emergence of technocracy. Finance capitalism was flawed, they argued. Profit-maximizing managers should, as such, be replaced by efficiency- and output-maximizing technology-aware civil servants.

Merit notwithstanding, the economics of abundance posed a serious threat to mainstream political economy, itself the outgrowth of an earlier political debate, and, perhaps more importantly, to society in general. Like Robert Owen a century before, Veblen and the Technocrats questioned the ability of a private, for-profit economies to produce at capacity.

Not surprisingly, the economics of abundance, born of energy and controversy, failed to make inroads into political economy. Today, nothing of it remains, not the role of energy in production, not the estimates of U.S. potential output in the early part of the century, not its views of downward price rigidity in the face of technological change. The reason is painfully obvious: to accept or to agree with any part of Technocracy was to accept all of it, lock, stock and barrel.

A good example of this is found in a "public policy pamphlet" by Aaron Director of the University of Chicago, entitled *The Economics of Technocracy* (Director, 1933). Riddled with sarcasm, "The Economics of Technocracy" was an attempt by a leading member of the U.S. economics profession to "debunk" the proposed new science of wealth. Take, for example, the opening sentences of the introduction, written by University of Chicago Press *Public Policy Pamplets* series editor Harry D. Gideonse: "Labor-saving machinery saves labor. This startling discovery of the technocrats has led them to important conclusions" (Director, 1933, 1). On page 4, the author, Aaron Director, attempted to discredit Howard Scott, one of Technocracy's founding members, by invoking his past ties to the I.W.W. (International Workers of the World).

Turning to more substantive issues, Director summarized Technocracy in terms of a series of six points.

1. The importance of energy: "Through the expenditure of energy we convert all raw materials into products that we consume and through it operate all the equipment that we use." This, of course, has always been familiar to us, except that it was stated in terms of work, and not of energy. The great merit of the latter term is the possibility of dragging in the Law of Conservation of Energy and this marrying physics to the social mechanism.

2. Energy can be measured, and the unit of measurement is always the same, while the dollar varies from time to time.

3. The chief distinction between our society and that of all previous societies is the much greater amount of energy which can be generated. This has always been recognized by the designation of our civilization as the machine era.

4. With every increase in the amount of mechanical energy the need for labor decreases.

5. The present depression marks the end of an era, since the increase in mechanical energy has at last become so great that, regardless of what happens, the need for human labor will rapidly decline.

6. Does it follow, therefore, that the price system must break down, and that only the engineers can run a mechanical civilization. (Director, 1933, 8)

He then proceeded to develop, using standard neoclassical analysis, each of these points. In keeping with the nineteenth century tradition of equating energy with machinery, he spoke in terms of "technical progress," not energy-deepening. This is then followed by a Ricardian-inspired analysis of the effects of "technical progress" on costs, wages and prices. Competition, he argued, is a sufficient condition for full employment.

On the other hand, the technocrats imply that a more scientific utilization of existing equipment would result in a much larger product. It is only necessary to insist that the number of engineers in industry far outweigh the number of economists, and if these engineers are to run industry in the future, they should be competent to point out methods of improving efficiency. It is not enough to hide behind a barrage of words. It should be patent to the most critical observer that the one thing which the individual enterprise under competitive conditions does strive for is to reduce its cost, regardless of the consequences on employment. (Director, 1933, 16)

Having concluded that "technical progress is not incompatible with full employment," he proceeds, in Chapter VII, to debunk the view that the Great Depression was the result of energy-based technological change. This, metaphorically speaking, is where the gloves came off. First, he, in the tradition of Say and Ricardo, ruled out underincome. Output, he argued, is identically equal to income, whether in the form of money or in kind.

If there were no commercial banking system, the national income would be distributed for consumption goods and the production of additional equipment in accordance with the desires of the community. The output of industry is equal to the income of the laborers employed in it and of the property owners whose capital is invested in it. Clearly, if entrepreneurs borrowed funds directly from the income receivers, they could not continue to produce capital equipment in excess of the amount which income receivers were willing to save. (Director, 1933, 21)

In short, according to Director, Technocracy offered nothing new, and, more importantly, suffered from the most elementary oversights and errors. Energy was nothing new, and, more importantly, presented no particular challenge to mainstream political economy. Technological progress, in this case, electric drive, increased, in a commensurate fashion, income, wages and profits. The causes of the Great Depression, he argued, lie elsewhere, notably in "the war, the resulting debts, and tariffs."

Despite its ignominious end, the various themes found in the economics of abundance continued to generate interest in political economy for years after, vindicating, as it it were, its scientific merit. For example, the role of energy in production and growth lived on after World War II in the form of growth accounting in general, and the "Solow residual" in particular (Beaudreau, 1995a, b, c, 1998). The role of downward price rigidity, as most know, can be found in the work of John M. Keynes (1936), Gardiner Means (1939), Paul

Sweezy (1939), and numerous others including recent New Keynesian macroeconomics (Mankiw and Romer, 1991).

CONCLUSIONS

The first half of the twentieth century saw things deteriorate further for political economy. In fact, one could go as far as to argue that were it not for Keynesian political economy with its user-friendly policy measures, there is every reason to believe that a major upheaval in social and economic organization would have occurred. Classical and neoclassical political economy were in shambles. The Great Depression remained an enigma. Many questions, few answers.

As I have attempted to show here, the chasm separating theory from reality, already wide, continued to widen. Belief in the virtues of the market as an equilibrating mechanism was shattered. Unemployment had become chronic, or so it seemed. High-throughput, mass-producing firms had chosen not to "flood" the market (?) and, in the process, had not provoked a generalized fall in product prices. Instead, as Veblen pointed out, they adjusted supply to demand, thus confirming the non-Walrasian nature of product markets.

By now, the problem was autoregressive, dating back to the early classical political economists' failure to identify, model and analyze the myriad aspects of inanimate energy-powered, high-throughput continuous-flow production processes. Neoclassical political economy, while successfully fending off radical political economists, failed to make significant advances in the study of such processes. Early twentieth-century political economists, in America and on the Continent, were then called upon to study what has to rank as one of the greatest quantitiative innovations in the history of material civilization, namely the electrification of industry, with a set of analytical tools and constructs best suited for studying, at best, the production processes of Neanderthals and Cromagnons.

As I have tried to show in this chapter, I am not the first to make such an observation. In the 1920s and 1930s, at the height of the Great Depression, scientists and engineers called for a wholesale revamping of political economy, one based on energy. The Continental Commitee on Technocracy, dismissed outright by political economists, stands as a testimony to man's irrepressible desire for truth, in spite of the many detractors. Clearly, something was terribly wrong.

While political economy continued to lack an empirically consistent model of production, the years that followed the Great Depression were nonetheless rich in theoretical developments, the large majority of which are related to high-throughput production processes. Most of these were in the area of industrial organization. Moreover, most were aimed at reexamining the workings of markets in the presence of a limited number of high-throughput producers.

In the next chapter, I examine the post–World War II period, a period characterized by massive energy-deepening in the form of increased electric power consumption per lower-level supervisor (worker). I show how the dialectic between neoclassical political economy and various revisionists continued unfettered. For example, it will be argued that the emergence of growth accounting was a response to this. Output and productivity, U.S. political economists noted, were far outdistancing growth in capital and labor, raising the myriad questions that dominate real business cycle analysis today. Productivity was increasing without a cause, or so it appeared.

NOTES

1. One could argue that muscular energy is also a power transmission technology, converting the the the chemical energy (adenosine triphosphates) found in carbohydrates and proteins into work (movement).

2. Nuclear power in this period is relatively insignificant. For example, in 1956, 10 million kilowatt hours of the net generation of electricity came from nuclear sources, which corresponds to 0.00209 of total net generation.

3. The Ford Motor Company's Highland Park plant, one could argue, marks the crossover from high-throughput continuous-flow production processes powered by either water or steam power, to extremely high-throughput continuous-flow production processes powered by electricity. Put differently, the looms and spinning jennies of the early nineteenth century, powered by steam, constituted high-throughput, continuous-flow production processes. The electric-powered stamping machines, the electric-powered material handling systems, the electric-powered assembly lines, on the other hand, constituted extremely high (in a comparative sense), continuous-flow production processes.

4. It need be pointed out that not all of this represents a net increase in energy consumption as electric drive had not completely displaced steam drive in industry.

5. It is worthwhile noting that Henry Ford and Edward A. Filene, like Robert Owen, were successful businessmen.

6. One could attribute this to the fact that the Ford Motor Company (FMC) assumed the role of both producer and merchant, the latter owing to the nature of the product (i.e., needing service). The FMC established a national—and international—network of dealerships.

7. For more on Ford and Filene's views on underincome, see Beaudreau (1996a), especially Chapters 2 and 7.

8. For more on the NIRA, see Beaudreau (1996a), Chapter 6.

9. Perhaps this explains the dominance of the United Kingdom in nineteenth century political economy and the near absence of Continental and North American political economy.

10. It need be pointed out that this is a fundamentally different argument than that presented here and in Beaudreau (1996a). While underincome implies underconsumption (in an absolute sense), underconsumption does not imply underincome. To

Tugwell, Wagner, Moulton, and others, output and income are identically equal. Where the problem arises, in their view, in with the functional distribution of the income in question.

4

Boom and Bust: Energy-Deepening in the Post–World War II Period

In modern mass production, as in modern mass distribution and modern transportation and communications, economies resulted more from speed than from size. It was not the size of the manufacturing establishment in terms of number of workers and the amount and value of productive equipment, but the velocity of throughput and the resulting increase in volume that permitted economies that lowered costs and increases output per worker and per machine.

—Alfred D. Chandler, Jr., *The Visible Hand, The Managerial Revolution in American Business*

INTRODUCTION

World War II was both a military and economic watershed. In 1939, U.S. GNP stood at $209.4 billion (constant 1958 dollars). By 1944, it had reached $361.3 billion, a 73 percent increase. In 1939, U.S. industry consumed 78,603 million kilowatt hours of electric power; by 1944, it was consuming 156,365 million kilowatt hours, a phenomenal 100 percent increase. Metaphorically speaking, the war had unleashed the potential that had been building throughout the early part of the century, putting the U.S. economy on a new, considerably higher growth path. The challenge, according to President Harry Truman, was staying on it. In his 1945 budget speech to the new Congress, he referred repeatedly to the country's "productive capacity," implicitly referring to the gap between actual and potential output:

The American people have learned during the war the measure of their productive capacity, and they will remember the experience in the peace to come. It is the responsibility of business enterprise to translate market opportunities into employment and production. It is the responsibility of the Government to hold open the door of opportunity and assure sustained markets. Then and only then can free enterprise provide jobs. (Senate Congressional Record, January 7, 1945)

The end of the war did not, however, mark the end of energy-deepening. In hindsight, what had happened during the war was but a preambule of things to come. In the decade from 1945 to 1955, total industrial consumption of electric power more than doubled, going from 146,261 million kilowatt hours in 1945 to 334 to 334,088 million kilowatt hours in 1955. From 1955 to 1965, it increased by another 60 percent. By 1965, the United States consumed more electric power than all other countries combined. Never before in the history of mankind had per-capita energy consumption increased so rapidly.

This "energy orgy" came to a sudden, unexpected end with the oil/energy crisis in the 1970s. Responding to the falling real oil prices, members of the Organization of Petroleum Exporting Countries (OPEC) orchestrated an artifical crisis in 1973, resulting in the quadrupling of oil and other energy prices. With this came the end of what had been over a century of declining real energy prices (Jorgenson, 1983). Per-worker energy consumption, monotone increasing for most of this century, stopped rising. Not surprisingly, productivity stopped growing.

This chapter examines the massive energy-deepening that characterized this period. As was the case in the mid-to-late nineteenth century, there is no new energy form or transmission technology per se; instead, the emphasis is on energy-deepening, defined as an increase in the consumption of a given type of energy—in this case, electric power—per unit time. As pointed out earlier, the nineteenth century witnessed a marked increase in horsepower per factory worker (see Table 2.5) the result of various improvements to steam engines (e.g., high-pressure steam engines, steam turbines). As in the previous chapter, the main focus will be on the relationship between the energy deepening of the post–World War II period and political economy. It will be shown that while these developments had little direct effect on political economy per se, they had important indirect effects, including the birth of growth accounting and, more recently, the wildfire interest in the productivity slowdown, and economic growth in general (e.g., real business cycle theory, endogenous growth theory).

Also, it will be argued that developments in labor law, especially the Wagner Act, which legalized collective bargaining, in consumer credit and in the financing of government expenditure had important macroeconomic implications. Specifically, they contributed in a nonnegligible way to resolving the problems of exchange and distribution as defined earlier. For example, by tying real wages to conventionally defined productivity (contemporaneously or lagged), collective bargaining removed the wage, and hence, money income inertia (underincome) referred to earlier. Rising productivity, the result of the massive energy-deepening of the 1950s and 1960s, resulted in higher nominal and real wages, higher money income, and consequently, higher output and expenditure. Merchants increased their demand for consumer and capital goods, contributing to an increase in firm profits. In combination with the increasing use of consumer credit, growing government expenditure, and increasing exports, the institution of collective bargaining solved, if not totally, then partially, the problem of underincome. For a short period in the history of material civilization, Western industrialized economies, specifically the United States, realized, almost instantaneously, the potential associated with energy-deepening. The energy crisis, however, put an abrupt end to this economic nirvana.

PRODUCTION, DISTRIBUTION, AND EXCHANGE IN THE POST–WORLD WAR II PERIOD

As far as data are concerned, the post–World War II period was a watershed of sorts. Prior to the Great Depression, economic data in the United States, and in most western industrialized democracies, were scant, if not altogether inexistent. This all changed with the rise of Keynesian macroeconomics. Specifically, governments began collecting detailed economic data, providing a wealth of information about production, exchange and distribution. In this section, these are used to study production, distribution and exchange in three Western industrialized economies, namely the United States, Germany and Japan, with particular emphasis on the manufacturing sector in the post–World War II period. At war's end, the first two were the leading consumers of electric power. The third, on the other hand, ranked far behind.

Electric Drive-Based Energy-Deepening and Manufacturing Productivity

By the end of World War II, electric motors had supplanted belting, shafting and gearing as the dominant energy transmission technology (Devine, 1990; Nye, 1990). Fossil fuels and hydraulic resources, however, remained the ultimate power source, in the United States, Germany and Japan, as well as in most other industrialized nations. While in the early part of the century, most manufacturing firms generated their own electric power, by the end of World War II, most were purchasing it from publically regulated electric power utilities. Referring to Table 3.1, we see that in 1945, electric utilities' installed generating capacity stood at 50,111,000 kilowatts, which, by 1955, had more than doubled to 114,472,000 kilowatts. By 1965, it had, once again, doubled, reaching 236,126,000 kilowatts. U.S. industrial generating capacity in this period increased, but at a considerably slower rate, going from 12,757,000 kilowatts in 1945 to 18,973,000 kilowatts.

Industrial power consumption increased at record rates in this period. Production processes were speeded up; throughput rates increased, resulting in higher plant output per period of time. What is particularly remarkable is the fact that most of this occurred with essentially the same capital and labor. For example, in the pulp and paper industry, existing paper machines turned faster, increasing productivity (Anderson, Bonsor and Beaudreau, 1982). According to business historian Alfred D. Chandler:

In modern mass production, as in modern mass distribution and modern transportation and communications, economies resulted more from speed than from size. It was not the size of the manufacturing establishment in terms of number of workers and the amount and value of productive equipment, but the velocity of throughput and the resulting increase in volume that permitted economies that lowered costs and increases output per worker and per machine. (Chandler, 1977, 244)

In earlier work (Beaudreau 1995a, b, c, 1998), I modeled what Chandler refers to as the "velocity of throughput" using a modified KLEMS production function, the KLEP (capital, labor and electric power) production function, and proceeded to estimate the relevant output elasticities directly using post–World War II input and output data for U.S., German and Japan manufacturing. These were then used in lieu of factor shares as the relevant weights in standard growth accounting exercises. Specifically, I assumed the existence of a well-behaved, twice differentiable, monotonic and quasi-concave production function (Equation 4.1) where $VA(t)$ = value added at time t, $EP(t)$ = electric power at time t, $L(t)$ = employment at time t, and $K(t)$ = capital at time t. Christensen and Jorgenson (1970) and Gollop and Jorgenson (1980) define the rate of growth of total factor productivity, $tfp = (dTFP(t)/dt)/TFP(t)$, as $tfp = va - s_{EP} \, ep - s_K \, k - s_L \, l$, where $va = (dVA(t)/dt)/VA(t)$, $ep = (dEP(t)/dt)/EP(t)$, $l = (dL(t)/dt)/L(t)$, and $k = (dK(t)/dt)/K(t)$, and s_i is the weighted average of the ith factor share over the discrete time interval $\forall \; i = EP, L, K$ (Gullickson and Harper, 1988).

$$VA(t) = F \, [EP(t), \, L(t), \, K(t)] \tag{4.1}$$

For the reasons outlined in Beaudreau (1996a, b, c, 1998), the relevant factor output elasticities were estimated directly (i.e., as opposed to indirectly using cost data). Specifically, data on value added, electric-power consumption, total employment and capital for U.S., German, and Japanese manufacturing were used to estimate the Cobb-Douglas KLEP production function: $VA(t) = EP(t)^{\beta_1} L(t)^{\beta_2} K(t)^{\beta_3}$.

Table 4.1
KLEP Output Elasticities: U.S., German, and Japanese Manufacturing

Dependent Variable: *VA*

Independent Variable	U.S. 1950–1984	Germany 1963–1988	Japan 1965–1988
EP	0.537244	0.747482	0.60559
	(26.551)	(3.135)	(3.017)
L	0.399727	0.121134	0.1976
	(18.231)	(2.332)	(1.847)
K	0.075049	0.131383	0.196748
	(2.768)	(0.543)	(1.608)
Constant	0.075049	0.046106	-0.019274
	(9.956)	(1.426)	(0.271)
R²	0.98438	0.95821	0.98314
F	1008.5140	229.2853	612.1780

Source: Beaudreau (1998), 98.

The estimated output elasticities for all three countries are presented in Table 4.1. What is particularly striking are the similarities across countries. In all three cases, electric-power consumption is, by far, the most important factor input, as evidenced by output elasticities of 0.537244, 0.747482 and 0.605599.

Pre– and Post–Energy Crisis Output Growth

Table 4.2 reports the relevant growth rates for manufacturing value added (*Q*), electric power (*EP*), labor (*L*) and capital (*K*), as well as the relevant fixed-weight aggregate input index (Θ) (Hisnanick and Kymm, 1992; Gullickson and Harper, 1988) for three time intervals: 1950–1984, 1950–1973, and 1974–1984.

Unlike previous studies that reported a nonnegligible gap between rates of output growth and rates of aggregate input growth (i.e., the Solow residual), these results show that growth in U.S., German and Japanese manufacturing value added is fully explained by growth in the relevant fixed-weight factor input growth indexes (Beaudreau 1995a, b, c, 1998). For the complete period 1950–1984, U.S. manufacturing value added increased at an average annual rate of 2.684 percent, while the aggregate input increased at 2.655 percent. For the first subperiod 1950–1973, it increased at 3.469, while the aggregate input increased at 3.472 percent. In the second subperiod, 1974–1984, it increased at an average annual rate of 0.121, while the aggregate input increased at 0.310.

Table 4.2
Output and Input Growth Rates: U.S., German, and Japanese Manufacturing

United States		1950–1984	1950–1973	1974–1984
	USVA	2.684	3.469	0.121
	USΘ*	2.674	3.472	0.310
	USEP	4.052	5.371	0.246
	USL	0.662	0.900	-0.091
	USK	3.694	3.614	3.400
Germany		1963–1988	1962–1973	1974–1988
	GERVA	2.462	6.522	1.486
	GERΘ	2.433	5.190	1.080
	GEREP	2.894	5.883	1.366
	GERL	-0.785	0.592	-0.938
	GERK	2.945	5.620	1.406
Japan		1965–1988	1965–1973	1974–1988
	JAPVA	3.826	8.844	3.099
	JAPΘ	3.566	9.856	1.538
	JAPEP	3.559	11.320	0.965
	JAPL	-0.082	2.297	-0.367
	JAPK	7.520	13.536	5.182

*$\Theta = \beta_1\, ep + \beta_2\, l + \beta_3\, k$, where β_1, β_2, and β_3 are the estimated coefficients.
Source: Beaudreau (1998), 99.

Chief among the causes of growth in U.S., German, and Japanese manufacturing value added is electric power consumption. In U.S. manufacturing, electric power consumption increased at an average annual rate of 4.052 percent over the period 1950–1984. Per-worker consumption of electric power in U.S. manufacturing in this period goes from 12,534 kilowatt hours in 1950 to 41,688 kilowatt hours in 1984, a total increase of 232 percent (U.S. Department of Commerce, various years). When multiplied by the relevant output elasticity (0.537244), the growth in electric power consumption in U.S. manufacturing accounts for 82 percent of overall output growth (2.17/2.68), corroborating the predictions of Newtonian production analysis. Prior to the energy crisis (i.e., 1973), electric power consumption in manufacturing increased at an average annual rate of 5.371 percent. Output increased at an average annual rate of 3.466 percent. Electric power consumption growth, it then follows, accounts for 83 percent of output growth (2.88/3.46). In the post–energy crisis period, electric power consumption increased at an average annual rate of 0.246, while output increased at an average annual rate of 0.121.

Pre- and Post–Energy Crisis Productivity Growth

Gullickson and Harper (1988) and Hisnanick and Kymm (1992) examined the sources of productivity growth in U.S. manufacturing using $lp = q - l$ (see Equation 4.2) as the measure of labor productivity.[1] In this section, I report a series of revised estimates of the role of electric power and capital in labor productivity in U.S., German and Japanese manufacturing. Referring to Table 4.3, we see that the rate of growth of labor productivity is, in all three cases, entirely explained by increasing electric power and capital intensities, defined here as $ep - l$, the shift away from labor to electric power, and $k - l$, the shift away from labor to capital.

$$lp = va - l = \beta_1 [ep - l] + \beta_3 [k - l] + tfp \qquad (4.2)$$

Over the entire sample period (1950–1984), U.S. labor productivity increased at an average annual rate of 2.022 percent. During this period, the electric-power-labor ratio increased at an average annual rate of 3.39 percent, which when multiplied by the relevant output elasticity (0.537244), yields a value of 1.820 percent, which measures the effects on labor productivity of the substitution of labor for electric power referred to by Dale Jorgenson (Jorgenson, 1983). Also, during this period, the capital-labor ratio increased at an average annual rate of 3.032, which when multiplied by the relevant output elasticity (0.075049) yields a value of 0.191, which measures the effects on labor productivity of the substitution of labor for capital. The sum of these two effects accounts for 99.5 percent of the growth in labor productivity in U.S. manufacturing (2.011/2.022).

Prior to the energy crisis, labor productivity increased at an average annual rate of 2.569 percent, of which 2.400 percent can be attributed to labor-electric power substitution (energy-deepening) and 0.170 percent can be attributed to labor-capital substitution. Together, these two effects overstate the overall increase in labor productivity by 1 percent. In the ensuing decade, labor productivity increased at an average annual rate of 0.212 percent, of which 0.180 percent can be attributed to labor-electric power substitution and 0.219 percent can be attributed to labor-capital substitution.

The Role of Capital and Labor in Growth Accounting

Traditional growth accounting, best associated with the work of Edward Denison, and Newtonian production analysis-based growth accounting (Beaudreau, 1998) are opposites. The former, Paleolithic in its view of production processes, attributes growth to capital, labor and a residual, while the latter attributes growth to energy consumption and innovations in second-law efficiency. The former views energy as an intermediate input, and, consequently, not productive in the physical sense; the latter views capital and labor as organizational inputs and, consequently, as not productive in the physical sense.

Table 4.3
Productivity Growth: U.S., German, and Japanese Manufacturing

United States		1950–1984	1950–1973	1974–1984
	uslp	2.022	2.569	0.212
	ustfp	0.010	-0.002	-0.1889
	$\beta_1(usep\text{-}usl)$	1.820	2.400	0.180
	$\beta_3(usk\text{-}usl)$	0.191	0.170	0.219
Germany		1963–1988	1963–1973	1974–1988
	gerlp	3.247	5.930	2.424
	gertfp	0.007	1.315	0.3942
	$\beta_1(gerep\text{-}gerl)$	2.750	3.954	1.722
	$\beta_3(gerk\text{-}gerl)$	0.489	0.660	0.307
Japan		1965–1988	1965–1973	1974–1988
	japlp	3.908	6.547	3.466
	japtfp	0.208	-1.126	1.567
	$\beta_1(japep\text{-}japl)$	2.204	5.463	0.806
	$\beta_3(japk\text{-}japl)$	1.495	2.210	1.091

Source: Beaudreau (1998), 101.

Unless it can somehow be shown that capital and labor are physically productive (i.e., are a source of energy) in modern production processes, reason dictates that the latter view should prevail. Capital and labor are to be viewed as organizational inputs.

NPA Growth Accounting

This simple finding has important implications for growth accounting. For example, it implies that to be theoretically consistent, the focus of growth accounting in general should be on two variables, energy and second-law efficiency, the latter being directly related to tools (capital) and upper- and lower-level supervision (labor). Tools and supervisors affect growth via their effect on η, second-law efficiency. Operationally, this implies that the basic Newtonian production function ($W(t) = \eta E(t)$) should be the theoretical basis of growth accounting. Accordingly, the rate of growth of work ($dW(t)/W(t)$) is equal to the sum of the rate of growth of second-law efficiency ($d\eta(t)/\eta(t)$), and the rate of growth of energy consumption ($dE(t)/E(t)$). This is formalized in terms of Equation 4.3.

$$dW(t)/W(t) = d\eta(t)/\eta(t) + dE(t)/E(t) \qquad (4.3)$$

Thus, the rate of growth of work (i.e., value added) is an increasing function of the rate of growth of second-law efficiency and the rate of growth of energy consumption. Table 4.4 presents the corresponding values for U.S., German and Japanese manufacturing. Second-law efficiency was defined as the ratio of value added to electric power consumption. We see, for example, that in U.S. manufacturing value added increased at a rate of 2.5625 percent from 1950 to 1984. Electric power consumption in this period increased at a rate of 3.9342 percent, while second-law efficiency decreased at a rate of 1.3203 percent. Manufacturing firms in all three countries were less able to extract work from each additional kilowatt hour (i.e., lower energy). Broken down into pre– and post–energy crisis subperiods, we see that in both, second-law efficiency decreased, albeit at a slower rate in the latter period. The corresponding values for German and Japanese manufacturing show that while second-law efficiency decreased from 1964 to 1988, it increased in Germany. Moreover, while the energy crisis failed to arrest the decline in second-law efficiency in U.S. manufacturing, it succeeded in Japanese manufacturing, where it went from an average annual decrease of 2.1835 from 1964 to 1973, to an average annual increase of 1.12975 from 1974 to 1988.

Table 4.4
NPA Output and Input Growth Rates: U.S., German, and Japanese Manufacturing

U.S.		1950–1984	1950–1973	1974–1984
	USVA	2.684	3.469	0.121
	USEP	4.052	5.371	0.246
	USη	-1.367	-1.902	-0.124
Germany		1963–1988	1963–1973	1974–1988
	GERVA	2.462	6.522	1.486
	GEREP	2.894	5.883	1.366
	GERη	-0.432	0.638	0.066
Japan		1965–1988	1965–1973	1974–1988
	JAPVA	3.826	8.844	3.099
	JAPEP	3.559	11.320	0.965
	JAPη	0.267	-2.479	2.134

Source: Beaudreau (1998), 103.

These results speak for themselves. The phenomenally high, uninterrupted growth in U.S., German and Japanese manufacturing in the post–World War II period was the result of energy-deepening in the form of increasing levels of electric power consumption per period of time. Factories turned out more and more output, the result of more and more electric power, confirming Alfred Chandler's views on productivity growth and its causes. This, however, came to an abrupt end in the 1970s with the energy crisis, as firms curtailed energy-deepening. Energy conservation became the norm. Electric power consumption growth fell dramatically, as did growth and productivity. The energy orgy was over, or so it appeared.

Electric-Drive-Based Energy-Deepening and the Problem of Exchange

Thus far, it has been shown that energy-deepening, whether the result of a new energy technology, or an increase in energy consumption for a given technology (e.g., high-pressure steam) resulted in the problem of underincome. At the firm level, the value of capacity output (i.e., output measured at full capacity) increased more than costs, which, aggregating across firms, resulted in the problem of underincome. Also, it has been shown that the repeal of the Corn Laws in 1846, the Smoot-Hawley Tariff Bill of 1929, and the National Industrial Recovery Act of 1933 were policy reactions to this very problem. In this section, it will be argued that a number of pre– and post–World War II developments in the U.S. economy contributed to lessening, and, at times, solving the problem of underincome. They are (1) the development of productivity-based collective bargaining, (2) the extensive growth of consumer credit and (3) the rise of the military-industrial complex. Together with rising exports (including such policy measures as the Marshall Plan), these developments increased wage and money income, thus resulting in thirty years of uninterrupted growth, characterized by collinear capacity, income and expenditure growth, all based on energy-deepening in the form of rising electric power consumption per lower-level supervisor.

The contribution of collective bargaining to resolving the problem of underincome should be obvious. As energy consumption per worker (lower-level supervisor) increased, productivity increased. As productivity increased, labor unions demanded higher nominal (and real) wages. This, in turn, increased the demand for trade credit on the part of firms, which, at the aggregate level, increased wage income. Rising wage income, in turn, led merchants to increase orders of goods and services, thus increasing firm profits.[2] Table 4.5, taken from Beaudreau (1998), presents data on real value added per production worker in U.S. manufacturing from 1947 to 1973, as well as the corresponding real salary levels per production worker (constant 1958 dollars). Column 3 is the ratio of the latter to the former, and measures, in large degree labor's (in this case, production workers') ability to appropriate energy-based rents. We see that from 1947 to 1973, productivity increased monotonically, as did production workers' take-home income. What is interesting to note is that throughout this period, the overall number of production workers in U.S. manufacturing increased monotonically. Collective bargaining, it therefore follows, had succeeded in doing what the market (producer-merchant exchange technology) had failed to do: increase real wages in response to rising productivity.

Table 4.5
Value Added and Earnings per Production Worker, U.S. Manufacturing, 1947–1973

Year	PW*	VAPW**	SALPW	Ratio
1947	11,917	8,355	3,401	0.407
1949	11,016	8,649	3,471	0.401
1950	11,778	9,500	3,662	0.385
1951	12,508	9,533	3,796	0.398
1952	12,706	9,818	3,936	0.400
1953	13,500	10,205	4,108	0.402
1954	12,372	10,557	4,022	0.381
1955	12,954	11,466	4,179	0.364
1956	13,131	11,740	4,216	0.359
1957	12,828	11,819	4,203	0.355
1958	11,681	12,117	4,246	0.350
1959	12,272	12,955	4,388	0.338
1960	12,209	13,002	4,404	0.338
1961	11,778	13,334	4,445	0.333
1962	12,126	13,957	4,609	0.330
1963	12,232	14,648	4,735	0.323
1964	12,403	15.279	4,878	0.319
1965	13,076	15,649	4,921	0.314
1966	13,826	15,930	4,969	0.311
1967	13,955	15,963	4,959	0.310
1968	14,041	16,599	5,094	0.306
1969	14,357	16,539	5,073	0.306
1970	13,528	16,415	5,008	0.305
1971	12,874	17,303	5,135	0.296
1972	13,527	17,963	5,353	0.298
1973	14,232	18,419	5,373	0.291

*000 **Constant 1958 dollars
Source: Beaudreau (1998), 139.

This triumph, however, was tempered by what appears to be a decline in production workers' bargaining power throughout this period. In 1947, the ratio of salary to value added stood at 0.407; however, by 1973, it had fallen to 0.2981. Thus, while production worker salaries had, via collective bargaining, tracked productivity, they received less in 1973, relatively speaking, than in 1947.

Table 4.6
Consumer Credit, United States, 1901–1968

Year	Consumer Credit*
1901	1.0
1912	2.9
1922	5.7
1929	8.6
1933	4.3
1939	7.8
1945	5.8
1946	8.5
1947	11.8
1948	14.7
1949	17.6
1950	21.8
1951	23.1
1952	27.9
1953	31.8
1954	32.9
1955	39.4
1956	43.1
1957	45.9
1958	46.1
1959	51.5
1960	56.1
1961	58.0
1962	63.8
1963	71.7
1964	80.3
1965	90.3
1966	97.5
1967	102.1
1968	113.2

*Billion current dollars.
Source: U.S. Department of Commerce (1975), Series F387.

The second contributing factor was the development of consumer credit, which, like higher exports, weakens the link between merchants' demand for credit and aggregate wage income. Aggregate merchants' orders would, as a result, no longer depend solely on aggregate wage income. Interestingly, large corporations such as General Motors, General Electric, Ford, Chrysler and

Westinghouse, were among the first to make extensive use of consumer credit.[3] This, I argue, is perfectly understandable given the extensive energy-deepening they had undergone, with the resulting massive increase in capacity. Referring to Table 4.6, we see that consumer credit increased by 470 percent from 1901 to 1945, and by 1,885 percent from 1945 to 1968. Clearly, consumer credit is, owing to the problem of underincome, an important macroeconomic instrument, increasing overall money income beyond that which would result from exchanges in the relevant factor markets only.

Another important factor was rising government expenditure, and, more importantly, the development of innovative payment (financing) techniques. Theoretically, tax-financed government expenditure does not increase overall money income, for what are obvious reasons. Briefly, it simply crowds out private expenditure (zero-sum game).[4] For government expenditure to increase money income, it must increase the overall level of outstanding credit. Historically, this was achieved in two ways. First, the Federal Reserve Act of 1913, by allowing the federal government to sell its liabilities to the newly created central bank (the "federal" reserve bank), created the "potential" for government expenditure-based increases in money income (via merchants). Money income was no longer limited to the demand for credit on the part of firms and exporters (not to mention, the suppliers of consumer credit). However, for this to increase net outstanding money income (credit), it had to somehow find its way into the economy (i.e., into firms' accounts receivable).

This, I maintain, was achieved by the massive increase in post–World War II government expenditure, financed, in large part, by the sale of government liabilities to the Federal Reserve Board. The key, as far as the problem of exchange is concerned, is the very way in which these monies (credit) made their way into the economy. Specifically, the federal government (e.g., the Department of Defense). acting as both consumer and merchant, began financing the day-to-day operations of its major suppliers, paying for the goods and services in question in an "up front" manner. That is, at the signing of the contract, the federal government would extend financing (credit) to the suppliers.

This practice (i.e., up-front financing) was, by this point in time, common in government contracts. John Francis Gorgel, for example, describes the U.S. federal government's dealings with "military-industrial firms" (MIFs) in the following terms:

The civilian firm's cash flow is a priority concern of management. Inability to finance work-in-progress until it is converted into finished, delivered goods and payments are received has been a principal cause of business failures. Management must anticipate its financing requirements and develop effective sources of money supply under conditions of substantial risk.

The DOD customer does not insist that its contractor face these uncertainties and problems. We find the possible alternatives described as follows:

To promote private financing, for example, the Government permits the contractor to assign his claim for payment. It may also guarantee his private loans in suitable cases. To reduce the need for such financing, the Government makes intermediate payments of two kinds: partial payments on fixed-price contracts and interim payments on cost-reimbursement procurements. These increase the contractor's cash flow from the contract; thus, they reduce the amount of working capital he must obtain from other sources.

The Government may also provide direct contract financing in appropriate instances. Customary progress payments are used most often. Unusual progress payments and advance payments are also available. All three may be used in any combination that is needed and justified by the financing regulations. (Gorgel, 1971, 67)

These three developments, I argue, contributed to resolving the problem of underincome in the post–World War II period, paving the way, so to speak, for three decades of phenomenal growth, unprecedented in the history of material civilization. Money income, no longer the sole responsibility of the nation's producers, increased commensurately (or almost) with productive capacity. Unfortunately, as I shall argue, political economists were, for the most part, oblivious to the role of these changes in resolving the problem of underincome.

Electric-Drive-Based Energy-Deepening and Income Distribution in U.S. Manufacturing

Like the shift from water, wind and muscular power to fire power, and the shift from fire power to electric power, the energy-deepening in the form of increasingly greater electric-power consumption in the post–World War II period resulted in significant energy rents, defined as the difference between the value of the marginal product of a kilowatt hour and its price.

As pointed out above, the right to bargain collectively and the closed-shop principle altered, in a nonnegligible way, the problem of distribution and the problem of exchange. Starting with the latter, rising productivity from higher electric power consumption per plant, worker or capital, would, almost automatically, result in higher real wages, thus solving, at least partially, the problem of energy-deepening-induced underincome. Unlike the first and second industrial revolutions where power innovations increased productive capacity without increasing money income, here, money income tracked productivity, albeit with a lag. This had important implications for the problem of distribution. Specifically, workers (i.e., supervisors) were able to capture a greater portion of these rents. Figuratively speaking, collective bargaining had killed "two birds with one stone," namely the problem of exchange and the problem of distribution. Labor income tracked productivity, which, as was shown above, increased dramatically in this period (that is, until the energy crisis). Income to capital increased too as evidenced by real stock price appreciation.

Table 4.4 presents data on production workers (PW), value added per production worker (VAPW), and salary per production worker (SALPW) for the period 1947 to 1973. We see that the number of production workers in U.S. manufacturing increased 19 percent in this period. Value added per production worker (lower-level supervisor) increased 120 percent, while salary per production worker increased 57 percent. What is particularly noteworthy is the collinear nature of the latter two series. From 1947, value added per production worker and salary per production worker increased in step, if not always in proportion. For example, in 1950, value added per production worker increased 9.8 percent, while salary per production worker increased 5.5 percent. Unlike the pre-Great Depression period where real wages remained relatively constant despite substantial productivity gains, here, wages and productivity increased in step.

ELECTRIC-DRIVE-BASED ENERGY-DEEPENING, EXCHANGE, AND DISTRIBUTION AS SEEN BY POLITICAL ECONOMISTS

By the end of World War II, mainstream political economy was in crisis. None of the received wisdom (i.e., theory) seemed relevant: not price theory, not wage theory, not monetary theory etcetera. Contributing to this state of crisis was the mercurial rise of Keynesian political economy (macro and micro). Traditional political economists, Marshallian in their approach to the world, had to deal with the General Theory and its many ramifications. Would government (e.g., the Full-Employment Act of 1946) supplant the market? Had markets failed? Were Marx, Engels and other nineteenth-century radicals right after all? Was capitalism inherently flawed? Ideology had returned with a vengeance.

Breaking the fall, metaphorically speaking, were the high growth rates that characterized this period. As shown above, growth rates reached new heights in the post–World War II period (1945–1973). Clearly, while something had gone terribly wrong in the 1920s and 1930s, the unprecedented growth of the 1940s, 1950s and 1960s had more than made up for it. Per-capita output. income, and expenditure increased at unprecedented over the course of this period, until, of course, the energy crisis.

In this section, I examine electric-drive-based energy-deepening—and its end in the 1970s—exchange and distribution as seen by political economists. It will be argued that unlike the early twentieth century, which had witnessed the development of new analytical approaches to production based on energy (Technocracy, The Brookings Institution approach to production, Social Credit, Frederick Soddy's Cartesian economics), the post–World War II period, despite being a period of unprecedented energy-deepening, was devoid of any such developments. Nor did it witness any developments in the theory of exchange and the theory of income distribution.

This only serves to beg the question, why? Why was it that in the midst of an energy revolution, political economy, the purported "science" of wealth, failed to even identify energy in general, and electric power in particular, as a key cause of growth? Why was it unable to identify the problem of exchange, and the problem of distribution? The answer, I purport, is "bad" science.

As pointed out above, the post–World War II period was one of crisis for political economy. On the one hand, output was growing at unprecedented—and unexplained—rates. Production theory was at a loss to explain why, the result of which was the birth of what Moses Abramovitz labelled the "measure of ignorance" (Solow residual). On the other hand, the Great Depression, and the chosen remedy, Keynesian-style government expenditure policies, continued to stir emotions in what had been throughout the nineteenth century, a political ideology, namely market-based political economy. The new debate pitted classical and neoclassical political economists (under the auspices of monetarism) against Keynesian political economists. At stake were a number of issues, including the causes of the Great Depression, the wisdom of the chosen solution (New Deal), the wisdom of the Full Employment Act of 1946, and the role of government in the economy. For three decades, political economists, whether of the classical/neoclassical or Keynesian persuasion, engaged in rhetorical debates, basing their arguments on a Paleolithic model of production—outdated by over three centuries—and a Paleolithic model of exchange (pre-merchant), an example of which is Don Patinkin's *Money, Interest and Prices*, published in 1965.

Bad science, I contend, is also to blame for the rise of formalism in post–World War II political economy. Take production theory, where the Paleolithic model of production referred to above was cloaked in new suits, including the Constant Elasticity of Substitution suit, the Translog suit, the Leontief suit, and the Cobb-Douglas suit. Throughout this period, formalism became (and continues to be) synonymous with "good" science. Today, professional journals are replete with formalizations of antiquated, Paleolithic production and exchange technologies. It comes as little surprise that paradoxes and ironies have become the norm, not the exception in political economy.

Electric-Drive-Based Energy-Deepening as Seen by Political Economists

While they ignored energy and the role of energy in the creation of wealth, political economists could not ignore the phenomenal growth in output in general, and output per worker (conventionally defined labor productivity) in this period. Among the first to acknowledge the existence of a divergence between conventionally used factor inputs (capital and labor) and output were Jan Tinbergen in Europe and Moses Abramovitz in the United States. Both had devised indexes of input and output growth, and uncovered, using post–World War I data, the presence of an unexplained, upward drift in output indexes. Abramovitz referred to this discrepancy as "our measure of ignorance."

Credit for the earliest explicit calculation belongs to Tinbergen, who in a 1942 paper, published in German, generalizes the Cobb-Douglas production function by adding an exponential trend to it, intended to represent various "technical developments". He computed the average value of this trend component, calling it a measure of "efficiency", for four countries: Germany, Great Britain, France, and the U.S., using the formula t = y − 2/3n − 1/3k, where y, n, and k are the average growth rates of output, labor and capital respectively, and the weights are taken explicitly from Douglas. Note how close this is to Solow who will let these weights change, shifting the index numbers from a fixed weight geometric to an approximate Divisia form. Nobody seems to have been aware of Tinbergen's paper in the U.S. until much later.

The developments in the U.S. originated primarily at the NBER where a program of constructing national income and "real" output series under the leadership of Simon Kuznets was expanded to include capital series for major sectors of the economy, with contributions by Creamer, Fabricant, Goldsmith, Tostlebe and others. (Griliches, 1995, 3)

Unfortunately, in spite of a half-century of work on growth since, our "measure of ignorance" has not decreased (Maddison, 1987; Gullickson and Harper, 1988; Aghion and Howitt, 1998). It has changed names, been cloaked in formal and informal models, been tested against every possible datum, yet, in the end, it stands as a living testimony to what by now were over two centuries of "bad" science.

Examples continue to abound in the professional journals. Take, for example, a recent article in *The Quarterly Journal of Economics* by Walter Nonneman and Patrick Vanhoudt, entitled "A Further Augmentation of the Solow Model and the Empirics of Economic Growth for OECD Countries," where production is modeled in terms of the following functional form:

$$Y_t = c\, L_t^{\,(1-\Sigma\,\alpha)}\, K_{1t}^{\,\alpha 1},\, K_{2t}^{\,\alpha 2},\, \ldots\ldots,\, K_{mt}^{\,\alpha m} \tag{4.3}$$

L is labor, and K_i is capital of type i. There are, altogether, m types of capital, including infrastructure, equipment, other physical capital, human capital and know-how. Clearly, political economists are, as far as modeling production is concerned, no further today than they were 200 years ago. All of Nonneman and Vanhoudt's inputs are organizational inputs, affecting productivity only indirectly through η, the level of second-law efficiency. Accordingly, improvements in any or all of these will affect output, but only marginally.

The Energy Crisis and Productivity as Seen by Political Economists

As pointed out earlier, the "energy orgy" of the post–World War II period came to an unexpected and unfortunate end in the mid-1970s with the OPEC-induced energy crisis. Energy prices doubled, tripled, and, eventually, quadrupled, pushing the West up along its demand curve for energy. Energy consumption stopped growing. In hindsight, one would think that, at long last, energy would get the attention it deserved. "Absence makes the heart grow fonder," as the saying goes. Figurately speaking, the hen that had laid the golden eggs (energy rents) for over two centuries was no more. As incredulous as it may appear, this was not to be, as evidenced by the continued absence of energy from production theory, my work (Beaudreau, 1995a, b, c, 1998) notwithstanding. Once again, the reasons are many. First, since energy had, up to then, not been defined as a factor input, the focus as far as production theory was concerned was not on energy per se, but rather, on the relationship between energy prices and the demand for capital and labor. For example, if energy and capital were found to complementary, then an increase in the price of the former will decrease the demand for the latter, reducing growth, and, quite possibly, in the short run, provoking a recession (Berndt and Wood, 1975).

To address these questions (complementarity-substitutability), Ernst Berndt and David O. Wood developed a new, all-inclusive production function, commonly known as the KLEMS production function (i.e., capital, labor, energy, materials and services). By eliminating the age-old distinction between factor inputs and intermediate inputs, Berndt and Wood cleared the way for the estimation of energy-labor and energy-capital, not to mention, energy-materials and energy-services, cross-elasticities.

One's first inclination is to laud what has to qualify as an important breakthrough, as far as the role of energy in production is concerned. After all, it took 200 years (from Smith's *Wealth of Nations* in 1776 to 1975) for energy to break the stranglehold held by capital and labor in production theory. Finally, energy had entered the select club of factor inputs. The irony, however, is that the select club was (is) no more. The distinction between intermediate input and factor input was blurred beyond recognition. Nothing was a factor input, and nothing was an intermediate input.

Further marring Berndt and Wood's contribution was the method used to estimate the various parameters (e.g., output-elasticities and cross-elasticities). Specifically, instead of using input and output data, they chose cost and factor share data. Implicit in the use of such data are the assumptions of constant returns to scale in production and competitive factor markets. It being the case that electric power is the dominant form of energy in manufacturing, and that the price of electric power is regulated, doing so introduces an important bias. Their results showed an energy output elasticity of 0.06 percent. Put plainly, energy was, for all intents and purposes, insignificant. Case closed.

When it was suggested that the energy crisis could lie at the root of the productivity and growth slowdown, Berndt's and Wood's energy output elasticity (and others') were cited as evidence to the contrary. Something as insignificant as energy in twentieth-century production processes could not possibly have halved the growth rate, and all but eliminated productivity growth, or so the story goes. In their comprehensive study of total factor productivity in U.S. manufacturing (the results are reproduced in Table 4.7), William Gullickson and Michael J. Harper, show, beyond a shadow of a doubt, that energy was not the cause.

Table 4.7
Gullickson and Harper's Estimates of Multifactor Productivity, 1949–1983

Period	Output	Aggregate input	Capital (K)	Labor (L)	Energy (E)	Materials (M)	Services (S)	KLEMS Productivity
1949–83	3.1	2.0	3.8	0.8	3.3	2.2	4.6	1.1
1949–73	4.2	2.7	3.9	1.5	5.1	3.1	5.4	1.5
1973–83	0.6	0.3	3.6	-1.0	-0.8	0.2	2.6	0.3

Source: Gullickson and Harper (1987), 22.

The Energy Agnostics

As if unswayed by either the methodology or the results of growth accounting, a small minority of political economists continued to study the role of energy in production. Among these, one finds Dale Jorgenson, Zvi Griliches and Nathan Rosenberg, and engineers-economists Sam H. Schurr, Calvin Burwell, Warren D. Devine, Jr., and Sidney Sonenblum. For example, in 1983, Dale Jorgenson published the results of a study of the role of electricity in technical change (i.e., whether they be electricity-using or not). Of the 35 sectors studied, 23 were found to be of the electricity-using type. Specifically, "the decline in electricity prices prior to 1973 prompted increased electrification via the substitution of electricity for other forms of energy, and through the substitution of energy for other inputs—especially labor (Jorgenson, 1983, 21). Electrification and energy- deepening in the form of higher levels of electricity consumption, he went on to conclude, played a fundamental role in productivity growth.

In similar work, Sidney Sonenblum shows that technological progress in manufacturing has been "related to the adoption and spread of production processes and modes of organization that are dependent on the use of electricity" (Sonenblum, 1990, 277). The downside, however, in Sonenblum and Jorgenson's work is the absence of a theory of production in which energy is explicitly incorporated. Oddly enough, energy, in this case, electricity, affects output indirectly through "technology." That is, via the A(t) scaler in the Cobb-Douglas production function. Habits die hard. The spirit of the neoclassical production function with its emphasis on capital and labor, and, to a lesser degree, on technology, is very much present in Jorgenson's work, and, indeed, in all post–energy crisis work on energy.

This, in brief, is where the economics profession stands today on the role of energy in production. Despite two epoch-defining energy innovations, two centuries of energy-deepening, and a cataclysmic "energy crisis," energy, the building block of the universe, remains very much the outsider, having no place at the table.

Post–World War II Energy-Deepening and the Problem of Exchange as Seen by Political Economists

As had been the case for over a century and a half, the problem of exchange as defined above was unbeknownst to political economists in the post–World War II period, and, consequently, was not studied. This is especially ironic in a period that witnessed a marked increase in interest in money and monetary theory. Beginning with Irving Fisher's work in the 1920s on prices and the quantity theory of money, the period following the Great Depression and World War II witnessed what many consider to be pathbreaking contributions in the field of monetary economics. Among these are Don Patinkin's "Money, Interest and Prices," which spawned a literature on money that, to this day, continues to grow. The problem, however, is that with few exceptions, monetary theory is about money, and not exchange. For example, in Patinkin's work, money enters as an argument in the representative agent's utility function. Some, however, have attempted to model exchange. Among these are Robert Clower and Peter Howitt who have attempted to model decentralized exchange technologies per se.

Notwithstanding these attempts at modeling exchange, political economists in general were oblivious to the role of the various innovations referred to earlier (collective bargaining, consumer credit, credit-financed government expenditure) in resolving the defining problem of the modern era, namely the problem of underincome. Previously, and as early as the 1920s, energy-deepening had increased potential output by more than costs, resulting in the problem of underincome. Now, with these changes (e.g., collective bargaining, consumer credit, government expenditure) in place, energy-based productivity growth would result in higher wages, costs and, consequently, money income, thus eliminating the problem. Ironically, mainstream political economy denounced collective bargaining and government expenditure as welfare decreasing.

Post–World War II Energy-Deepening and the Problem of Distribution as Seen by Political Economists

The problem of distribution, as defined in Chapter 1, is absent in this period, owing, in large measure to (1) the absence of a theory of production incorporating energy, and (2) consequently, the absence of the very notion of energy rents, in this case, electric power rents. Because output is defined solely in terms of labor and capital, it followed that higher wages and profits would be attributed to higher intrinsic labor and capital productivity.

As for trade unions, the relevant analytical framework adopted by political economists was Marshallian in origin, with the demand for labor being dictated by the marginal productivity of labor schedule, and the supply of labor, by worker preferences for work and leisure. Higher wages, its therefore follows, would lead to a decrease in the quantity demanded for labor, *ceteris paribus*. The marginal product of labor being a decreasing function of employment, a higher wage would force firms to decrease employment (Blanchflower, Oswald and Sanfey, 1996; Van Reenen, 1996).

As far as policy was concerned, the upshot of this literature was predictable: unions are private goods and social bads. Unionized workers enjoy higher wages; however, unionization reduces employment, and increases unemployment.

The Detractors

There were, of course, a number of detractors in this period, the most celebrated of whom was John K. Galbraith, who provided what I feel is an accurate, albeit incomplete, portrait of the developments in the post–World War II period. Taking his cue from developments in the 1920s and 1930s, notably, the rise of the large corporation, Berle and Means' *The Modern Corporation and Private Property*, published in 1932, and the New Deals (I and II), he modeled the development of labor unions and government in bargaining terms, specifically, in terms of "coutervailing power" (Galbraith, 1952). By the end of the Great Depression, economic power in the U.S. economy was concentrated in the hands of what he mistakingly referred to as "Technocrats," but which, in actual fact, were the profit-maximizing managers of large corporations. In the spirit of President Herbert C. Hoover's notion of the "associative state," Rexford Tugwell's notion of the "planned economy," and the National Industrial Recovery Act of 1933, Galbraith pushed the idea of "countervailing" powers (i.e., to that of large corporations). The emergence of "big" government and "big" unions, were, in his view, positive developments in the bigger scheme of things (i.e., the social bargaining game).

The operation of countervailing power is to be seen with the greatest clarity in the labor market where it is also most fully developed. Because of his comparatively immobility, the indivdual worker has long been highly vulnerable to private economic power. The customer of any particular steel mill . . . could always take himself elsewhere if he felt he was being overcharged. . . . The worker had no comparable freedom if he felt he was being underpaid. . . . As late as the early twenties, the steel industry worked a twelve-hour day and seventy-two-hour week with an incredible twenty-four-hour stint every fortnight when the shift changed. No such power is exercised today and for the reason that its earlier exercise stimulated the counterreaction that brought it to an end. (Galbraith, 1952, 114)

This is consistent with the bargaining model of income distribution found in Beaudreau (1998) and reproduced in Chapter 1. The owners of capital and labor—and government—bargain over the distribution of the income pie. Where it differs, however, is with regard to the underlying model of production. While Galbraith refers repeatedly to the role of science in economic progress and growth, he, like his orthodox counterparts, was unable to pinpoint the exact causes of growth. In short, like Paul Samuelson and Milton Friedman, he was working with a model of Paleolithic production processes, devoid of all inanimate energy, and in which labor and capital are seen as physically productive. Understandably, any reference to redistribution (from capital to labor) was seen as an attack on private property (i.e., value of marginal product).

CONCLUSIONS

While rich in formalism—relative to the early twentieth century and all of the nineteenth century—political economy in the post–World War II period suffered, in my view, a number of setbacks. The first is the disappearance of alternative theories of production (e.g., cranks and heretics), especially those purporting to include energy as a factor input. As shown earlier, the early twentieth century, and to a lesser degree, the nineteenth century, were characterized by scientific dissent, oftentimes over the appropriate view of production. The Technocracy movement is a case in point, as is Chemistry Nobel prize-winner Frederick Soddy's attempt at constructing an alternative theory of wealth, Cartesian economics. Notwithstanding Nicholas Georgescu-Roegen's work, production theory, not to mention exchange theory, in this period is overtly singular, and this despite being fraught with failure (e.g., Solow residual). Clearly, developments in political economy in this period were variety (diversity) reducing, which as I argued in Beaudreau (1996b) is a welfare-reducing strategy.

Is this any different from the nineteenth and early twentieth centuries? The answer is both yes and no. Starting with the latter, political economy in this period continues to be policy based, with Keynesian political economy dictating the intellectual agenda from 1945 to 1980, and with Marshallian political economy doing likewise since. By Marshallian political economy, it should be understood Reaganomics, the Monetarist Counterrevolution, Monetarism, Real Business Cycle Theory and Growth Theory.

Ironically, the dominant model of production today, used notably in the burgeoning field of growth accounting, differs little from that contained in Adam Smith's *An Inquiry into the Nature and Causes of the Wealth of Nations*; yet production processes differ markedly, as evidenced by growing automation, and what economist Jeremy Rifkin refers to as the "end of work."

NOTES

1. As pointed out earlier, this view of productivity is archaic. Labor is not productive in the physical sense; instead, it is productive in the organizational sense. As such, labor productivity is analogous to management productivity.

2. Higher sales revenue (from merchants) allowed firms to clear outstanding credit notes (for variable inputs), and, in the end, earn higher profits.

3. In each of these cases, the distinction between producer and merchant is blurred, as each controls the relevant distribution network (e.g., automobile dealerships).

4. This is formally known as "crowding out."

5

Growth without Growth: The Post–Energy Crisis Period

In 1974, Robert Solow presented a model suggesting that a constant level of economic growth could be sustained indefinitely, in principle, provided that the elasticity of substitution of capital and labor (taken together) for exhaustible resources is greater than unity. . . . In fact, most of the theoretical work being done by economists at the time ignored the implications of the basic laws of thermodynamics. Economic theorists, at least briefly, seem to have reinvented the perpetual motion machine, an idea that seems very hard to kill.

—Robert U. Ayres and Indira Nair, "Thermodynamics and Economics"

INTRODUCTION

In the previous three chapters, the analysis focused on "positive" energy-related innovations, whether in the form of a new power source, a new power transmission technology or energy-deepening per se, as the primary force behind the study of political economy, and, paradoxically, as its bane, contributing to its downfall. In this chapter, I continue my critique of political economy by examining an altogether different scenario, one devoid of new energy forms and of energy-deepening per se: the "post–energy crisis period," which runs from the early 1980s to the present.

This period is particularly interesting, not to mention revealing, for a number of reasons, not the least of which is the continued widespread use of theoretically and empirically irrelevant models of production and exchange. For example, production continued—and continues—to be studied in terms of models in which labor and capital are the relevant factor inputs, when, as a number of writers (Jeremy Rifkin, William Greider) have shown, Western industrialized economies are moving toward a laborless (animate supervisor-less) society. Also, traditional neoclassical models have been and continue to be used to study the effects of information (e.g., computers) on productivity, despite being devoid of information (as a factor).

Perhaps the greatest interest, however, arises from the area of growth, specifically growth theory (Romer, 1986; Maddison, 1987; Grossman and Helpman, 1992; Aghion and Howitt, 1998). As shown earlier, the energy crisis, by ending two centuries of energy-deepening, brought to a close the era of high growth rates (conventional and labor productivity). Growth rates were halved; productivity growth fell dramatically. Ironically, while the profession has yet to understand two centuries of growth (McCloskey, 1994), it has now taken on the "heroic" task of recreating a past it does not understand.

The chapter is organized as follows. First, using Newtonian production analysis and the bargaining model of distribution, I examine the "fallout" of the energy crisis, consisting of lower energy consumption growth, lower labor productivity growth and the resulting "profit squeeze." As argued in Beaudreau (1998), higher energy prices, in combination with higher real wages, "squeezed" profits in the 1970s and early 1980s.[1] Profit-maximizing firms responded by (1) accelerating the rate of automation in the workplace (replacing animate lower-level supervisors with inanimate ones), and (2) where not technically feasible, moving production offshore. Not surprisingly, this has contributed to higher earnings, and, consequently, higher share prices. Lastly, I examine the macroeconomic consequences of increasing automation and offshore production using the model of exchange described in Chapter 1. Falling nominal wages at the aggregate level raise the problem of underincome. Given that merchants base their orders on aggregate wage income, it stands to reason that, *ceteris paribus*, output will fall as will profits.

As in the previous chapters, this will be followed by an examination of the profession's response to these issues. Not surprisingly, it fares no better than previously. In fact, one could argue that it fares worse, given the absence of a "radical" fringe like the Technocracy movement.[2] As I shall show here, the recent emphasis on R&D and education as growth panacea is misfounded, as is the hype surrounding the current information age. Information is not, was not, and never will be physically productive.

POST–1973 OUTPUT GROWTH, DISTRIBUTION, AND EXCHANGE

The centuries-old "energy orgy," characterized by ever-increasing levels of energy consumption, came to an abrupt, and more importantly, unexpected end with the energy crisis of the 1970s. Per-capita energy consumption stopped growing, as did per capita income, and consequently the standard (matierial) of living. As such, the current generation of lower- and upper-level supervisors (conventional labor) cannot expect to do better than their parents. Per-capita income growth, predicated on per-capita energy consumption growth, has, for all intents and purposes, ended. Barring some unforeseen development in energy technology (e.g., the development of commercially viable, environmentally friendly energy from nuclear fusion), there is every reason to believe that low—in the limit, zero—energy-consumption growth and consequently, low-productivity growth, will be with us for a long, long time, and this, in spite of the much-touted information revolution currently in swing.

This section examines the problems of post–energy crisis output growth, distribution and exchange using the framework developed in Chapter 1. The starting point is the productivity slowdown described in the previous chapter. Higher energy prices in the 1970s, in combination with the foreboding specter of even higher prices in the future, brought the centuries-old process of energy-deepening to a halt. Productivity growth (conventionally-defined) ceased as a result. At the microlevel, firms faced higher energy and labor costs, the latter owing to workers' expectations. In light of this, the analysis of the post–energy crisis period begins with an in-depth look at firms' responses to the energy crisis.

Output Growth in the Post–Energy Crisis Period

As Dale Jorgenson has argued, the energy deepening of the twentieth century in the form of higher and higher electric power consumption per worker was largely the result of a falling real price of electricity.

Our empirical results strongly confirm the hypothesis advanced by Schurr and Rosenberg that electrification and productivity growth are related in a wide range of industries. Schurr et al. (1979) show that the price of electricity fell in real terms through 1971. This decline in real electricity prices has promoted electrification through the substitution of electricity for other forms of energy and through the substitution of energy for other inputs—especially for labor input. In addition, the decline in the real price of electricity has stimulated the growth of productivity in a wide range of industries. The spread of electrification and rapid growth of productivity through the early 1970s are both associated with a decline in real electricity prices. This decline was made possible in part by advances in the thermal efficiency of electricity generation. (Jorgenson, 1983, 21)

Throughout this period, falling real prices prompted process engineers in these industries to devise new, more energy-intensive production processes, the defining feature of which was what Alfred Chandler referred to as "higher velocity of throughput" (speed). Production processes were speeded up, with the result that conventionally defined productivity increased monotonically in the period. In the process, lower- and upper-level supervisors were called upon to supervise increasing quantities of energy, and, consequently, of work. This "idyllic" situation came to a sudden and unexpected halt with the energy crises of the 1970s. Energy prices stopped falling and began rising, with the expected results on developments in production technology. Table 5.1 presents pre– and post–energy crisis electric-power consumption growth rates for U.S., German, and Japanese manufacturing. In short, energy-deepening, the principal cause of production-line speed-ups, ended with the energy crisis. More important, however, is the fact that, from this point on, energy conservation (energy-shallowing) became the overriding concern in process engineering.

Table 5.1
Electric Power Consumption Growth Rates: U.S., German, and Japanese Manufacturing

U.S.				
		1950–1984	1950–1973	1974–1984
	USEP	4.052	5.371	0.246
Germany				
		1963–1988	1962–1973	1974–1988
	GEREP	2.894	5.883	1.366
Japan				
		1965–1988	1965–1973	1974–1988
	JAPEP	3.559	11.320	0.965

Source: Beaudreau (1998).

The U.S. pulp and paper industry is a case in point. Higher energy prices, and, more importantly, the uncertainty over future energy prices have altered fundamentally the role of energy deepening in this industry, as evidenced by its post-energy crisis obsession with energy efficiency/energy. In his introductory remarks to a TAPPI (Technical Association of the Pulp and Paper Industry) volume devoted to *Energy Engineering and Management in the Pulp and Paper Industry*, editor Matthew J. Coleman explains:

The basic resources needed to make paper are wood, water and energy. While fiber sources can change, it is not practical to make paper without water and energy. Electricity, coal, and fuel oil are the primary purchased sources of energy, with bark and hog fuel the primary indigenous sources of fuel available to mills. Whether a mill purchases all its power, or is able to generate its own using waste for fuel, the large amounts of energy used in the pulping and papermaking process have maintained the need for efficient energy management.

In North America during the past decade, the pulp and paper industry has made great strides toward energy independence. The availability of waste and bark for boiler fuel has focused the strategies of fully-integrated mills into more efficient use of these energy resources, while for non-integrated mills and many European mills, the management emphasis has been on better energy efficiency and conservation.

Mills which practice the best methods of energy recovery and management will benefit the most from the current instabilities in the world oil markets. The current price rise of oil is a reminder of how delicate the balance is between production and consumption of that particular fuel. Price increases in fuel oil can trigger increases in electrical power cost, and increase the substitution value of fuels such as coal, bark, and waste wood. (Coleman, 1991, i)

Evidence that the energy crisis and its aftershocks, especially the lingering uncertainty, have affected production processes in the pulp and paper industry is provided by Heikko Mannisto, vice president of EKONO Inc., Bellevue, Washington, who, in the same volume, describes just how energy price increases have "drastically" changed mill design.

Because of the energy crisis in the early 1970's, energy conservation became one of the key issues in the North Amercian pulp and paper industry, and most companies initiated millwide studies on how to reduce energy consumption. Because the mills had been designed and built for low energy costs, there were suddenly more conservation measures that had a high or reasonable payback than many companies could manage. (Mannisto, 1991, 21)

As this example clearly shows, the emphasis in manufacturing (U.S., German, and especially Japanese) has shifted from maximizing throughput (velocity) to maximizing second-law efficiency (η). Theoretically speaking, this involves lowering energy consumption levels in production processes closer to their theoretical minimums. More energy-intensive production processes (i.e., higher throughput) are, in spite of lower real energy prices, no longer an option, owing in large measure to the pervading uncertainty over energy prices. That energy prices have fallen in real terms over the past decade is immaterial. The emphasis is, and no doubt will continue to be, on increasing energy efficiency.

The Problem of Distribution

In addition to ending over two centuries of energy-deepening, the energy crises of the 1970s ended what had been, as pointed out in the previous chapter, a period of labor peace (1945–1975). From 1945 on, energy-deepening had generated energy rents, which, through the process of collective bargaining, were shared among the owners of organization inputs (capital and labor). With falling real energy prices leading to ever-increasing energy consumption levels per lower-level supervisor, energy rents increased monotonically, as did real wages and earnings. However, the energy crisis (higher energy prices and uncertain future prices) brought this "nirvanic" state of affairs to an end. Productivity growth ceased, as did three decades of "labor peace."

Contributing to the deteriorating state of labor relations were two factors. First, there were higher energy prices, which violated the various incentive constraints in the relevant cooperative bargaining problem (Equation 1.6 in Chapter 1). To reach a new bargaining solution, either real wages or real earnings would have to fall; otherwise, bargaining would break down. Second, there was the problem of workers' real-wage growth expectations. Throughout most of the post–World War II era, real wages in manufacturing had increased monotonically, the result of thirty years of uninterrupted energy-deepening. Workers (lower-level supervisors) in the 1970s, it therefore follows, had come to expect annual real wage increases. The combination of these two factors, I argue, explains the industrial strife of the 1970s, 1980s and, to a certain extent, of the 1990s. Firm earnings and profits were being squeezed by both the owners of energy and the owners of labor.

Firms responded, albeit with a lag, in a number of ways. In the mid-to-late 1970s, they held their ground, resisting demands for higher wages (real and nominal). In time, however, they turned to other means. Higher energy prices and the specter of even higher prices, in combination with increased labor militancy, led to (1) increased automation and (2) offshore production, especially in low-wage countries (Beaudreau, 1998).

Perhaps the best way to understand this is in terms of energy rents, specifically in terms of labor and capital's share of energy rents. Like the owners of lower-level supervisory inputs, the owners of capital had enjoyed, from the post–World War II period on, rising earnings. The energy crisis, and the ensuing "energy-rent clawback," turned positive energy-rent growth rates negative (see Equation 1.6). Profit-maximizing firms, intent on returning to pre–energy crisis earnings levels and growth rates, responded by precipitating the conversion to automated lower-level supervision (more feasible owing to the microchip), and, in industries where not feasible, moved production offshore.

Increasing Automation: Replacing Animate Lower-Level Supervision with Inanimate Forms

As shown in the previous two chapters, developments in power drive technology—specifically, the development of steam and electric power—altered fundamentally the nature of work. Specifically, laborers (exerting human muscular force) were metamorphosed into lower-level supervisors (machine operatives). Ironically, in these changes, especially the development of electric power, were the seeds of further changes, changes that would, in time, render the newly created supervisors also redundant, namely, the advent of microelectronics (i.e., computer chips). As early as 1968, David Landes described the resulting changes as follows:

Seen from the hindsight of the mid-twentieth century, scientific management was the natural sequence to the process of mechanization that constituted the heart of the Industrial Revolution: first, the substitution of machines and inaninate power for human skills and strength; then the conversion of the operative into an automaton to match and keep pace with his equipment. The third stage is now upon us: automation—the replacement of man by machines that think as well as do. How far and fast the new technique will go; whether, in combination with atomic power, it will mean a second (or third) Industrial Revolution, it is still too early to say. But it is some consolation to think that it is apparently easier to make machines like man than to turn man into machine. (Landes, 1969, 322)

While the development of control technologies in general and microelectronics in particular predates the energy crisis by over two decades, the energy crisis, nonetheless, played an important role in the diffusion of such technologies. As pointed out above, the energy crisis violated firms' cost constraint. While most political economists predicted a decrease in the demand for energy and an increase in the demand for labor, just the reverse happened.

Figure 5.1
U.S. Current-Cost Net Stock of Fixed Private Capital, 1959–1995

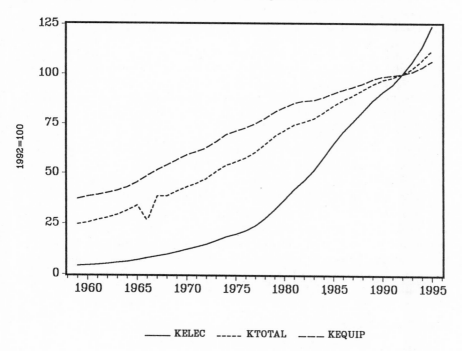

Source: U.S. Department of Commerce (1997), 79.

The demand for labor decreased, while the demand for capital (broadly defined) increased—and this, in spite of the observed energy-capital complementarity (Berndt and Wood, 1975). As it turned out, manufacturing firms reacted to the energy crisis by increasing their demand for control technologies, and reducing their demand for labor. Analytically speaking, they substituted inanimate forms of supervision for animate ones. This is illustrated in Figure 5.1 which plots the current-cost net stock of fixed private capital in the United States, broken down in to three categories (total capital (KTOTAL), equipment (KEQUIP), and information processing and related equipment (KELEC)) against time (1959–1995). We see that prior to the first energy crisis (1973), the three series were collinear; however, after 1973, the information processing and related equipment (KELEC) series literally "takes off," outpacing the other two by a large margin. This development is of paramount importance in the history of production technology. It marked the triumph of man's genius over man. Homo sapiens had recreated himself completely (energy and organization) in virtual form. Engineers applauded the development. Some predicted yet another "industrial revolution."

The advent of microcomputers since the beginning of the 1970's has brought a new dimension to power electronics and drive technology. The impact of this evolution is as significant as the advent of power semiconductor devices in the 1950's. In the forthcoming *industrial revolution,* that is the "computerized automation of factories," microcomputers will not only provide intelligence to higher level factory automation, but will play a vital role in the control of lower-level power electronics and motion control systems. Microcomputers have now been accepted universally for the control of power electronic and drive systems. It is interesting to note that both the ends of the power-electronics spectrum are digital: one provides the brain, and the other provides the muscle. (Bose, 1987, 148)

Table 5.2 presents time-series data on value added and production workers in U.S. manufacturing from 1958 to 1993. We see that prior to the energy crisis, lower-level supervisors, shown here as production workers, increased in step with value added. In 1958, there were 11,681,000 production workers in U.S. manufacturing. By 1973, their numbers had increased to 14,232,800, a 22 percent increase. Throughout the energy crisis (i.e., after 1973), their numbers dwindled. By 1993, they had fallen to 11,731,700, an 18 percent decrease. Value added, however, had increased by 18 percent. Clearly, animate lower-level supervisors are becoming increasingly redundant in manufacturing processes (Rifkin, 1995; Greider, 1997).

Freer World Trade

Starting with the Reciprocal Trade Agreements Act of 1934, aimed at undoing at least some of the damage done by the ruinous Smoot-Hawley Tariff Act of 1930, governments of most Western industrialized nations have

Table 5.2
Value Added and Production Workers, U.S. Manufacturing, 1958–1993

Year	Value Added*	Production Workers*
1958	141,540	11,681
1959	158,991	12,272
1960	158,759	12,209
1961	157,056	11,778
1962	169,254	12,126
1963	179,181	12,232
1964	189,516	12,403
1965	204,634	13,076
1966	220,263	13,826
1967	222,775	13,955
1968	233,081	14,041
1969	237,288	14,357
1970	222,061	13,528
1971	222,777	12,874
1972	243,014	13,527
1973	262,166	14,232
1974	263,522	13,927
1975	236,131	12,568
1976	258,058	13,052
1977	277,342	13,691
1978	289,430	14,228
1979	295,774	14,537
1980	253,612	13,900
1981	264,489	13,542
1982	245,229	12,400
1983	254,285	12,203
1984	271,887	12,572
1985	267,039	12,174
1986	269,336	11,765
1987	293,838	12,242
1988	306,262	12,404
1989	303,866	12,341
1991	281,617	11,513
1992	296,596	11,648
1993	300,294	11,731

Source: U.S. Department of Commerce (various years). (*000)

moved, albeit at times slowly, in the direction of freer world trade. Whether multilateral (i.e., via the General Agreement on Tariffs and Trade [GATT] or regional trading agreements) or bilateral in nature, they have worked toward reducing and eventually eliminating tariff and nontariff barriers. This process, however, assumed altogether new proportions in the aftermath of the two energy crises. The United States is a case in point. A protectionist nation for most of its history, it became a champion of unfettered free trade in raw materials, energy and finished goods and services. What is particularly noteworthy—but not surprising—is the unprecedented support shown by large U.S. corporations for free trade. Prior to the energy crisis, free trade with "low-wage countries" was, in general, seen as a "social bad"; suddenly, however, it became a "social good." Why? The reason, I submit, is relatively straightforward: higher energy costs, higher real wages and lower profits. Free trade would reverse all three.

As such, free trade had little, if nothing, to do with the win-win, comparative advantage-based forms of unobstructed trade found in international trade text books, and everything to do with restoring a ravaged bottom line, one ravaged by the end of the "energy nirvana" referred to above. As had been the case in Smith and Ricardo's day, free trade was a cog in a bigger wheel, namely that of lower labor costs, higher earnings, higher savings, higher investment and higher economic growth.

Throughout this period, producers that had, throughout the twentieth century, fought long and hard against low-cost imports were—and are currently—busily rationalizing their operations, transferring labor-intensive processes offshore. Why the change of behavior? Once again, the answer lies in the energy deepening of the pre-1973 era. Prior to the energy crisis, large U.S. corporations (read: shareholders) could count on increasing energy rents, the result of ongoing energy-deepening, to pay out higher and higher wages and, more importantly, higher and higher dividends. Foreign competition from low-wage countries was unwelcomed for obvious reasons. By paying out higher and higher wages, these same firms maintained that they were responsible for the level of demand (making the market), and consequently, should be entitled to the lion's share of the market. This all changed with the end of energy-deepening. Low-wages went from vice to virtue in little less than a decade.

With the end of energy-deepening (the beginning of energy stasis), the problem of distribution became truly dialectic. Labor's loss of energy rents has been capital's gain. Real wages in Western industrialized democracies have decreased, while earnings have increased. The proverbial income pie has stopped growing. Now, profit growth could only be achieved at the expense of labor costs.

This is borne out by the data. Consider, for example, the behavior of the Dow Jones Industrial average from 1980 to 1994. In 1980, the Dow Jones Industrial Average stood at 891.1. By 1994, it had climbed to 3794.2. In constant 1958 dollars, it went from 310.71 in 1980 to 712.15 in 1993, a 129 percent increase. In 1980, production and nonproduction workers' share of U.S. manufacturing value added stood at 46.75 percent; by 1994, it had fallen to 36.31 percent. Figure 5.2 illustrates the inverse relationship that exists between labor's share of value added and stock prices, highlighting the dialectic nature of income distribution in the post–energy crisis period.

Figure 5.2
Stock Prices and Labor's Income Share, 1980–1993

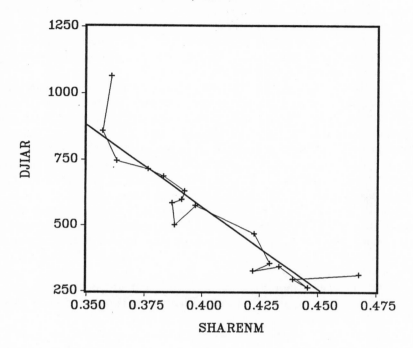

Throughout much of this century, stock prices tracked, for the most part, the increases in energy-based rents. Energy-deepening in U.S. manufacturing resulted in rents that were shared between the owners of capital and the owners of labor. The energy crises of the 1970s put an end to energy-deepening. Throughout the early 1980s, stock prices remained relatively constant. However, from roughly 1985 to 1993, they began increasing on the strength of a marked decrease in labor's share of energy rents. The owners of capital were able to renew with growing profits and earnings via increasing automation and offshore production. The point of the matter, however, is that the underlying causes of the recent increases in stock prices (i.e., since the early 1980s) are qualitatively different from those increases that characterized most of this century. Once the energy-rent pie had stopped growing, increased profits could only be achieved at labor's expense.

The Problem of Exchange

As argued in the previous chapter, the advent of collective bargaining in the post–World War II period contributed to solving the centuries-old problem of exchange. Post–World War II energy-deepening led to higher productivity, which, in turn, led to higher real wages, and, consequently, higher profits. Money income tracked productive capacity. As it turns out, this all changed in the post–energy crisis period. Factory automation and offshore production, by reducing labor costs, reduced the level of money income (credit), thus raising the specter of the problem of underincome.

To illustrate the exchange-related risks (underincome) of automation, consider the following hypothetical case. Suppose that all U.S. manufacturing firms were to automate their production processes, the result of which was to decrease labor costs to zero. What would happen? I submit that trading, and consequently, production, would break down. Remember that profits are a residual form of income, paid from sales revenues (consumption and capital goods). As merchants' orders for consumption and, consequently, capital goods, decrease, so too will producers' sales revenues.

Admittedly, this is an extreme case scenario. However, it illustrates the problem at hand. The more firms reduce labor costs (i.e., up-front costs), the less money income they create, and consequently, the less money income there is, in aggregate. Short-run profits may rise; however, in the long run, if all firms behave similarily, profits (i.e., money) will fall. As pointed out in Chapter 9 of Beaudreau (1998), the problem is akin to the prisoner's dilemma. If one firm automates or relocalizes offshore, then its profits rise; if all firms do it, then profits fall.

It is important to note, however, that profits in kind (i.e., the goods and services controlled by shareholders) will increase; in fact, they will command all of the output. The problem, however, is that it will have no exchange value, and, undoubtedly, no use value.

GROWTH WITHOUT GROWTH, AUTOMATION, FREER TRADE, AND THE PROBLEMS OF EXCHANGE AND DISTRIBUTION AS SEEN BY POLITICAL ECONOMISTS

How has the economics profession responded to these three related developments? How has it reponded to the productivity slowdown, to increasing automation in the workplace, and to freer world trade? The answer, in one word, is poorly. The reasons are many, but one stands out, namely the continued absence of a theoretically and empirically consistent theory of production. As I have shown elsewhere (Beaudreau, 1998), this lacuna has stymied any and all attempts at understanding the productivity slowdown, as well as the role of information, and hence, information-related technologies, in production in general.

Today, the results are there for everyone to see. At a time in our history when basic production theory should be the least concern, it is, as evidenced by recent work in growth, the main concern. Robert M. Solow, for example, referred to a "wildfire revival of interest in growth theory" to describe recent developments (Solow, 1994, 45). The current debate pitting disciples of the Solow–Swan, neoclassical approach to growth against the more recent, increasing returns to scale (i.e., AK) approach, popularlized by Paul Romer, is further evidence of the intellectual bankruptcy of political economy as "the" science of wealth. For over a century, physicists and engineers have known that tools are not productive in the physical sense, yet political economists continue, to this very day, to put them at the center of their analysis.

What is particularly disturbing about recent developments in growth theory, I submit, is the continued absence of diversity in the growth research program. Unlike political economy in the early twentieth century, which witnessed the development of new, alternative approaches to "the science of wealth," the current period is devoid of "relevant alternatives," however far-fetched they may appear. Unlike the pure and applied sciences which allow for nonmainstream thought and ideas, political economy had been disturbingly insular. This, one could argue, is a welfare-decreasing strategy (Beaudreau, 1996b). As Edwin Mansfield et al. pointed out in his 1971 book *Research and Innovation in the Modern Corporation,* diversity in research programs is welfare increasing.

Many R&D projects use parallel approaches to help cope with uncertainty. For example, in the development of the atomic bomb, there were several methods of making fissionable materials, and no consensus existed among scientists as to which of these alternatives was most promising. To make sure that the best one was not discarded, all methods were pursued in parallel. The wisdom of this decision was indicated by the fact that the method that was the first to produce appreciable quantitites of fissionable material was one that had been considered relatively unpromising early in the development program. (Mansfield et al., 1971, 10)

The Problem of Growth as Seen by Political Economists

How has the economics profession responded to the problem of growth, as described above. Before addressing this question, a few remarks are in order. First, it bears reminding that the problem of growth is as old as political economy itself. Adam Smith's primary concern, as evidenced by the title of his *magnum opus,* was the "causes of the wealth of nations." Few, however, were those who followed in his footsteps. Classical, radical and neoclassical political economists were, as shown earlier, more concerned with distribution than with wealth production. Likewise, monetarists and Keynesians in the post–World War II period were more concerned with full employment than with wealth production per se. This indifference, however, came to an end with the recent "wildfire interest" in economic growth.

This, I maintain, is essential to understanding the profession's response to the "problem of growth." First, the paucity of work on growth in the past has made for the current situation in which surprisingly little is known. This can, in part, be attributed to the "parametric" view of technology that has characterized production theory from William Cobb's and Paul Douglas' first analytical production function in 1928. Technology is determined exogenously.

As growth rates in the mid-to-late 1980s failed to return to their pre-1973 levels, it became painfully obvious that our knowledge of the A in AK approach was inadequate, and, consequently, in need of a major overhaul. The profession responded in two ways. The first was in terms of what are today referred to as AK models, popularized by Paul Romer (1986). The second was in terms of Schumpeterian models of innovation (Aghion and Howitt, 1998).

Implicit in both is the view that technology—at least in so far as aggregate growth is concerned—is a social phenomena. Growth rates in Western industrialized economies are not the result of an individual process or product innovation, but of an agglomeration of such innovations, each having a common cause, whether it be higher education, more basic research or novel "General Purpose Technologies." Both approaches should as such be seen for what they are, namely attempts at mapping the *social* DNA of innovation. In their work on innovation hierarchies, Elhanan Helpman and Manuel Trajtenberg describe "General Purpose Technologies," as follows:

In any given "era" there typically exist a handful of technologies that play a far-reaching role in fostering technical change in a wide range of user sectors, thereby bringing about sustained and pervasive productivity gains. The steam engine during the first industrial revolution, electricity in the early part of this century and microelectronics in the past two decades are widely thought to have played such a role. (Helpman and Trajtenberg, 1994, 1)

Still in its early infancy, this literature has yet to generate testable, and indeed, tested predictions. In fact, it is my view that this literature, being based on a Paleolithic model of production, will fail to produce any important breakthroughs. As I have maintained throughout this book, political economy has, for over 200 years, worked with an archaic model of production. Capital and labor are not physically productive factor inputs, but, rather, are organization inputs, affecting η, the level of second-law efficiency. Until these simple facts, common knowledge in production engineering and in elementary physics, are integrated into production theory, there will be little hope that the work now under way will explain the past, understand the present and predict the future. In other words, there is little hope that these models will shed light on "the" issue of the 1980s and 1990s, the productivity slowdown.

Automation and Freer Trade as Seen by Political Economists

I begin with automation. At the risk of sounding repetitive, the main problem in so far as the literature on information-based technologies is concerned, is the absence of a model of production sufficiently general to include, in a meaningful way, information as a factor of production. As it now stands, information is lumped into what is commonly referred to as "technology," the A in AK. More information, it therefore follows, renders capital—including human capital—and labor more productive.

This is best illustrated by recent work on computers and productivity. A good example of this is Lehr and Lichtenberg's recent work on computers and prodcutivity growth in U.S. federal government agencies (Lehr and Lichtenberg 1996). Not knowing just how to handle computers analytically, they do what "neoclassical apologists" have done for decades, namely, include them as a separate input in production functions, and proceed to estimate the relevant output elasticities. They find a value of 0.06 for the computer-output elasticity and interpret it as evidence that computers are, in fact, productive.

Further, the absence of an empirically consistent model of production has distorted the debate over the role of information and automation at the firm and at the aggregate level. As pointed out earlier, since the end of energy-deepening (1973–1980), firms have resorted to automation and offshore production to increase profits and earnings. Most engineers know perfectly well that information has never been, is not, and never will be productive in the physical sense. They also know that labor costs constitute (constituted) the single most important cost factor, and that assuming a 65/35 wage/profit split, a 1 percent decrease in labor costs results in a 2 percent increase in profits.

In spite of this, there is a widely held view that automation and information will, eventually, lead to higher productivity. Paul David's view on information and productivity is a case in point. Responding to the apparent failure of "new information technologies" to increase growth and productivity, he pointed to the presence of significant diffusion lags. In "The Dynamo and the Computer: An Historical Perspective on the Modern Productivity Paradox," he described the effects of another important innovation, the electrification of industry in the early part of the century, were not instantaneous, but rather were diffused over a long, somewhat protracted period. The effects of the information revolution now upon Western industrialized economies, he surmises, will be felt over time.

But, even these cautionary qualifications serve only to further reinforce one of the main thrusts of the dynamo analogy. They suggest the existence of special difficulties in the commercialization of novel (information) technologies that need to be overcome before the mass of information-users can benefit in their roles as producers, and do so in ways reflected by our traditional, market-oriented indicators of productivity. (David, 1990, 360)

The extent to which the engineering (read: business) and political economy professions differ with regard to the effects of automation is best seen in the professional journals. From roughly the 1970s, automation has spawned an extensive literature in engineering, engineering economics and production economics. Professional journals such as the *International Journal of Production Research* and the *International Journal of Production Economics*, to name but two, are replete with work dealing with automation. Titles such as "Automated Productivity Line Design with Flexible Unreliable Machines for Profit Maximization" convey both the purpose and essence of this literature.

Political economy has also spawned a literature on automation. See, for example, Mark Doms', Timothy Dunne's and Kenneth Troske's recent article in *The Quarterly Journal of Economics* for a list of the relevant articles. What is particularly interesting to note about this literature is (1) its insular nature, having no link(s) to the engineering literature, and (2) its labor-centricity. Both of these, I maintain, can be traced to the underlying model of production. That political economists and engineers today are unable to find common ground is not surprising given their widely diverging views of production processes, the former focusing on organizational variables, the latter on energy. Presently, any rapprochement appears unlikely. Political economy's labor-centricity, I maintain, owes to the absence of a model of production explicitly incorporating information. Labor acts as an anchor, relating automation to something political economists are familiar with. What is ironic is the fact that automation has, is and will continue to eliminate labor (lower-level supervisors) from the workplace, just as inanimate energy sources eliminated labor in the nineteenth and twentieth centuries.

As for the move toward freer trade, begun in the mid-1980s, it too is studied using models that, in my view, are irrelevant. The question of causality is lost in trade theorists' centuries-old plea, begun by Ricardo, for free trade. The globalization of the world economy, characterized by a shift of manufacturing away from the North and to the South, is, as such, viewed as an organic development. Why corporations that had previously invested and created hundreds of thousands of jobs in the North, and who, throughout this century, opposed free trade with low-wage countries, pushed for free trade is a question not even raised.

As such, trade theorists and trade economists in general are at a loss when it comes time to rationalizing the current move toward globalization and freer world trade. For example, in response to the question, why did globalization "take off" in the mid-1980s, the most common response is "developments in information technology," allowing for cheaper and quicker international communication.

Automation, Free Trade, and the Problem of Distribution as Seen by Political Economists

The economics profession's response to automation and freer trade as they relate to the problem of income distribution is, in my view, a good example of its political nature (i.e., having little to do with science). Declining real wages in Western industrialized nations, combined with increasing unemployment, offshore production and the breakdown of the welfare state, are seen as cathartic events, whose purpose it is to restore Western industrialized economies to their "natural" state, disturbed by the appearance of unions and the welfare state in the post–Great Depression period, not to mention restrictive tariff legislation in the post–Smoot-Hawley era.

Unions and government, its main pundits maintain, by distorting prices and hence resource allocation, contributed to the downfall, which, in this case, consists of the productivity slowdown and the productivity paradox. Only by exorcizing both could growth and prosperity resume. This, I argue, is the underlying logos of what many refer to as "new economic liberalism." Lower real wages, higher unemployment, offshore production etcetera, are, as such, the costs of having violated the *deus ex machina*, known as the market. Increasingly skewed income distribution, political economists and governments maintain, is a necessary precondition for growth. In short, we are back to David Ricardo and the classical political economists. Growth requires savings, and savings require profits and profits require fewer workers (automation) and/or less-costly workers (offshore production).

Automation, Free Trade, and the Problem of Exchange as Seen by Political Economists

To the economics profession, this remains a non-issue. The debate over Say's Law is little more than a historical curiosity. Supply creates money income and money income creates demand. A decrease in labor costs, whether due to automation or offshore relocalization, results in a corresponding increase in profits. Consequently, total money income remains constant.

There are, however, some exceptions. John Culbertson of the University of Wisconsin, for example, argues that free-trade with low-wage countries is pure "folly." He bases his argument on what he refers to as the "importance of demand and markets."

Our present-day ecnomics fails to recognize the importance of demand and markets—and thus exagerates what production alone can accomplish. Yet a nation's productive capacities are decisively limited by the levels and kinds of its domestic demand and its access to foreign markets. But in the United States, we persistently fail to see the importance of our vast, propserous and acessible domestic market. We don't appreciate the key role that the demand side of our deomestic market has played generating growth for our country. (Culbertson, 1986, 123)

Moving production offshore, according to Culbertson, will reduce money income, especially wage income, thus reducing overall demand and hence overall output.

CONCLUSIONS

As I have attempted to show in this chapter, the twentieth century will end in much the same way as the nineteenth century, namely in a state of energy stasis. As pointed out in Chapter 2, by the 1890s, the per-capita level of energy consumption in Great Britain and the rest of the Western world had reached its maximum—that is, with the then-existing power transmission technology, namely shafting, belting and gearing. This, however, is where the similarities end. Unlike today where the possibilities of a new energy form or transmission technology appear to be limited, the end of the nineteenth century was characterized by important developments in electro-magnetics, which, as shown in Chapter 3, ushered in three-quarters of a century of energy-deepening, productivity growth and rising material well-being. Such is not the case at the time of writing. In fact, if anything, the emphasis, since the energy crisis, has been on energy "shallowing" in the form of conservation. There is nothing fundamentally wrong with conservation per se; however, it must be clearly understood that one cannot have more with less, that one cannot have "growth without growth." That is, society cannot have more output (i.e., work) with less energy. To think otherwise is to violate the basic laws of thermodynamics.

Another important difference is in the area of organization, specifically developments in "organization" technology. As shown in this chapter, developments in inanimate, computer-based lower-level forms of supervision have altered and continue to alter the nature of what is commonly referred to as "work." Alfred Marshall's "one woman" managing "four or more looms" has been replaced by a control unit. Clearly, while not yet extinct, it is but a matter of time before animate lower-level supervisors become a thing of the past, only to be found in history books and museums.

As I have argued in this chapter, the economics profession has failed to identify, let alone analyze, the fundamental, paradigm changes of the last two decades. This owes, I believe, less to a lack of will or intention, than to the presence of an outdated, archaic, model of production activity. As I have argued throughout this book, this shortcoming is autoregressive, having its roots in the classical political economists' failure to include "fire power" in their analysis of production. As I have attempted to show in this chapter, were mainstream political economists to have a model like the one presented in Chapter 1, then the myriad forces now shaping the present and, ultimately, the future would be better understood.

NOTES

1. Formally, I refer to this as the "energy-rent clawback." Energy rents which, until then, had been shared by capital and labor, were clawed back by the owners of energy (OPEC countries).

2. Incidentally, the Technocrats had predicted what Jeremy Rifkin refers to as the "end of work," some 60 years ago.

Conclusions

As pointed out in the Introduction, it is generally held that the study of political economy was the direct result of the introduction of machinery in the late eighteenth/early nineteenth century, and the ensuing industrialization. This explains why, among other things, political economy is overwhelmingly British in its origins. While this is, in my view, an accurate description of the origins of political economy, it is, unfortunately, incomplete. According to classical mechanics, machinery is not not productive per se, not being a source of energy/force. Rather, it "is used to change the magnitude, direction and point of application of required forces in order to make tasks easier." (Betts, 1989, 172). The key factor input in the industrial revolution was energy, or "required forces" as Betts refers to it. Invoking transitivity, it follows that energy in general, and innovations in energy use in particular—not machinery—are responsible for the rise of political economy. Innovations in Homo sapiens' use of energy, it therefore follows, are key to understanding modern political economy.

In this book, I have argued that while innovations in energy were at the root of the industrial revolution, and, indeed, of the myriad changes thrust upon Western society ever since (e.g., electrification and subsequent energy deepening), they were, from very early on, overlooked, with the result that, today, energy is altogether absent from the literature on production, growth, distribution etcetera. The results, as I have shown throughout this book, have been catastrophic, to say the least. The failure to accurately model the role of energy in production, in growth and in distribution, has contributed, and continues to contribute, to the "fall" of political economy as the science of wealth. Today, paradoxes, puzzles and pitfalls are the realm of political economy. Two hundred years after Adam Smith's pathbreaking work, we are no further in our quest to understand the "nature and causes of the wealth of nations."

By way of a conclusion, I examine the reasons for this sad, even tragic, state of affairs. Tragic for the simple reason that, from very early on (i.e., from Robert Owen), attempts were made to steer the logos of political economy on to a more scientific footing. These were described at considerable length in Chapters 2 and 3. The question, it therefore follows, is why mainstream political economy, in which are included the classics, utopians, radicals, neoclassics and Keynesians, chose to ignore the "cranks and heretics" of the nineteenth and twentieth centuries? Why was Technocracy ignored? Why was Thornstein Veblen's work ignored? Why was Frederick Soddy's work on Cartesian economics ignored? Why was Stuart Chase's economics of abundance ignored? Why was Rexford G. Tugwell ostracized from the profession, as were John A. Hobson and Scott Nearing?

While unicausal explanations are no longer in vogue, I, after having examined the evidence, choose to nonetheless offer one here. The reason, I believe, owes principally to their normative analysis, specifically to calls for either increased government intervention or for a total overhaul of the "for-profit economy." Most of these writers were not professional political economists, but rather, were businessmen, engineers or politicians. Motivating them was the perceived-of inability of the U.K. and U.S. economies to produce at its new higher capacity (i.e., as defined by the new technologies). The reasons offered differed widely as did the solutions. Where they converged, however, is in their views of the role of energy in productivity growth. Almost invariably, the works in question begin with a description of the increases in productive capacity that had resulted from either a new energy source, a new transmission technology (electricity) or energy-deepening. This is followed by a description of the reason(s) for the "failed transition(s)," and, lastly, with the corresponding policy solutions. For example, in Henry Ford's case, the problem was the failure of wages to rise and prices to fall, and the solution was an increase in nominal wages accompanied by a fall in nominal prices. In Clifford H. Douglas' case, the problem was underincome and the monopolistic nature of the private banking system (i.e., restricting the amount of credit), and the solution was the issuance of "social" credit. In the case of Technocracy, the problem was the failure of income to increase in step with productive capacity, and the solution was the complete overhaul of the exchange process, including the exchange medium and the price system.

The "radical" nature of the proposed solutions, I argue, is what doomed the literature in question. Perhaps the best way to understand this is in terms of the notion of "tied sales," found in industrial organization. Specifically, by subscribing to Technocratic notions of substantial energy-based increases in potential output, one would have implicitly subscribed to the Technocratic solutions, including the radical reorganization of exchange and prices. Likewise, if one were sympathetic to the problems as defined by Clifford H.

Douglas, then, by association, one would have sympathized with the solution of issuing "phoney money."

Good science, it follows, was overlooked for what were essentially political reasons. Important advances in production theory, especially, with regard to the role of energy, were ignored. "Radical" political economists were ostracized. To agree with their positive analysis was to agree with their normative analysis. More importantly, to discredit their normative analysis, one had to, as much as possible, discredit their positive analysis. Doubt as to the validity of their proposed solutions had to be quashed. A good example of this is the policy pamphlet published by the University of Chicago entitled *The Economics of Technocracy*, referred to earlier. Written by Professor Aaron Director, with an introduction by Harry D. Gideonse, it set out to discredit "Technocracy."

That the contributions of "radical" political economists were summarily dismissed does not, however, come as a surprise, given the decidedly political nature of political economy. Critics of Robert Owen, John A. Hobson, Thomas Malthus, Thornstein Veblen, Rexford Tugwell, Howard Scott, Stuart Chase and the others sought, in most cases, to dismiss what in their eyes were "radical" solutions, paying little attention to the scientific merit of their work (positive contributions). Perhaps the best example of this is Thornstein Veblen who, today, is best remembered for his work on "conspicuous consumption," his work on the failings of the price system and its eventual replacement by an army of engineers, having been struck from the collective memory of political economy.

The overtly political nature of political economy over the course of the last two centuries, has, as shown throughout this book, contributed to its downfall. Important contributions were ignored. Good science was sacrificed on the alter of ideology. The results are there for everyone to see. Two centuries after Adam Smith's *An Inquiry into the Nature and Causes of the Wealth of Nations*, we are no closer to understanding the process of growth, as evidenced by the current "productivity slowdown," and "productivity paradox."

Until political economy rejects ideology (right-wing and left-wing) in favor of science, paradoxes and puzzles will abound. Similarly, until political economy sees energy for what it is (the source of all work), and capital and labor for what they are (organizational inputs), paradoxes and puzzles will abound. Lastly, until political economy recognizes economic activity as a subset of the larger set of entropic processes (i.e., those in the universe), paradoxes and puzzles will abound. I would like to conclude with a quote from Nobel prize-winning chemist-turned-economist, Frederick Soddy:

At the risk of being redundant, let me illustrate what I mean by the question "How do men live?" by asking what makes a railroad train go. In one sense or another, credit for the achievement may be claimed by the so-called "engine-driver," the guard, the signalman, the manager, the capitalist, the share-holder,—or, again, by the scientific pioneers who discovered the nature of fire, by the inventors who harnessed it, by labour which built the railroad and the train. The fact remains that all of them by their collective effort could not drive the train. The real engine-driver is the coal. So, in the present state of science, the answer to the question how men live, or how anything lives, or how inanimate nature lives, in the sense in which we speak of the life of a waterfall or of any other manifestation of continued liveliness, is, with few and unimportant exceptions, "By sunshine." Switch off the sun and a world would result lifeless, not only in the sense of animate life, but also in respect of by far the greater part of the life of inanimate nature. (Soddy, 1924, 4)

Appendix 1

A Treatise on Energy and Price Theory

In this treatise, I examine the historical relationship between energy in general, and energy innovations in particular, and price theory. It will be argued that, despite the inability of classical, Marxian, and neoclassical political economists to accurately model the role of inanimate energy in production, energy in general and energy innovations in particular played a key role in the development of price theory. For example, the labor theory of value is, in its simplest form, shown to be an energy theory of value. Also, the decline of Marshallian price theory in the 1920s, 1930s, and 1940s, and the rise of imperfect competition as the dominant model of pricing, are shown to be, in large part, the result of the emergence of electric-powered, high-throughput mass production techniques in the United Kingdom and the United States.

The clash between Marshallian price theory and the theory of imperfect competition, as defined by Joan Robinson and Edward Chamberlin's work on monopolistic competition, I go on to show, dates back to the early nineteenth century with the work of Nassau Senior and John Stuart Mill on cost conditions in "manufactures." Specifically, according to Senior and Mill, costs are decidedly nonconvex in nature. The resulting debate over pricing, I go on to argue, is rooted in what, in essence, are sectorial differences (agriculture versus manufactures). Increasing marginal costs were the lot of agriculture, especially British agriculture, while decreasing marginal costs (or constant) were the lot of British manufacturing.

As was the case in Chapters 2–5, the approach taken here is counterfactual. First, using the model of production developed in Beaudreau (1998) and reproduced in Chapter 1, I outline a basic energy theory of value, not unlike the one envisioned by Howard Scott in his work on Technocracy. Specifically, relative prices are determined by relative energy consumption, broadly defined to include energy and organization inputs. This will then serve as a guide to the various developments in price theory over the course of the past two centuries.

AN ENERGY THEORY OF VALUE

My starting point is the model of production activity found in Newtonian production analysis (NPA). Specifically, value added is increasing in energy consumption and second-law efficiency, the latter being determined by organizational variables, notably supervision and tools. Recall that energy and energy alone is productive in the physical sense; tools and supervision affect value added through second-law efficiency. However, one could argue that tools and supervision are, in essence, energy forms. Tools consist of embodied energy and raw materials (e.g., iron, copper, lead etcetera) (Bullard and Herendeen, 1975; van Engelenberg et al., 1994). Supervision is a cerebral activity which, like all other bodily functions, is energy based.

Suppose for the moment that the energy content of tools and supervision per unit time is known. For example, a lower-level supervisor (machine operative) consumes 2,500 calories per day. I shall refer to these as indirect energy requirements—as opposed to direct energy requirements. Direct energy requirements are those referred to in Chapters 2 to 5. Combining the direct and indirect energy requirements, and introducing time into the analysis, provides for an elementary theory of value based on energy. Suppose that the going rate of interest (price of time) is 5 percent. Assuming no depreciation, one could argue that the cost of capital per period of time is simply the interest rate, expressed in percentage terms, multiplied by the amount of energy embodied in capital (measured in say kilowatt hours). The total costs of the firm per period of time, it therefore follows, consist of the sum of the direct energy consumed (kilowatt hours) per period time (animate and inanimate) and the indirect energy consumed per period time, consisting of the "supervisory" energy and the cost of capital. The average cost, it then follows, is defined as the total cost divided by output, while the marginal cost is the derivative of total costs with respect to output.

Within this framework, the more energy (direct and indirect) is required to produce a good/service, the higher its price. More specifically, *ceteris paribus*, the more capital is required, the greater is the indirect amount of energy required (i.e., to produce tools), and, hence, the greater is its price, relative to other goods/services.

This simple framework has many advantages. Take, for example, the issue of factor substitution. The advent of the steam engine, according to classical political economists (Smith, Ricardo, Mill), decreased unit costs and, as shown in Chapter 2, product prices. Theoretically speaking (thermodynamics), energy costs (i.e., the amount of energy required to do work) can only decrease if second-law efficiency increases. That is, the relevant process approaches its theoretical minimum amount of energy required for production. The question, it therefore follows, is whether steam engine-based production increased second-law efficiency, and, if so, by how much? Nonenergy-based theories of value (classical, radical and neoclassical) ignore such issues. Monetary costs, not real energy costs, constitute the basis of comparison. As such, given the prices for labor (high), machinery and coal, the shift from animate energy to inanimate energy that was the conversion to steam power, may lead to lower money costs, when, in actual fact, real costs (direct and indirect energy costs) may be either higher, lower or identical. As it turned out, British society was substituting high-priced animate energy (muscle power) for low-priced, inanimate energy. From a "money cost" point of view, a miracle of sorts will appear to have occurred. After all, more output is obtained at a lower cost. This, it bears noting, violates most laws of physics.

A similar argument can be invoked in the current debate over automation. As pointed out in Chapter 4, inanimate energy-powered control systems are taking the place of animate human supervision (computers replacing workers). Again, this is seen as decreasing costs, when, in fact, there is no evidence that less indirect energy is necessary—or, for that matter, second-law efficiency has increased.[1] Lower real costs, it bears reminding, can only be achieved via higher second-law efficiency.

The problem with the practice of cost-based pricing (from Smith to the present), as it turns out, is the presence of price-distorting energy rents. As argued in Beaudreau (1998) and in Chapter 1, the bulk of payments to capital and labor today are energy rents, defined as the difference between the value of energy productivity and its price. As such, it makes perfect sense for managers (upper-level supervisors) to substitute control systems for animate supervision given the fact that the bulk of workers' earnings are energy rents.

Case Studies: The Agricultural and Manufacturing Sectors

To better understand the energy theory of value outlined here, I now turn to two case studies, agriculture and manufacturing. First, I describe in some detail the relevant production processes, and then I discuss the relevant cost structure, expressed in energy units.

Agriculture

As pointed out in Chapter 2, while the object of classical political economy was to analyze the changes thrust upon the United Kingdom by the manufacturing sector, the agricultural sector continued to play an important role in the resulting literature. Population growth in the United Kingdom in combination with various trade restrictions (e.g., Corn Laws) had increased the demand for domestically-produced foodstuffs, forcing U.K. farmers, using what essentially were Neolithic production techniques, to till less and less fertile lands (owned by the lords), the result of which was higher food prices over time. Ricardo's theory of rents, and the classical theory of supply (price elastic), were by-products of this development. To better understand agriculture, and, consequently, to better compare it with say the manufacturing sector, a little background (technical) is in order.

Broadly speaking, agriculture can be defined as the human activity of organizing and supervising the biological process of photosynthesis, whereby energy in the form of solar radiation, trapped by chlorophyll, powers a series of chemical reactions involving carbon dioxide and hydrogen, the result of which is a sugar called glucose, which, in turn, constitutes the energy supply for growth and a source of building materials for the walls of plant cells. The latter, in turn, is the basis of multicellular life forms, of which Homo sapiens-sapiens is a prime example. Technically, neither the farmers themselves nor the sources of energy used to till, enrich or otherwise alter the soil, are directly productive; instead, these activities are to be viewed as organizational in nature. As such, farmers are not productive in the physical sense (i.e., transforming carbon dioxide into starch, sugar and oxygen), but, instead, are productive in the organizational sense. That is, they organize agricultural activity by (1) choosing the crop and (2) preparing the soil (e.g., plowing, harrowing, fertilizing, irrigating etcetera).

Affecting the rate at which solar radiation can transform carbon dioxide into starch, sugar and oxygen are (1) the characteristics of the soil and (2) the effort provided by the farmer. Poor soil, that is, with little organic matter (nitrogen, phosphates), yields less output *ceteris paribus* (i.e., for the same amount of energy).

In an ideal world, the relative price of food should reflect its relative energy content, say to manufactures. Included in this would be the direct and indirect energy required to produce, say, a bushel of wheat, or a gross of tomatoes. Poorer soil conditions, by reducing the yield, *ceteris paribus*, would lead to higher prices. Such a development would, theoretically speaking, have less to do with the productivity of energy than it would with the absence of adequate feedstocks (e.g., phosphates, water etcetera). Ricardian rents, in an agricultural setting, should as such be viewed as a feedstock problem, and not as a productivity problem, per se. In other words, the energy is there; what isn't are the relevant feedstocks (nitrogen, phosphates, water etcetera).

Such a view stands in contrast with observed pricing practices in agriculture. Because solar radiation is a free good, it does not enter the various pricing equations, which is somewhat paradoxical given its import in the actual production process as described above. Consequently, the output is appropriated entirely by the owners of the feedstocks and the owners of the organizational inputs (tools and supervision).

Manufacturing

Manufacturing activity is, in essence, identical to agricultural activity. Substitute animate and inanimate (direct) energy for solar radiation, and the various industrial feedstocks (i.e., intermediate inputs) for nitrogen, phosphates etcetera, and one gets manufacturing. Interestingly enough, most animate and inanimate energy (fossil fuels, hydraulic resources, wind power) is solar-radiation based (Soddy, 1924; Odum and Odum, 1976). The one important difference is the fact that here, the energy source is not a free good; instead, it is governed by property rights. The second important difference is the fact that energy consumption in manufacturing is variable.[2] Machine speeds, as shown in this book, can and have been increased. Historically, this is perhaps the single most important difference between agriculture and manufacturing. By increasing energy consumption (i.e., energy-deepening), Homo sapiens-sapiens has increased output and, consequently, the level of material civilization. Interestingly enough, advances in the chemical industry, largely made possible by energy-related innovations, have benefited the agricultural sector. Specifically, chemical fertilizers have allowed for increasingly higher yields. Thus, while energy deepening has not occurred in the process of photosynthesis, it has nonetheless benefited agriculture by virtually eliminating feedstock shortages, the chief constraint facing modern-day agriculture.

Energy and Classical Price Theory

At first blush, classical price theory, with its emphasis on labor as the source of value, would appear to have little in common with the energy theory of value outlined above. After all, there is no mention of energy, supervision, tools etcetera. Such a view, however, would be erroneous. In fact, it can be reasonably argued that classical price theory is, in fact, a primitive energy theory of value.

To see why, let us return to Equation 1.3 in Chapter 1, reproduced here as Equation A1.1. Prior to the introduction of water- or steam-powered machinery, work, $W(t)$, was an increasing function of animate, muscular energy, defined as $E_a(t)$, at time t. The greater the amount of animate energy, the greater the work. η, in this case, measures the corresponding level of second-law efficiency, determined, in large measure, by the quality of tools (e.g., looms, spinning wheels, knives, shovels, spades etcetera). Equation A1.1, it therefore follows, describes production processes prior to the steam age (or, generally, the inanimate energy age):

$$W(t) = \eta \ [S(t),T(t)] \ E(t) \tag{A1.1}$$

I submit that the labor theory of value, as outlined by Adam Smith and David Ricardo, is a variant on Equation A1.1. Drawing from Ricardo's work on international trade, which, also, is founded on the labor theory of value, η, the level of second-law efficiency, is, in the labor theory of value, the average product of labor, labor being a form of animate, muscular energy. In both Newtonian production analysis and the labor theory of value, capital (tools) is not productive. Clearly, in this regard, the classical political economists were right: tools are not productive in the physical sense, but rather, are productive in the organizational sense.

Adam Smith's detailed description of value theory in a hunter-gatherer (i.e., Paleolithic) society captures this well:

In that early and rude state of society which procedes both the accumulation of stock and the appropriation of land, the proportion between the quantities of labour necessary for acquiring different objects seems to be the only circumstance which can afford any rule for exchanging them for another one. If, among a nation of hunters, for example, it usually costs twice the labour to kill a beaver which it does to kill a deer, one beaver should naturally exchange for or be worth two deer. It is natural that what is usually the produce of two days' or two hours; labour, should be worth double of what is usually the produce of one day's or one hour's labour. (Smith, 1990 [1776], 23)

As such, the problem with the labor theory of value lies not with its internal logic, but rather, with its specificity, namely as a model of Paleolithic production processes. Had Smith and Ricardo used it to describe prehistoric economies, then problems would not have arisen. The problem is that they, along with classical political economists in general, used it to describe production in the presence of inanimate energy forms, in this case, steam power. To argue that capital (tools and inanimate energy forms) was not productive at a time when labor had been reduced to a supervisory input, made little sense.

This raises other questions. For example, why did Smith and Ricardo stand pat? Why did they not attempt to incorporate steam power into their analysis? Clearly, these are questions that require more space than I can devote to them here. However, the most plausible answer, in my view, lies with their motives. As pointed out earlier, neither saw himself as a theorist in the contemporary sense of an individual scholar whose purpose is to model the natural or moral world. Rather, both were moved to put pen to paper to address what they considered to be impediments to steam-engine-powered growth, the "extent of the market" in the case of Smith, and higher food prices

Energy and the Neoclassical Price Theory

It is fair to say that by the 1870s, the labor theory of value found itself at an important crossroads. Empirically, with the intensive use of inanimate energy (steam power) in British industry, the idea that labor was the source of all value was less and less attractive. Politically, it had, as argued in Chapter 2, landed classical political economy and the merchant class, of which Ricardo had been a leading advocate, in hot water, so to speak. Specifically, the labor theory of value, born of classical political economy, had become the rallying cry of utopian and radical political economy. Since labor was the source of all value, it only followed that it receive all of the product.

Clearly, classical political economy had to respond. The *status quo* was unacceptable. Theoretically, a number of options existed. For example, classical political economists could have chosen to dispense with the labor theory of value, and adopt an energy theory of value based on the then-emerging "energetics" movement. Human animate energy would be replaced by inanimate, fossil fuel-based energy. Labor would have joined capital as nonphysically productive factor inputs (organization inputs). Or, capital, which, at the time, consisted of inanimate energy-powered simple and composite tools, could have been be raised to the status of physically productive inputs, thus diffusing the impending crisis.

As most readers will by now have surmised, the likes of William Stanley Jevons, Alfred Marshall and Leon Walras opted for the latter solution. Empirically, the chasm that separated production and, consequently, value theory from classical mechanics and thermodynamics, was, as a result, widened even further. Tools and supervisors (lower-level) were now physically productive, and energy was nowhere to be found. Politically, factor payments to capital could now be rationalized in terms of what, to most, was hard science. Capital productivity was likened to second-law efficiency functions, which, as most engineers know, are quasi-concave.

This, I maintain, was an unfortunate turn of events. Instead of removing labor from the list of productive inputs (in the sense defined above), neoclassical political economist made matters worse by adding yet another nonproductive input to the list of productive inputs. As the adage goes, "two wrongs don't make a right. This was especially true here.

The result was a theory of pricing (neoclassical pricing theory) based on nonproductive (in the physical sense) inputs. Pricing had no direct bearing to energy, force and, ultimately, work; the only relationship was indirect via the historical collinearity (decreasing over time) of capital and energy consumption (Beaudreau, 1998).

The Dissenters

Judging from the sheer amount of work coming out of Great Britain in the nineteenth century, it is fair to say that political economy as a branch of inquiry was a distinctly British phenomenon. Put differently, Great Britain was the dominant player, dictating for the most part the development of the science—if, of course, science there was. Scarcity was, throughout the nineteenth century, a key preoccupation of British political economists. Events such as the U.S. Civil War, and the cessation of cotton imports from the U.S. South further accentuated the problem of scarcity, and, consequently, the notion that prices both of foodstuffs and textiles, Great Britain's principal export, would rise over time.

Great Britain's predicament, however, was not shared by every nation. Conditions in the United States, for example, were just the opposite. The opening up of the Midwest to farming, both of foodstuffs and cotton, the increasing use of steam power, and the development and spread of the new power transmission technology that was electricity ushered in a period of seemingly unlimited optimism. Abundance, not scarcity, best describes the conditions that prevailed in the United States in the late nineteenth century.

Among the first political economists to realize this was Professor Simon N. Patten of the University of Pennsylvania, according to whom the problem the United States faced was not that of managing scarcity, but rather, that of managing abundance.

That Patten was among the first to question the underlying logos of political economy, British in its origins, owes, I believe, to a number of factors, not the least of which was the fact that he found himself at the University of Pennsylvania, in the heart of the keystone state, a highly industrialized state rich in fossil fuels. One could argue that from Patten's vantage point, scarcity was a non-issue.

Energy and the Modern Theory of Value

While U.S. political economy was characterized by a revisionist movement, headed by Patten at Pennsylvania, it remained firmly British in its movements. Upward-sloping supply curves, both short- and long-run, are ubiquitous. Scarcity is the dominant feature, as illustrated by Marshall's contribution to price theory.

That U.S. political economists did not openly reject neoclassical political economy in favor of Patten-style political economy is a question that, in and of itself, is worthy of further study. After all, as shown earlier, at the end of the nineteenth century, the United States was hit by an energy shock in the form of electric power that ushered in the second industrial revolution. As pointed out earlier, the advent of high-throughput, electric-powered continuous-flow mass production, and the commercialization of the internal combustion engine, the United States had lifted and pushed as far back as one could see both the agricultural and manufacturing constraint. Scarcity would, for the next century, remain a theoretical concept, far removed from reality.

Ironically, the first salvo aimed at neoclassical price theory, especially Marshallian price theory, was British in origin, and came in the period following World War I. The war had, in textbook fashion, increased prices in the United Kingdom, and the United States. Estimates show that between 1913 and 1920, prices increased 195 percent in the United Kingdom and 117 percent in the United States. After the war, most believed that prices would fall to their pre–World War I levels, thus permitting the United Kingdom, the hub of the world financial system, to return to the gold standard, at prewar parities. Such, however, was not the case. While prices had been flexible upward, they appeared to be inflexible downward. This, as it turns out, did not augur well for Marshallian price theory. In what was its first real empirical test, it had come up short. It is perhaps useful to note that Marshallian price theory was, at the time, relatively new, dating back a mere twenty years to 1890. Clearly, profit-maximizing firms did not set price equal to marginal cost, the latter being a function of labor productivity.

With the benefit of hindsight, Nassau Senior and John Stuart Mill had come back to haunt Marshall and neoclassical political economy. Marshallian political economy, born of agriculture and scarcity, had failed to capture the behavior of high-throughput, continuous-flow-based manufacturing firms, which, at the time, were becoming commonplace. The revolt was widespread, and is chronicled in the pages of the *Economic Journal*, where the heretics found refuge. Throughout the post–World War I period (1917–1940), it abounded with work, most of it critical, on price theory. The main emphasis is on increasing returns and decreasing costs à la Senior and Mill.

Out of this came the foundations of modern price theory, referred to as industrial organization, where perfect competition as well as monopoly give way to imperfect competition, oligopoly and duopoly. Characterizing this literature is the ubiquitous presence of economies of scale. From Edward Chamberlin and Joan Robinson's work on monopolistic competition, to Gardiner Means notion of "administered price," to Edward Mason and Joseph Bain's Structure-Conduct-Performance framework, economies of scale loom large. In fact, one could argue that industrial organization is the economics of "large-scale production," and consequently, of abundance.

If one equates abundance with energy, then it can be argued that energy had, although indirectly, entered mainstream political economy. Decreasing costs, economies of scale, imperfect competition and industrial organization in general were the result of the increasing presence of high-throughput, continuous-flow mass production techniques in U.K., and especially U.S. industry.

To some, this was not enough. While developments in energy technology underlie the second industrial revolution, energy was nowhere to be found. Production theory was devoid of energy, as was price theory. This, in combination with the Great Depression, is what prompted a group of social-minded engineers and scientists to break with traditional political economy, and found a science of wealth based on elementary physics (mechanics and thermodynamics), namely, the Continental Committee on Technocracy. If prices were to convey relative scarcity, they argued, then they should be based on the one scarce resource, namely energy. The more energy, measured in kilowatt hours, Joules, calories or kilocalories, required to produce a good, *ceteris paribus*, the greater is its price, and vice-versa. According to William Akin:

At the core of Scott's vision was an energy theory of value. Since the basic measure common to the production of all goods and services was energy, he reasoned that the sole scientific foundation for the monetary system was also energy. Essentially, he wished to determine the value of goods by the physical cost of production. This cost was the amount of energy, measured in terms of ergs, consumed in the production of goods and services.

The first step in his scheme would be to determine the amount of energy, both human and machine, available for production, over and above that required for the operation and maintenance of physical equipment. Then energy certificates equivalent to the net energy figure, would be divided equally among all members of society. (Akin, 1977, 84)

CONCLUSIONS

If one accepts the view of the price system as a set of signals conveying the notion of scarcity and opportunity cost, and one also accepts the view that energy is the ultimate factor input (both as usable energy and as the ultimate source of organization), then one invariably must accept the energy theory of value as constituting the only theoretically consistent price system. Since everything can be reduced to energy, the energy theory of value provides the only emprically relevant model of prices.

In this treatise, I have argued that while price theory from Adam Smith to Edward S. Mason has, for the most part, been devoid of energy, energy in general, and energy innovations in particular, have motivated most of its major developments. The labor theory of value, I argue, is, in essence, an energy theory of value, labor being an energy source in prefatory system times (i.e., the domestic system).

It is my view that price theory in its current incarnation is on its last leg. The reasons are many, but one in particular stands out, namely the continuing marginalization of labor as a factor input (Rifkin, 1995; Greider, 1997). As I have shown here, value theory went from unicausal (labor) to bicausal (labor and capital). Now, with recent developments in control technology, there is the risk that it revert to unicausality, with capital, a nonproductive factor, as its only cause. An energy theory of value, based on relative direct and indirect energy inputs, combined with an energy theory of distribution *à la* Howard Scott, would, in my opinion, solve the problem of optimal allocation as well as that of income distribution. In fact, with regard to the latter, it would provide what the neoclassical political economists sought, namely a positive theory of distribution.

NOTES

1. It should be noted that overall supervision energy requirements will decrease as the cost of maintaining human life will have been replaced with the cost of maintaining say a microcomputer.

2. One could argue that this is also true in agriculture (hydroponic methods, greenhouses etcetera).

Appendix 2

A Treatise on Energy and Money

By money, it should be understood media of exchange per se, and not the exchange technologies described in Chapter 1. For example, specie, bills of exchange, promissory notes, credit and, more recently, credit cards are examples of money, while barter and the producer-merchant exchange environment are examples of exchange technologies. In Chapter 2, it was argued that energy innovations, specifically, the introduction of the steam engine, altered the exchange technology in late eighteenth century/early nineteenth-century Great Britain. Specifically, producers began to coordinate production activity in a market setting, as opposed to a family setting. Labor and other variable inputs were then purchased in the market place. More importantly, producers would now demand money/credit/finance to carry out their activities.

In this treatise on energy and money, it shall be argued that the various energy innovations examined in this book underlie a number of significant developments in both the demand for and supply of exchange media. Specifically, it will be argued that innovations in energy consumption in industry, lying a the root of innovations in output, were and are largely responsible for innovations in the demand for money. Also, it will be argued that innovations in energy consumption, by contributing to the "division of labor" (in actual fact, the transformation of labor from energy source and supervisor, to mere supervisor (machine operative), and, hence, altering the geographical localization of industry (upstream and downstream producers and suppliers) contributed in a nonneglligble way to the emergence of standardized, national currencies. Specifically, it is argued that the joint occurrences of the development of central banking in England in the nineteenth century and the first industrial revolution, and, secondly, the development of central banking in the United States in the early twentieth century, and the second industrial revolutions, were not coincidental. These two energy shocks, by increasing throughput rates and productivity, contributed to increasing the geographical scope of production, which, in turn, contributed to the demand for, and supply of, standardized, national currencies.

These ideas will be developed as follows. First, I examine the relationship between energy and the demand for money, focusing, in large part, on the British (nineteenth century) and American (twentieth century) experiences. Second, I examine the various innovations in money supply over the course of the past two centuries, paying particular attention to the role of government expenditure. Specifically, it will be shown that by financing its purchases of military supplies with security-based credit (bank notes), the U.S. government altered the very nature of exchange. Instead of financing the production of military supplies by way of traditional bank credit, large U.S. concerns (the military in the military-industrial complex) obtained advances from the federal government. Also examined is the role of consumer credit in resolving the problem of exchange, specifically, the problem of underincome. Lastly, I examine the writings of two monetary heretics, notably Henry Ford, who as early as 1912 called for the creation of an energy standard and the abandonment of the gold standard, and, of Technocrat Howard Scott, who, like Ford, called for the creation of an energy monetary and price standard.

ENERGY AND THE DEMAND FOR MONEY

At first blush, the idea of relating the demand for money to energy use or energy consumption appears somewhat far-fetched. After all, up until now, the demand for money has been linked to more traditional macroeconomic variables such as actual income, permanent income, and wealth, to mention a few (Friedman and Schwartz, 1963; Laidler, 1977). Consider, however, the following. As Harold Moulton pointed out some 60 years ago, money plays a fundamental role in the productive process, one which has, unfortunately, been ignored in favor of the exchange process.

When money is spoken of as a medium of exchange, one usually has in mind the exchange of consumers' goods. For convenience of exposition, economic treatises have commonly been divided into four parts, devoted respectively to consumption, production, exchange, and distribution. Money is treated under exchange, and its chief function is usually regarded as that of effecting the exchange of goods that have already been produced and are in the market awaiting transfer to the hands of those who are to consume them. But if one is to appreciate fully the significance of money under a capitalistic regime it is necessary to consider the part that it plays in the productive as well as in the exchange process. Exchange of consumers' goods is not to be excluded; but the role of money in getting goods ready to be exchanged as completed products must be included.

Modern business is almost universally conducted through the use of money. With money, the manufacturer purchases the materials needed for the construction of his plant; with money, he employs an administrative staff to manage his business; and with money he purchases the raw materials and supplies and employs the labor force required to operate the business. . . . In short, practically the entire productive process is nowadays organized and operated through the use of money. (Moulton, 1938, 21)

In fact, I go further than Moulton and argue that, in industrialized economies, it is through its role in the productive process that money acquires its role in the exchange process. For example, when workers are paid a salary, the productive and exchange roles of money are being brought into play. Specifically, workers exchange their supervisory skills in return for credit (medium of exchange), which, in turn, is then exchanged for final (or intermediate) goods.

$$W(t) = \eta \, [T(t),S(t)] \, E(t) \qquad\qquad (A2.1)$$

Accordingly, the demand for money in industrialized economies is an increasing function of the planned level of output (value added), which, in turn, is via Equation 1.3 in Chapter 1 (reproduced here as Equation A2.1) an increasing function of the level of planned energy consumption. Producers demand money to finance their variable costs, while merchants demand money to finance their purchases from producers. It follows that for every dollar of output, the total demand for money will be in excess of one dollar.[1] Thus, by transitivity, the demand for money is intimately related to the level of energy consumption. This is formalized in terms of Equation A2.2, where κ is an institutional constant (producers and merchants), the determinants of which include various firm and industry attributes. For example, the more an industry is vertically integrated, the less is its producers' demand for credit as interdivision profits become a bookkeeping entry as opposed to a financial entity (payment).

$$M(t) = \kappa \, [\eta \, [T(t),S(t)] \, E(t)] \qquad\qquad (A2.2)$$

Chronologically speaking, in the factory system, money precedes output. Producers must have access to credit/finance to begin production. In this sense, one could argue that money causes income, for without money (trade credit, specie, bills of exchange), trade and hence production, could not take place. By contrast, in primitive economies (low energy consumption per capita), output, choronologically speaking, can precede money.

Energy, Geographical Dispersion, and Money

Under the domestic system, merchants—typically from cities and towns—
—contracted with farmers for the production of, and transformation of cotton,
wool and linen (putting out). Geographically speaking, the whole of the
activity was typically confined to a well-defined—and oftentimes, restricted—geographical area (call it the region). Transactions, for the most part, were
mediated using promissory notes and bills of exchange. As such, suppliers
would be remunerated in the form of bank notes drawn upon bills of exchange.
Bills of exchange would be discounted by the banks, the proceeds of which
would constitute the bank's revenue.

The First Industrial Revolution

As it turned out, the shift from the domestic system to the factory system in
Great Britain in the late eighteenth and early nineteenth century provoked a
number of nonnegligible changes in British banking, and, hence, in the British
money supply. First, there were scale effects. The shift from animate human
power to inanimate water and steam power in the textiles industry, as shown in
Chapter 2 of this book, resulted in a manifold increase in production. Second,
there was the demand for credit by producers. Whereas before, producers
coordinated production within the confines of the family farm (i.e., cottage),
now they would coordinate it within a market setting, one requiring a means of
exchange.

The money supply, consisting of bank credit, promissory notes, bills of
exchange and coins, was, for the most part, demand-determined, being directly
tied to the activities of producers and merchants. For example, an increase in
the planned level of output in the textile sector would result in an increase in
the demand for the relevant feedstocks, which would, in turn, lead to an
increase in outstanding bills of exchange and promissory notes. In short, the
supply of money was, for all intents and purposes, infinitely elastic.

Clearly, in an ideal world where the supply of goods creates a commensurate
level of income (money) and income creates a commensurate demand on the
part of merchants, such a system would operate flawlessly. Planned increases
in output would lead to higher money income as firms traded in intermediate
goods, energy, labor and capital. Merchants would, in turn, increase their
orders of goods and services from firms. Aggregate supply would equal
aggregate income, which, in turn, would equal aggregate demand. The
problem, as showed in Chapter 2 of the book, is that the nineteenth-century
U.K. economy was less than ideal, the problem of underincome being present
from the inception of the factory system. This, inevitably, led to commercial
crises as increases in aggregate demand, based on increases in aggregate
income, were less than increases in aggregate supply.

The commercial crises of 1825 and 1836 provoked a nation-wide discussion about the role of money and bank policy. Were private, note-issuing banks responsible? Had they issued too many notes (to producers or to merchants), thus contributing to the crisis? Sould they be regulated? If so, then how? Such were the questions debated between two schools of thought, the "banking school" and the "currency school." The former held that note issuing banks were not responsible for the crises, and, what's more, the growth of notes was collinear with the growth of economic activity. This was an early version of the "real-bills doctrine," which held that for each bill of exchange issued, there was a corresponding real asset, be it wool, thread, cloth, cutlery, tools etcetera. The currency school, however, focused on the underlying incentive structure, specifically on the seemingly unlimited arbitrage opportunities banks faced. The cost of issuing notes was relatively low, while the corresponding revenue was high, making it extremely profitable. Herein lay the cause of commercial crises, members of this school argued.

As it turns out, the currency school won out over the banking school. The Bank Charter Act of 1844 regulated the note issue in a number of ways. For example, it prevented existing banks from increasing their note issue after 1844. Unfortunately, but not surprisingly, the Bank Charter Act of 1844 did little to end commercial crises. If anything, the debate between the banking school and the currency school showed, beyond a shadow of a doubt, that the government and the financial sector had, by 1844, not understood the innerworkings of a high-energy consumption-based industrial economy.

Second, there is the question of the "optimal currency zone." That is, what is the optimal geographical entity for a single currency? Prior to the industrial revolution, since trade was, in general, confined to a given, somewhat limited region, information problems were negligible. Note-issuing local or regional banks sufficed, so to speak. Bank notes rarely circulated outside of the region. This, however, was no longer true in the early nineteenth century. As pointed out earlier, steam-power was synonymous with high-throughput levels. Factories operating around the clock processed (transformed) infinitely more cotton, wool and linen than was the case in the domestic system. Raw materials, it therefore follows, had to be imported from neighboring regions and counties, not to mention countries.

Notes drawn on local banks used by merchants (firms) in neighboring counties, regions and countries were more risky. Was the bank soluable? For example, would a Glasgow wool merchant readily accept a bank note from the First Bank of Leeds? Clearly, the system of regional banks that had served Great Britain well in the preindustrial period was ill-suited to the highly integrated British economy that had resulted from the industrial revolution. What was needed, it follows, was a national currency, or, at the very least, a means of mitigating the risk inherent in a regionalized fractional banking system.

The Bank Charter Act of 1844 addressed these concerns. Existing banks could not increase the quantity of notes they had in use. From 1844 on, the Bank of England would be the sole issuer of new notes.

In conclusion, the first industrial revolution, by increasing throughput rates, led to important changes in the British banking system, and, consequently, in the supply of money in Great Britain. Higher throughput rates increased the demand for feedstocks (cotton, wool and linen), which, in turn, increased interregional trade in Britain, and, in time, led to the creation of a national currency and a central bank (Bank of England).

High-Powered Money, Banking, and the Supply of Money

The first and second industrial revolutions led to a marked increase in the demand for exchange media (promissory notes, bills of exchange, credit). The demand for intermediate goods and labor and energy increased, increasing the demand for exchange media. Similarly, merchants' demand for consumption and capital goods increased, thus increasing their demand for exchange media. In a world of commodity-based money, the demand for say gold would increase, thus increasing its price and, in the long run, its supply. Should the supply not be perfectly elastic, it stands to reason that prices in the economy would fall. In a world of credit-based money, the demand for credit would increase, prompting banks to increase supply. Should the supply of credit increase in proportion, then it stands to reason that prices would remain relatively constant.

By the late eighteenth century, exchange media in Great Britain consisted of commodity-based as well as credit-based money. Gold was the commodity of choice, while credit notes, bills of exchange, and promissory notes were the credit instruments of choice. In this section, I examine various issues pertaining to the supply of exchange media in the first and second industrial revolutions. The latter being the result of energy innovations, it follows that the causality will run from energy to the supply of money. Among the issues examined is the question of what I shall refer to as the optimal "bridge," in reference to the underlying nature of credit. Credit in a merchant or industrial setting is a *bridge* of sorts, spanning the period in time between payments (intermediate goods, variable costs) and receipts (revenue). Another way of seeing it is as a proxy commodity. While goods are in the process of being produced, proxy commodities are issued, and used to remunerate intermediate goods suppliers and the owners of the variable factor inputs. These are then used to purchase the goods and services in question. The relevant question, it therefore follows, is the optimal length of the bridge. Should it be 30, 60, 90, 120 days? Should a credit-issuing institution extend credit to a firm/merchant whose final output is 360 days in the making? That is, whose output will only "hit" the market in one year?

The Optimal Bridge Length

The question of the "optimal bridge" is perhaps the most important, yet overlooked aspects of credit-based economies. The reasons for this are many. One, however, stands out, namely the problem of the optimal quantity of exchange media (money). It being the case that credit (bills of exchange, promissory notes) are relatively costless to produce, it follows that there exists the possibility of overissue. Banks can discount bills for which the goods/services in question do not yet exist, or extend credit over an extended period of time. Should this occur, then the possibility of inflation arises. The volume of outstanding credit, in this case, exceeds the value of output, resulting in upward pressure on prices.

Consider the following. Suppose a Wicksellian-style economy devoid of intermediate goods, and in which all production processes, being roundabout, require 90 days. If factor payments (i.e., to labor) are made on a weekly basis, it stands to reason that the supply of money (credit) and, consequently, the demand for goods will be greater than the supply of goods. In fact, for a period of 90 days the supply of goods will be zero, as goods are in "process" so to speak. Clearly, as numerous nineteenth century political economists pointed out, in such a world, some of current production (e.g., food) has to be put aside (saved) for future (delayed) consumption. The longer are production processes (the more roundabout), the more savings is required.

This serves to highlight what I believe is the main issue in credit-based exchange environments, namely, determining the optimal supply of credit for a given set of heterogeneous production processes. What are the relevant guidelines? Where does one put the limit on financing roundabout processes? At 120 days, at 240 days or at 360 days?

Such were the issues confronting the British government in the early nineteenth century. Should the supply of credit be demand-determined (i.e., by producers' and merchants' demand for trade credit), or should it be fixed by government decree? Should the latter be chosen, then the question of optimal regulation arises. How should the "optimal" quantity of money be determined, and who should do it?

As pointed out earlier, the debate over rules pitted the "banking school" against the "currency school," the former arguing for what, in essence, amounted to "free banking" and the latter arguing for a form of government regulation, specifically by way of reserve requirements. The proponents of the banking school maintained that because there is a real component to every credit instrument, there was no risk of overissue. This has since become known as the "real-bills doctrine." The proponents of the currency school, on the other hand, maintained that the commercial crises of the 1830s and 1840s were the result of bankers' largesse, having overissued credit.

More so than anything else, this debate highlighted the primitive state of political economy in the first half of the nineteenth century, and the toll this exacted on the U.K. economy. Clearly, members of the currency school were aware of real possibility of bank overissue. Banks could, at least theoretically, discount bills coming due years later. To them, some form of regulation was needed. The problem, however, was chosing the proper guidelines. As it turned out, the only guideline considered was tying credit to gold. In the Bank Charter Act of 1844, gold reserves were introduced.

In hindsight, it is clear that the choice of gold was a poor one. A relic of the Neolithic era, precious metal-based currency was unsuited to an era of unprecedented output, income and expenditure growth. Growth in nineteenth-century Britain, and twentieth-century America made it abundantly clear that gold would not do the trick, so to speak. Given their desire to limit growth of exchange media to the rate of growth of output, it follows that a more judicious choice would have been to tie credit to the supply of energy, in this case, the supply of coal.

Government Expenditure and the Medium of Exchange

In a pure-credit Wicksellian-style economy, producers finance their day-to-day transactions via bank credit. Variable and fixed costs are covered by drawing down credit levels (bank notes and/or cheques). Revenues from sales to merchants, which accrue afterward, are then used to reimburse (payoff) the outstanding liability. The important point is that for each dollar of revenue, there is a comparable amount of bank credit, and consequently, a comparable firm liability. This, however, is not the case if the buyer (consumer) finances production. That is, if the buyer undertakes to finance the production of the good/service. For example, consider the case of a government ordering custom-made F-18 fighter jets, and paying up front, that is, at the time the contract is signed.

While this may appear to be an inconsequential detail, it is of great import to the money supply process, especially if the government in question has the constituional right to sell its liabilities to its central bank. The reasons are straightforward. First, firms dealing with the government are likely to be less dependent upon private banks to finance production. Monies provided by the buyer can and will be used to pay suppliers and cover variable costs. Second, sales and profits will be guaranteed, by contrast with firms in the private sector. Third, firm profits will be in the form of high-powered money, and not in the form of credit. Clearly, if the firms in question deposit their earnings in the private banking system, then there will be an increase in the level of high-powered money, potentially leading to credit inflation. On the other hand, these firms could use the proceeds to finance subsequent rounds of production, or, more interestingly, go into the banking business themselves. The important point is that purchaser-financed production, as described here, alters the essential nature of financial transactions in firms. Specifically, firms no longer depend on bills of exchange, promissory notes, or various other credit instruments, but rather are "self-financed."

It is my contention that the joint occurrence of the passage of the Federal Reserve Act of 1913 in the United States and the massive government expenditure incurred by the federal government in World War I, altered fundamentally the nature of short-term business finance in the United States, especially among large corporations. The Federal Reserve Act of 1913, by allowing the government to sell its liabilities to the newly created central bank (the "federal" reserve bank), created a potential for purchaser-financed—in this case, federal government-financed—production. World War I fulfilled this potential with rising levels of government expenditure (purchase of tanks, fighter planes etcetera). As has been documented elsewhere, these purchases were financed by the Federal Reserve. More importantly, as is the norm as far as government contracts go, monies were paid to the various suppliers---mostly large industrial concerns—when the orders were placed (at the signing of the contracts).

This practice (i.e., paying up front) is common in government contracts. John Francis Gorgel, for example, describes the U.S. federal government's dealings with "military industrial firms" (MIFs) in the following terms:

The civilian firm's cash flow is a priority concern of management. Inability to finance work-in-progress until it is converted into finished, delivered goods and payments are received has been a principal cause of business failures. Management must anticipate its financing requirements and develop effective sources of money supply under conditions of substantial risk.

The DOD customer does not insist that its contractor face these uncertainties and problems. We find the possible alternatives described as follows:

To promote private financing, for example, the Government permits the contractor to assign his claim for payment. It may also guarantee his private loans in suitable cases. To reduce the need for such financing, the Government makes intermediate payments of two kinds: partial payments on fixed-price contracts and interim payments on cost-reimbursement procurements. These increase the contractor's cash flow from the contract; thus, they reduce the amount of working capital he must obtain from other sources.

The Government may also provide direct contract financing in appropriate instances. Customary progress payments are used most often. Unusual progress payments and advance payments are also available. All three may be used in any combination that is needed and justified by the financing regulations. (Gorgel, 1971, 67)

Hence, the greater were a firm's dealings with the federal government in the World War I period, the greater was the likelihood that it could finance itself from internal sources—as opposed to the private banking system. Evidence of this was first provided by Frederich A. Lutz in a study entitled *Corporate Cash*

Balances, 1914–1943, where he refers to the near absence of bank credit in large manufacturing corporations:

During the decade of the twenties, bank credit was of little importance for large manufacturing corporations; bank debt, measured by notes payable, was reduced sharply throughout that period. In 1929, the year before "free" cash began to accumulate, 27 companies out of our sample of 45 large manufacturing corporations had no notes payable. Therefore, when these concerns became liquid the paying off of bank debt did not provide an outlet for their excess funds. Total notes payable of the other 19 companies in 1929 amounted to 2.6 percent of their combined total assets. By 1931, the payable of 8 of these companies had been reduced to zero, and those remaining 10, to 0.7 percent. By 1931 the absolute amount of notes payable for the entire group of corporations had declined to 21 percent of the 1929 level. Thus the great liquidity which corporations built up after 1929 was accompanied by an almost complete disappearance of bank debt. (Lutz, 1945, 52)

Thus, in conclusion, the government expenditure occasioned by World Wars I and World War II, in combination with the various programs of the New Deal (I and II) altered fundamentally, the nature of business short-term finance in the United States. Bank credit, the bane of nineteenth century industrialists, had, for all intents and purposes, disappeared, to be replaced by internal funds and "free cash flows." Put differently, firms became banks unto themselves, owing, in large measure, to the high-powered money tendered to them by the federal government.

Monetary Heretics

As pointed out above, the problem of regulating the supply of fiduciary (fiat) money dominated the monetary debate for over a century. Energy-driven economic growth in the nineteenth and twentieth centuries increased the demands placed upon the banking system to provide the necessary media of exchange (to producers and merchants). The triumph of the "currency school" over the "banking school" in Great Britain, and the ensuing Bank Charter Act of 1844, resulted in the establishment of the gold standard, with its inherent restrictions on the supply of credit. The United States followed a similar path, adopting reserve requirements in an attempt to prevent credit inflation.

The second industrial revolution, by increasing the demand for bank credit, raised the problem of money (medium of exchange) again. Would enough gold and/or government securities be available to enable banks the wherewithal to extend their liabilities (credit)? Would the supply of gold/government securities limit growth?

In 1914, Henry Ford, the father of electric-powered, high-throughput, continuous-flow mass production, proposed a solution to the problem, namely replacing the gold standard with an energy standard. Money (credit) should be backed by energy. That is, the supply of money should be tied to the supply of energy. In this way, he argued, there could be neither a dearth nor an oversupply of money (credit). Given that energy constitutes the basis of all economic activity (or so thought Ford), it follows that an increase in energy supply creates a potential for greater output and income. By tying money (credit) to, say, the total amount of energy used in the economy (industry), then the monetary problem (surplus or dearth) would disappear.

Another monetary heretic was Howard Scott, one of the founding members of the Continental Committee on Technocracy, and a leading exponent of technocracy in the 1930s. As pointed out in the Treatise on Energy and Price Theory, Scott envisaged an energy theory of value, coupled with an energy-based exchange technology, namely the issuing of "energy certificates."

This energy system of value would serve as the means of adjusting production to use by establishing a stable non-negotiable monetary system. The first step in his scheme would be to determine the amount of energy, both human and machine, available for production, over and above that required for the operation and maintenance of the physical equipment. Then, "energy certificates," equivalent to the net energy figure, would be divided equally among all members of society. Scott hardly paused to justify his radical egalitarian division, noting only that "physical science could not justify special privilege." Under his proposed arrangement, individuals would be free to spend their income in the marketplace. In fact, they would be required to do so.... To accomplish this, the "energy certificates" would be nonnegotiable, nontransferable, and void after the "time its takes for a complete cycle of the operating and production procedures to be completed." In this way, consumers would be required to spend all their exchange notes or lose them, thus purchasing, or using up all that was produced. The consumers' buying patterns, moreover, would indicate what society used and, therefore, what should be produced. (Akin, 1977, 85)

Analogous in many ways to Robert Owen's labor-certificate-based exchange technology, Scott's energy-certificate exchange technology sought to replace credit, real-bills, and gold in conventional fractional reserve currencies with energy. The supply of money, as such, would be limited by the supply of energy. Similarly, the rate of growth of the money supply would be limited—and determined—by the rate of growth of energy.

CONCLUSIONS

As argued throughout the first five chapters of this book, output is an increasing function of energy consumption. Since the demand for money is traditionally seen as an increasing function of output, it stands to reason that the demand for money could be seen as an increasing function of energy consumption. The more energy Western industrialized economies consumed, the greater their output, and the greater the demand for exchange media.

As I have tried to show here, the failure on the part of early nineteenth century political economists to identify the role of energy in production, and the choice of gold by governments as the reserve base in the private banking system resulted in a series of problems, which culminated with the suspension of the gold standard in the post–World War II period. While the gold-standard had provided sufficient liquidity to the world economy in the nineteenth century, it was clear, at the outset of the twentieth century that, barring massive price deflation, it could not generate reserves at a sufficient rate, prompting calls by some to replace it with, among other things, an energy standard. Such calls went unheeded. Instead, by mid-century, the gold standard had been replaced by a gold-dollar standard (Bretton Woods). By 1973, the system was in tatters, owing in large measure to the U.S. governments decision to finance the Vietnam war at the Federal Reserve. In hindsight, had the United States—and, indeed, the rest of the world—heeded Howard Scott's plan for an "energy standard," then three decades of price inflation could have been avoided.

NOTE

1. Take, for example, the case of a standard CRS Cobb-Douglas production function with an α value of 0.7. In this case, the demand for money on the part of the producer will be \$0.70 per dollar output, while the demand for credit on the part of the merchant (retailer) will be one dollar. Thus, one dollar of output will require \$1.70 of money, spaced out over time.

Bibliography

Aghion, Philippe, and Peter Howitt. *Endogenous Growth Theory.* Cambridge, MA: MIT Press, 1998.

Akin, William E. *Technocracy and the American Dream, The Technocratic Movement, 1900–1941.* Berkeley, CA: University of California Press, 1977.

Alterman, Jack. A Historical Perspective on Changes in U.S. Energy-Output Ratios, Bulletin EA-3997. Palo Alto, CA: Electric Power Research Institute, 1985.

Alting, Leo. *Manufacturing Engineering Processes.* New York, NY: Marcel Decker Inc., 1994.

Anderson, F. J., N. C. Bonsor, and B. C. Beaudreau. *The Economic Future of the Forest Products Industry in Northern Ontario.* Royal Commission on the Northern Environment, Thunder Bay, Ontario, 1982.

Ayres, Robert U., and Indira Nair. "Thermodynamics and Economics." *Physics Today* 1984, 62–71.

Babbage, Charles. *The Economy of Machinery and Manufacturing.* London: C. Knight, 1832.

Baily, Martin N. and Robert J. Gordon. "The Productivity Slowdown, Measurement Issues, and the Explosion of Computer Power." *Brookings Papers on Economic Activity* 2, 1988, 347–420.

Baines, E. *The History of the Cotton Manufactures.* London, 1835.

Barro, Robert J. and Xavier Sala-i-Martin. *Economic Growth.* New York, NY: McGraw-Hill, 1995.

Beaudreau, Bernard C. "The Impact of Electric Power on Productivity: The Case of U.S. Manufacturing 1958–1984." *Energy Economics* 17(3), 1995a, 231–236.

Beaudreau, Bernard C. "The Impact of Electric Power on Productivity: The Case of Japanese Manufacturing 1965–1988." Working Paper, Department of Economics, Université Laval, 1995b.

Beaudreau, Bernard C. "The Impact of Electric Power on Productivity: The Case of German Manufacturing 1963–1988." Working Paper, Department of Economics, Université Laval, 1995c.

Beaudreau, Bernard C. "Newtonian Production Processes," Working Paper, Department of Economics, Université Laval, 1995d.

Beaudreau, Bernard C. *Mass Production, The Stock Market Crash, and The Great Depression: The Macroeconomics of Electrification.* Westport, CT: Greenwood Press, 1996a.

Beaudreau, Bernard C. "R&D: To Compete or to Cooperate." *Economics of Innovation and New Technology* 4, 1996b, 173–186.

Beaudreau, Bernard C. *Energy and Organization: Growth and Distribution Reexamined.* Westport, CT: Greenwood Press, 1998.

Beiser, Arthur. *Modern Technical Physics.* Menlo Park, CA: The Benjamin/Cummings Publishing Company 1983.

Bental, Benjamin and Benjamin Eden. "Money and Inventories in an Economy with Uncertain and Sequential Trade." *Journal of Monetary Economics* 37 1996, 445–459.

Berg, Maxine. *The Machinery Question and the Making of Political Economy.* Cambridge: Cambridge University Press, 1980.

Berndt, Ernst and David O. Wood. "Technology, Prices and the Derived Demand for Energy." *The Review of Economics and Statistics* August 1975, 259–268.

Betts. John E. *Essentials of Applied Physics.* Englewood Cliffs, NJ: Prentice-Hall, 1989.

Birnie, Arthur. *An Economic History of Europe 1760–1930.* New York, NY: The Dial Press, 1930.

Blair, John M. "Does Large-Scale Eneterprise Result in Lower Costs?" *American Economic Review* 38, 1948, 121–152.

Blanchflower, David G., Andrew J. Oswald, and Peter Sanfey. "Wages, Profits, and Rent Sharing." *Quarterly Journal of Economics* 60(1), 1996, 227–251.

Bose, Bismal K. "Introduction to Microcomputer Control." in Bose, Bismal K. ed., *Microcomputer Control of Power Electronics and Drives.* New York: IEEE Press, 1987.

Bresnahan, Timothy and Manuel Trajtenberg. "General Purpose Technologies: Engines of Growth?" National Bureau of Economic Research Working Paper No. 4148, August 1992.

Bullard, Clark W., and Robert A. Herendeen. "The Energy Cost of Goods and Services." *Energy Policy* December 1975, 268–278.

Butt, John. *Robert Owen: Prince of Cotton.* Newton Abbott: David and Charles, 1971.

Chase, Stuart. *The Economics of Abundance.* New York: Macmillan Company, 1934.

Challoner, Jack, *Energy.* London: Darling Kindersley, 1993.

Chandler, Alfred D., Jr. *The Visible Hand, The Managerial Revolution in American Business.* Cambridge, MA: Harvard University Press, 1977.

Christensen, L. R., and D. W. Jorgenson. "U.S. Real Product and Real Factor Input." *The Review of Income and Wealth,* 1970.

Clark, J. Maurice, *Studies in the Economics of Overhead Costs.* Chicago, IL: University of Chicago Press, 1923.

Clapham, J. H. "Of Empty Economic Boxes." *Economic Journal* 32, 1922, 305–314.

Cleveland, Cutler J., Costanza, R., Hall, Charles, and Kaufmann, R. "Energy and the U.S. Economy: A Biophysical Perspective." *Science* 225, 1984, 890–897.

Clower, Robert. "A Reconsideration of the Microfoundations of Monetary Theory." *Western Economic Journal* 1967, 1–19.

Clower, Robert, and Peter Howitt. "Keynes and the Classics: An End of Century View." in Ahiakpor, James C. W. ed., *Keynes and the Classics Reconsidered.* Boston, MA: Kluwer, 1998.

Cobb, Charles, and Paul Douglas. "A Theory of Production." *American Economic Review* 18, 1928, 139–165.

Coleman, Matthew J. ed., *Energy Engineering and Management in the Pulp and Paper Industry.* Atlanta, GA: TAPPI, 1991.

Copithorne, Lawrence W. "A Neoclassical Perspective on Natural Resource-Led Regional Economic Growth." Economic Council of Canada, Discussion Paper no. 92, 1977.

Crafts, Nicholas. *"Forging Ahead and Falling Behind: The Rise and Relative Decline of the First Industrial Nation." Journal of Economic Perspectives* 12(2), 193–210.

Culbertson, John M. "The Folly of Free-Trade." *Harvard Business Review* 1986, 122–128.

David, Paul A. "The Dynamo and the Computer: An Historical Perspective on the Modern Productivity Paradox." *American Economic Review, Papers and Proceedings* May, 1990, 355–361.

Dean, Joel. "Cost-Structures of Enterprises and Break-Even Charts." *American Economic Review* 38, 1948, 153–164.

Denison, Edward F. *The Sources of Economic Growth in the United States and the Alternatives Before Us.* New York, NY: Committee for Economic Development, 1962.

Denison, Edward F. *Trends in American Economic Growth 1929–1982.* Washington, DC.: The Brookings Institution, 1985.

Devine, Warren D. "Electricity in Information Management: The Evolution of Electronic Control," in Schurr, Sam H. et al. eds., *Electricity in the American Economy.* Westport CT: Greenwood Press, 1990.

Dimand, Robert W. "Cranks, Heretics and Macroeconomics in the 1930's." *History of Economic Review* 16, 1991, 11–30.

Director, Aaron. *The Economics of Technocracy.* Chicago, IL: The University of Chicago Press, 1933.

Doms, Mark, Timothy Dunne and Kenneth R. Troske. "Workers, Wages and Technology." *Quarterly Journal of Economics* 112, 253–289.

Douglas, Clifford H. *Social Credit.* New York, NY: Norton and Company, 1933.

Douglas, Clifford H. *The Monopoly of Credit.* Liverpool: K.R.P. Publications, 1951.

Du Boff, Richard B. "The Introduction of Electric Power in American Manufacturing," *Economic History Review* 1967, 509–518.

Du Boff, Richard B. *Electrical Power in American Manufacturing, 1889–1958.* New York, NY: Arno Press, 1979.

Eden, Benjamin. "The Adjustment of Prices to Monetary Shocks when Trade is Uncertain and Sequential." *Journal of Political Economy* 102 1994, 493–509.

Edgeworth, Francis Y. *Mathematical Psychics.* London: Kegan Paul, 1881.

Fielden, John. "National Regeneration." in Carpenter, Kenneth E. ed., *The Factory Act of 1833.* New York, NY: Arno Press, 1972.

Filene, Edward A. *Successful Living in This Machine Age.* New York: Simon and Schuster, 1931.

Fischer, Stanley. "Money and the Production Function" *Economic Inquiry* 12 1974, 517–533.

Fisher, Clyde Ohlin. "An Issue in Economic Theory: Rate of Wages and the Use of Machinery." *American Economic Review* 13(4) 1923, 654–655.

Fisher, Irving. *The Purchasing Power of Money.* New York, NY: MacMillan, 1911.

Fisher, Irving. *The Stock Market Crash and After.* New York: Macmillan, 1930.

Floud, Roderick and McCloskey, Donald, eds., *The Economic History of Britain Since 1700, Volume 1: 1700–1860.* Cambridge: Cambridge University Press, 1994.

Ford, Henry. "Mass Production." *Encyclopaedia Britannica* 13, 1926, 821–823.

Friedman, Milton and Anna J. Schwartz. *A Monetary History of the United States 1867–1960.* New York: National Bureau of Economic Research, 1963.

Galbraith, J.K. *American Capitalism, The Concept of Countervailing Power.* New Brunswick, NJ: Transaction Publishers, 1952.

Georgescu-Roegen, Nicholas. *The Entropy Law and the Economic Process.* Cambridge, MA: Harvard University Press, 1971.

Gollop, F.M., and Jorgenson, D.W. "U.S. Productivity Growth by Industry, 1948–1973." in Kendrick, J.W., and Vaccara, B.N. eds., *New Developments in Productivity Measurement and Analysis.* Chicago: National Bureau of Economic Research, 1980.

Gordon, Robert J. "Supply Shocks and Monetary Policy Revisited." *American Economic Review* 74(2) 1984, 38–43.

Gorgel, John Francis. "A Theory of the Military-Industrial Firm." in Seymour Melman, ed., *The War Economy of the United States.* New York: St. Martin's Press, 1971.

Graham, Frank D. "Relation of Wage Rates to the Use of Machinery." *American Economic Review* 16(3) 1926, 434–442.

Greider, William. *One World Ready or Not, The Maniac Logic of Global Capitalism.* New York, NY: Simon and Schuster, 1997.

Griliches, Zvi. "The Discovery of the Residual: An Historical Note." National Bureau of Economic Research, Working Paper 5348, 1995.

Grossman, Gene, and Elhanan Helpman. *Innovation and Growth in the Global Economy.* Cambridge, MA: MIT Press, 1991.

Gullickson, William and Michael J. Harper. "Multifactor Productivity in U.S. Manufacturing, 1949–1983." *Monthly Labor Review* 1988, 18–28.

Harley, C. Knick. "Reassessing the Industrial Revolution: A Macro View." in Moykr, Joel. ed., *The British Industrial Revolution: An Economic Perspective.* Oxford: Westview Press, 1993, 171–226.

Hayek, Friedrich A. *Prices and Production.* London: George Routledge and Sons, 1935.

Hayes, H. Gordon. "Rate of Wages and the Use of Machinery." *American Economic Review* 13(3) 1923, 461–465.

Hayes, H. Gordon. "Rate of Wages and the Use of Machinery: Further Comment." *American Economic Review* 13(4) 1923, 655–657.

Helpman, Elhanan and Manuel Trajtenberg. "A Time to Sow and a Time to Reap: Growth Based on General Purpose Technologies." National Bureau of Economic Research Working Paper No. 4854, September 1994.

Helpman, Elhanan. ed., *General Purpose Technologies and Economic Growth.* Cambridge, MA: MIT Press, 1998.

Hills, Richard L. *Power in the Industrial Revolution.* Manchester: Manchester University Press, 1970.

Hills, Richard L. *Power from Steam, A History of the Stationary Steam Engine.* Cambridge: Cambridge University Press, 1989.

Hisnanick, John J., and Kymm, Kern "The Impact of Disaggregated Energy on Productivity." *Energy Economics* 1992, 274–278.

Hollander, Samuel. *The Economics of Adam Smith.* Toronto: University of Toronto Press, 1973.

Hollander, Samuel. *Classical Economics.* New York, NY: Basil Blackwell, 1987.

Honeyman, Katrina. *Origins of Entreprise: Business Leadership in the Industrial Revolution.* Manchester: Manchester University Press, 1982.

Hounshell, David A. *From the American System to Mass Production 1800–1932: The Development of Manufacturing Technology in the United States.* Baltimore: The Johns Hopkins University Press, 1984.

Hulten, Charles R. "Growth Accounting When Technical Change is Embodied in Capital." *American Economic Review* September 1992, 964–980.

Hunt, E. K., "Simon N. Patten's Contributions to Economics." *Journal of Economic Issues* 4(4), December 1970, 38–55.

Inglis, Brian. *Men of Conscience.* New York, NY: The Macmillan Company, 1971.

Jevons, W. S. *The Coal Question.* London: Macmillan and Co., 1865.

Jevons, W. S. *The Theory of Political Economy.* London: Pelican Books, 1871.

Johnson, H. G. "The Efficiency and Welfare Implications of International Corporations." in Kindleberger, C.P. ed., *The International Corporation.* Cambridge, MA: MIT Press, 1970.

Jorgenson, D. W. "Energy Prices and Productivity Growth." in Schurr, S. *et al.* eds., *Energy, Productivity, and Economic Growth.* Cambridge, MA: Oelgeschlager, Gunn, and Hain, 1983.

Jorgenson, D. W. The Role of Energy in Productivity Growth, in Kendrick, J.W. ed., *International Comparisons of Productivity and Causes of the Slowdown.* Cambridge, MA: MIT Press, 1981.

Jorgenson, D. W. and B. Fraumeni. "Relative Prices and Technical Change." in Berndt, E.R. and B. Field. eds., *Modeling and Measuring Natural Resource Substitution.* Cambridge, MA: MIT Press, 1981.

Kahn, Alfred E. *The Economics of Regulation: Principles and Institutions.* Cambridge, MA: MIT Press, 1988.

Kelley, Charles R. *Manual and Automatic Control, A Theory of Manual Control and its Application to Manual and to Automatic Systems.* New York, NY: John Wiley and Sons, 1968.

Keynes, John M. *The General Theory of Employment, Interest and Money.* London: Macmillan, 1936.

King, Williford I. "Circulating Capital: Its Nature and Relation to the Public Welfare." *American Economic Review* 10(4), 1920, 738–754.

Knight, F. H. *Risk, Uncertainty and Profit.* Chicago: University of Chicago Press, 1921.

Lacey, Robert. *Ford: The Men and the Machine.* Boston: Little, Brown and Company, 1986.

Laidler, David. *The Demand for Money: Theories and Evidence.* New York: Dun-Donnelley, 1977.

Laidler, David. *Taking Money Seriously and Other Essays.* Cambridge, MA: MIT Press, 1990.

Landes, David S. *The Unbound Prometheus, Technological change and industrial development in Western Europe from 1750 to the present.* Cambridge: Cambridge University Press, 1969.

Lehr, William and Frank R. Lichtenberg "Computer Use and Productivity Growth in Federal Government Agencies." National Bureau of Economic Research, Working Paper 5616, 1996.

Leibenstein, H. "Entrepreneurship and Development." *American Economic Review* 58, 72–83.

Lloyd George, David. *Coal and Power Report.* London: Hodder and Stoughton, 1924.

Lloyd-Jones, Roger and M. J. Lewis. *Manchester and the Age of the Factory, The Business Structure of Cottonopolis in the Industrial Revolution.* London: Croom Helm, 1988.

Lutz, Frederich A. *Corporate Cash Balances, 1914–1943.* New York, NY: National Bureau of Economic Research, 1945.

Maddison, Angus. "Growth Slowdown in Advanced Capitalist Economies: Techniques of Quantitative Assessment." *Journal of Economic Literature* 25(2), 1987, 649–698.

Malthus, T. R. *Principles of Political Economy Considered with a View to Their Practical Application.* New York: Augustus M. Kelley, 1951 [1827].

Mankiw, N. G. and D. Romer. *New Keynesian Economics.* Cambridge, MA: MIT Press, 1991.

Mankiw, N. G., D. Romer, and D. Weil. "Contributions to the Empirics of Economic Growth," *Quarterly Journal of Economics* 107(2) 1992, 407–438.

Mannisto, Heikki. "Who can afford to save energy?" in Coleman, Matthew J. ed., *Energy Engineering and Management in the Pulp and Paper Industry.* Atlanta, GA: TAPPI, 1991.

Mansfield, E., J. Rapoport, J. Schnee, S. Wagner, and M. Hamburger. *Research and Innovation in the Modern Corporation.* New York, NY: W. W. Norton and Co., 1971.

Marshall, Alfred. *Principles of Economics.* 8th Ed. London: MacMillan, 1890.

Marx, Karl, *Capital.* New York, NY: The Modern Library, 1906 [1867].

Mathias, Peter. *The First Industrial Nation: An Economic History of Britain 1700–1914.* London: Methusen & Co., 1969.

Means, Gardiner. "The Growth in the Realtive Importance of the Large Corporation in American Economic Life." *American Economic Review* 21, 1931, 10–42.

Means, Gardiner. *The Structure of the U.S. Economy.* Washington, DC: U.S. Government Printing Office for the National resource Committee, 1939.

Merrill, Milton R. *Reed Smoot: Apostle in Politics.* Logan, UT: Utah State Press, 1990.

Mirowski, Philip. "Energy and Energetics in Economic Theory: A Review Essay," *Journal of Economic Issues* 22(3), 1988, 811–830.

Mirowski, Philip. *More Heat Than Light, Economics as Social Physics, Physics as Nature's Economics.* Cambridge: Cambridge University Press, 1989.

Mitchell, B. R. *British Historical Statistics.* Cambridge: Cambridge University Press, 1988.

Moulton, Harold G. *Financial Organization and the Economic System.* New York: McGraw-Hill, 1938.

Mowery, D. C., and N. Rosenberg. *Technology and the Pursuit of Economic Growth.* Cambridge: Cambridge University Press, 1989.

Musson, A. E. "Industrial Motive Power in the United Kingdom, 1800–70." *Economic History Review* 29, 1976, 415–439.

National Bureau of Economic Research. *Recent Economic Changes in the United States.* New York, NY: McGraw Hill, 1929.

Newcomb, Simon. *Principles of Economics.* New York: Augustus Kelley, 1886.

Nonneman, Walter, and Patrick Vanhoudt. "A Further Augmentation of the Solow Model and the Empirics of Economic Growth for OECD Countries." *Quarterly Journal of Economics* 1997, 112, 943–953.

Nye, David E. *Electrifying America: Social Meaning of a New Technology.* Cambridge, MA: MIT Press, 1990.

Odum, H. T., and E. C. Odum. *Energy Basis for Man and Nature.* New York, NY: McGraw-Hill, 1976.

Ormerod, Paul. *The Death of Economics.* New York, NY: John Wiley and Sons, 1997.

Owen, Robert. *The Life of Robert Owen.* London: Cass, 1967.

Owen, Robert. *A New View of Society and Other Writings.* London: J.M. Dent and Sons, Ltd., 1927.

Patinkin, Don. *Money, Interest and Prices.* New York, NY: Harper and Row, 1965.

Pigou, Arthur C. "The Value of Money." *Quarterly Journal of Economics* 37(4), 1917, 38–65.

Prescott, Edward C. "Needed: A Theory of Total Factor Productivity." *International Economic Review* 39(3), 1998.

Pullen, J. M., and G. O. Smith. "Major Douglas and Social Credit: A Reappraisal." *History of Political Economy* 29, 1997, 219–273.

Rabinbach, Anson. *The Human Motor: Energy, Fatigue and the Origins of Modernity.* New York, NY: Basic Books, 1990.

Ricardo, David. *The Principles of Political Economy and Taxation.* New York, NY: Everyman's Library, 1965.

Rifkin, Jeremy. *The End of Work.* New York, NY: G. P. Putnam's Sons, 1995.

Romer, Paul M. "Increasing Returns and Long-Run Growth." *Journal of Political Economy* 94, 1986, 1002–1037.

Romer, Paul M. "Crazy Explanations for the Productivity Slowdown." *NBER Macroeconomics Annual 1987* 1987, 163–202.

Romer, Paul M. "Endogenous Technological Change." *Journal of Political Economy* 98, 1990, s71–s102.

Romer, Paul M. "The Origins of Endogenous Growth." *Journal of Economic Perspectives* 8, 1994, 3–22.

Rosenberg, Nathan. *Technology and American Economic Growth.* Armonk, NY: M.E. Sharpe, 1972.

Rosenberg, N. "The Effects of Energy Supply Characteristics on Technology and Economic Growth," in Schurr, S. et al. eds., *Energy, Productivity and Economic Growth.* Cambridge, MA: Oelgeschager, Gunn and Hain, 1983.

Rosenberg, Nathan, and L.E. Birdzell, Jr. *How the West Grew Rich: The Transformation of the Industrial World.* New York, NY: Basic Books, 1986.

Rotemberg, Julio, and Michael Woodford. "Imperfect Competition and the Effects of Energy Price Increases on Economic Activity." National Bureau of Economic Research, Working Paper 5634, 1996.

Ruth, Matthias. *Integrating Economics, Ecology and Thermodynamics.* Dordrecht: Kluwer Academic Publishers, 1993.

Ruth, Matthias, and Clark W. Bullard. "Information, Production and Utility." *Energy Policy* October 1993, 1059–1067.

Schurr, S.H., and Netschert, B. *Energy in the American Economy, 1850-1975.* Baltimore, MD: Johns Hopkins University Press, 1960.

Schurr, S., J. Darmstadler, H. Perry, W. Ramsay, and M. Russell. *Energy in America's Future.* Baltimore, MD: Johns Hopkins Press, 1979.

Schurr, S., C. Burwell, W. Devine, and S. Sonenblum. *Electricity in the American Economy: Agents of Technological Progress.* Westport, CT: Greenwood Press, 1990.

Scott, Howard et al. *Introduction to Technocracy.* New York, NY: The John Day Company, 1933.

Self, Sir Henry, and Elizabeth M. Watson. *Electricity Supply in Great Britain.* London: Allen and Unwin, 1952.

Shapiro, Seymour. *Capital and the Cotton Industry in the Industrial Revolution.* Ithaca, NY: Cornell University Press, 1967.

Simon, Herbert. *The Sciences of the Artificial.* Cambridge, MA: MIT Press, 1996.

Sinclair, Upton. *The Autobiography of Upton Sinclair.* New York, NY: Harcourt, Brace and World, 1962.

Sismonde de Sismondi, Jean-Charles Léonard. Nouveaux principes d'économie politique. Paris: Calmann-Lévy, 1970 [1819].

Smith, Adam. *An Inquiry into the Nature and Causes of the Wealth of Nations.* Chicago: Encyclopaedia Britannica, 1990 [1776].

Sobel, Robert. *The Age of Giant Corporations, A Mciroeconomic History of American Business 1914–1970.* Westport, CT: Greenwood Press, 1972.

Soddy, Frederick. *Cartesian Economics, The Bearing of Physical Sciences upon State Stewardship.* London: Hendersons, 1924.

Solow, Robert M. "The Economics of Resources or the Resources of Economics." *American Economic Review* 64(2), 1974, 1–14.

Solow, Robert M. "Perspectives on Growth Theory." *Journal of Economic Perspectives* 8, 1994, 45–54.

Sowell, Thomas. *Say's Law, An Historical Analysis.* Princeton, NJ: Princeton University Press, 1972.

Spreng, Daniel T. "Possibilities for Substitution between Energy, Time, and Information." *Energy Policy*, 1993, 13–23.

Stearns, Peter. *The Industrial Revolution in World History.* Boulder, CO: Westview Press, 1993.

Stern, David I. "Energy and Economic Growth in the USA." *Energy Economics* April 1993, 137–151.

Stocking, Collis A. "Modern Advertising and Economic Theory." *American Economic Review* 21, 1931, 43–55.

Sweezy, Paul M. "Demand under Conditions of Oligopoly." *Journal of Political Economy* 47, 1939, 568–573.

Tatom, J. "Potential Output and the Recent Productivity Decline." *Economic Review of the Federal Reserve Bank of St-Louis* 64, 1982, 3–15.

Thomas, Woodlief. "The Economic Significance of the Increased Efficiency of American Industry." *American Economic Review* 18, 1928, 122–138.

Tugwell, Rexford G. *Industry's Coming of Age.* New York, NY: Columbia University Press, 1927.

Tugwell, Rexford G. *The Industrial Discipline and the Governmental Arts.* New York, NY: Columbia University Press, 1933.

Tylecote, Mabel. *The Mechanics Institutes of Lancashire and Yorkshire before 1851.* Manchester: Manchester University Press, 1957.

Tyron, F.G. "An Index of Consumption of Fuels and Water Power." *Journal of the American Statistical Association* 22, 1927, 271–282.

United Nations. Industrial Statistics Yearbook 1984. New York, NY: United Nations, 1960–1988.

U.S. Department of Commerce. *Annual Survey of Manufactures.* Washington, DC: Bureau of the Census, various years.

U.S. Department of Commerce. *Historical Statistics of the U.S.: Colonial Times to 1970, Bicentennial Edition.* Washington, DC: Bureau of the Census, 1975.

U.S. Department of Commerce. *Survey of Current Business.* Washington, DC: Bureau of Economic Analysis, various years.

van Engelenburg, B. C. W., T. F. M. van Rossum, K. Blok, and K. Vringer. "Calculating the Energy requirements of Household Purchases." *Energy Policy* 22(8) 1994, 648–656.

Van Reenen, John. "The Creation and Capture of Rents: Wages and Innovation in a Panel of U.K. Companies." *Quarterly Journal of Economics* 61(1), 1996, 195–226.

Varian, Hal R. *Microeconomic Analysis.* New York, NY: Norton, 1992.

Veblen, Thornstein. *The Engineers and the Price System.* New York, NY: Augustus M. Kelley, 1965 [1921].

von Schulze-Gaevernitz, G. *The Cotton Trade in England and on the Continent.* London: Simpkin, Marshall, Hamilton, and Kent, 1895.

von Tunzelmann, G. N. *Steam Power and Bristish Industrialization to 1860.* Oxford: Clarendon Press, 1978.

Wicksell, Knut. *Interest and Prices, A Study of the Causes Regulating the Value of Money.* London: Macmillan and Co, 1936 [1898].

Wicksteed, Phillip. *An Essay on the Coordintaion of the Law of Production.* London: Macmillan, 1894.

Whitaker, J. K. *The Early Writings of Alfred Marshall, 1867–1890.* New York, NY: The Free Press, 1975.

White, Horace G. "A Review of Monopolistic and Imperfect Competition Theories." *American Economic Review* 26, 1936, 637–649.

Woirol, Gregory R., *The Technological Unemployment and Structural Unemployment Debates.* Westport, CT: Greenwood Press, 1996.

Woolf, Arthur G. "Electricity, Productivity and Labor Saving: American Manufacturing, 1900–1929." *Explorations in Economic History* 21, 1984, 176–191.

Wright, Gavin. "The Origins of American Industrial Success, 1879–1940." *American Economic Review* 80(4), 1990, 651–668.

Index

Abramovitz, Moses, 148.
Aghion, Philippe, 4, 158, 170.
Agricultrure, United Kingdom, 111.
Akin, William E., 190, 203.
Alting, Leo, 7.
Arkwright, Richard, 40; spinning jenny, 46.
Automation, 158, 162–164, 168, 171–173.
Ayres, Robert U., 18, 157.

Babbage, Charles, 86.
Bain, Joseph, 118, 189.
Baines, E., 48.
Bank of England, 51.
Bargaining, 30–33; and energy rents, 33; power, 32; with outside options, 31–32; without outside options, 32.
Barro, Robert, 4.
Barter, see Exchange technology.
Beaudreau, Bernard, 3, 7, 9, 19, 20, 28, 57, 83, 88, 101, 132, 136–138, 142, 150, 183.
Beiser, Arthur, 11.
Berg, Maxine, 1–2, 38.
Berle, Adolf, 153.
Berndt, Ernst, 150.
Betts, John E., 2, 11, 177.
Blanchflower, David G., 153.

Bonsor, N. C., 136.
Bose, Bismal K., 164.
Boulton, Matthew, 41.
Bresnahan, Timothy, 85.
Bullard, Clark W., 182.
Burwell, Calvin, 151.

Cannon, William, 55.
Cantillon, Richard, 89.
Capital, 2, 9; circulating, 20.
Carboniferous era, 45.
Cartesian economics, see Soddy, Frederick.
Challoner, Jack, 1.
Chamberlin, Edward, 117, 181.
Chandler, Alfred D., 133, 136, 142, 159.
Chase, Stuart, 110–111, 114.
Christensen, L. R., 136.
Clapham, J. H., 117.
Clark, John Maurice, 119–120, 125.
Classical mechanics, 80, 177.
Clower, Robert, 22, 152.
Coal consumption, United Kingdom, 43.
Cobb, Charles, 20.
Coleman, Matthew J., 160.
Collective bargaining, 134, 142, 152.
Consumer credit, 144–145, 152.
Continental Committee on Technocracy, see Technocracy.

Control devices, 31.
Corn Laws, 52, 53, 88, 183; repeal of,
    52, 142.
Cotton industry, United Kingdom, 42.
Crafts, Nicholas, 84.
Credit, *see* Exchange technologies.
Culbertson, John, 173.
Currency school, 197.

David, Paul, 171–172.
Demand for credit, 24–25, 27, 40; and
    energy, 194–195.
Demand for money, *see* Demand for
    credit.
Denison, Edward, 112, 139.
Detroit Edison Illuminating Company,
    101.
Devine, Warren D., Jr., 96–97, 112, 135,
    151.
Director, Aaron, 128–129, 179.
Distribution, *see* Income distribution.
Domestic system, 4, 7, 20, 38, 47, 60.
Doms, Mark, 172.
Douglas, Clifford H., 122–124, 178.
Douglas, Paul, 20.
Dow Jones Industrial Average, 166–167.
Dunne, Timothy, 172.

Economics of abundance, 126–127.
Economics of scarcity, 112–114.
Edgeworth, Francis Y., 79.
Electric motors, 92.
Electricity, 87.
Energy: animate, 8–10; deepening, 3; in
    economic analysis, 2; efficiency, 106;
    inanimate, 8–10; innovation, 4; rents,
    8, 27, 33, 69, 82; transmission
    technology, 92.
Energy crisis, 135, 149, 163; and firm
    behavior, 162–166.
Engineering literature, 172.
Entropic processes: anthropomorphic, 8,
    13; naturally occurring, 8, 13.
Exchange, problem of, 49.
Exchange technology: barter, 23;
    cash-in-advance constraint, 22; and
    foreign trade, 54; merchant, 8;
    producer-merchant, 8, 22–24, 67, 77,

92, 105, 135; Walrasian, 70.

Factor input: capital, 2, 12; complements,
    4, 17; substitutes, 17; in U.S.
    manufacturing, 136–138.
Factory system, 7, 20, 38, 47, 60.
Federal Reserve Act of 1913, 145.
Federal Reserve Board, 113, 145.
Fielden, John, 52–53, 55–57, 71.
Filene, Edward A., 106, 109–110,
    131–132.
Fire power, 2–3, 7, 38, 61, 87.
Fischer, Stanley, 35.
Fisher, Clyde Ohlin, 126.
Fisher, Irving, 112–113, 121.
Floud, Roderick, 84.
Force, *see* Energy.
Ford, Henry, 92, 108, 132, 178; on mass
    production, 102.
Ford Motor Company, 101–103;
    Highland Park plant, 131.
Free trade, United Kingdom, 53–54.
Friedman, Milton, 154, 194.
Full Employment Act of 1946, 148.

Galbraith, John K., 153–154.
Gathering-in system, 38–41.
General Electric Company, 17, 137.
General Motors, 137.
General purpose technology, 85, 170.
Georgescu-Roegen, Nicholas, 154.
German manufacturing, *see* Manufactur-
    ing.
Germany, 135.
Gideonse, Harry D., 128, 179.
Gold standard, 118.
Gollop, F. M., 136.
Gorgel, John Francis, 145–146, 201.
Graham, Frank D., 126.
Great Depression, 119, 126–127, 130,
    148, 189.
Greider, William, 158, 164, 190.
Griliches, Zvi, 149.
Grossman, Gene, 158.
Growth, slowdown, 137–138.
Growth accounting: Newtonian
    production analysis, 140–142; role of
    capital and labor, 139–142.

Grundy, Joseph R., 106.
Gullickson, William, 136, 139, 149, 151.

Harper, Michael J., 136–137, 139, 149, 151.
Hayes, H. Gordon, 126.
Helpman, Elhanan, 85, 158, 170.
Herendeen, Robert A., 182.
Hills, Richard, 41.
Hisnanick, John J., 137, 139.
Hobson, John A., 178.
Hockley Brook, 41.
Hollander, Samuel, 62–63, 67–68, 89.
Homo sapiens, 8; neanderthalensis, 91; sapiens, 91.
Honeyman, Katrina, 41–42.
Hounshell, David, 102–103.
Howitt, Peter, 4, 152, 158, 170.
Hoover, Herbert C., 97, 106.
Human body, obsolescence of, 34.
Hydraulic press, 12.

Inclined plane, 12.
Income distribution, 27; bargaining model, 5, 8, 30; classical, 8, 27, 82–83; functional, 126, 132; Marxian, 8, 28; neoclassical, 8, 27; Newtonian production analysis, 28–29; U.S. manufacturing 146–147.
Industrial organization, 117–188.
Industrial revolution: first, 4; second, 4.
Innovation, 2.
Institute of Economics, 113.
Inverse wage-profit relationship, 68.

Japan, 135; manufacturing, 136.
Jevons, Stanley W., 5, 79, 81.
Jorgenson, Dale, 85, 134, 139, 151, 154.

Keynes, John M., 121–122.
King, Williford, 121.
KLEMS, *see* Production function.
KLEP, *see* Production function.
Knight, Frank, 27.
Kymm, Kern, 137, 139.

Labor, 9; cheap, 173; market, 56; productivity, 19–20.

Laidler, David, 22, 162–163, 194.
Landes, David, 94.
Law of Markets, *see* Say's law.
Lehr, William, 171.
Leibenstein, Harvey, 14; managerial taxonomy, 14–15.
Lever, 12.
Lichtenberg, Frank R., 171.
Lloyd George, David, 109.
Lloyd Jones, Roger, 88.
Longston, William, 46.
Lutz, Frederich, 201–202.

Machinery, 69, 71; and labor demand, 71; operatives, 4; steam-powered, 48.
Maddison, Angus, 149, 158.
Malthus, Thomas Robert, 66, 174.
Manager, *see* Supervision.
Mannisto, Heikki, 161.
Manufacturing: Germany, 136–142; Japan, 136–142; United States, 136–143.
Marshall, Alfred, 14, 16, 47–49, 80, 89, 110, 125, 174; price theory, 117.
Marx, Karl, 3, 76–78, 86, 109.
Mason, Edward, 189.
Mass production, 119.
McCloskey, Donald, 84, 158.
Means, Gardiner, 153.
Merchant, *see* Exchange technology.
Military-industrial producers, 145.
Mill, John Stuart, 181, 189.
Mirowski, Philip, 79, 89.
Mokyr, Joel, 84.
Moral philosophers, 4, 7, 38, 58.
Moulton, Harold, 24, 132, 195.
Musson, A. E., 84, 88.

Nair, Indira, 157.
Nash bargaining solution, 32.
National Industrial Recovery Act of 1933, 92, 106, 153.
National Regeneration Society, 52–53.
Natural philosophers, 4.
Neanderthal man, *see* Homo sapiens, neanderthalensis.
Neolithic era, 58; production processes, 118.

New Deal, 117.
New York Edison Company, 97.
Newcomb, Simon, 16.
Newton, Sir Isaac, physics, 9.
Newtonian production analysis (NPA),
4–5, 138–139, 182.
Nonneman, Walter, 149.
Nye, David E., 17, 96, 98–99, 101, 135.

Odum, E. C., 185.
Odum, H. T., 185.
Offshore production, 142–143, 156, 172.
Oil crisis, *see* Energy crisis.
Organization, 12; definition, 13.
Organization for Economic Cooperation
and Development (OECD), 149.
Organization of Petroleum Exporting
Countries (OPEC), 4, 134.
Oswald, Andrew J., 153.
Overproduction, 71.
Owen, Robert, 3, 37, 72–75, 78, 86, 178.

Paleolithic era, 8, 10, 15, 61.
Patinkin, Don, 22, 148.
Patten, Simon N., 92.
Perpetual motion machine, 157.
Photosynthesis, 184.
Pigou, Arthur, 118, 121.
Political economy: classical, 2, 38, 49,
58, 70; Marxian, 38, 70; neoclassical,
38, 70, 80; radical, 38.
Power, *see* Energy.
Prisoner's dilemma, 168.
Production function: Cobb-Douglas, 136;
general Newtonian, 14; KLEMS,
150; KLEP, 20, 136; neoclassical,
18, 160.
Productivity: capital, 11, 20; energy,
19–30; German manufacturing,
135–140; growth, 4; Japanese
manufacturing, 139–140; labor, 20;
NPA measures, 19–20; organization,
20; paradox, 84; slowdown, 4, 84;
speed, 46, 94, 198; tool, 20; U.S.
manufacturing, 139–140, 142–143.
Pulp and paper industry, U. S., 160.
Putting-out system, *see* Domestic system.

Rabinbach, Anson, 34, 80.
Rautenstrauch, Walter, 93.
Reciprocal Trade Agreements Act of
1934, 164.
Rent sharing, 134.
Research and development, 2.
Ricardo, David, 3, 58, 61, 65, 67, 69,
125; and machinery, 69.
Rifkin, Jeremy, 158, 164, 175, 190.
Robinson, Joan, 117, 181.
Romer, Paul, 85, 158, 170.
Rosenberg, Nathan, 91, 96.

Saint-Simon, Claude Henri de, 128.
Sala-i-Martin, Xavier, 4.
Samuelson, Paul, 154.
Sanfey, Peter, 153.
Santayana, George, 87.
Say, Jean-Baptiste, 67.
Say's law, 173.
Schurr, Sam A., 151.
Schwartz, Anna, 194.
Scott, Howard, 93, 115.
Second-law efficiency, 11, 34.
Second-law of motion, 8, 158.
Self, Sir Henry, 99.
Senior, Nassau, 181, 189.
Sismonde de Sismondi, Jean-Charles
Léonard, 65–67; dynamic period
analysis, 65–66.
Sloan, Matthew S., 97.
Smith, Adam, 3, 41, 63–64, 67, 85, 125,
164–165, 177, 186; on circulating
capital, 63–64; on machinery, 60–61;
on specialization, 60–61.
Smoot-Hawley Tariff Act of 1933, see
Smoot-Hawley Tariff Bill of 1929.
Smoot-Hawley Tariff Bill of 1929,
92–93, 106, 142, 164.
Sobel, Robert, 119.
Social credit, 122.
Soddy, Frederick, 10–11, 93, 154, 178,
180, 185.
Soho manufactory, 41.
Solow, Robert, 17, 169.
Solow residual, 4, 148, 154.
Sonenblum, Sidney, 151.
Sowell, Thomas, 67, 121.

Speed, *see* Productivity.
Speedups, *see* Productivity.
Spinners, 7.
Spreng, Daniel T., 4, 15, 63.
Sraffa, Piero, 117.
Steam: engine 8, 70; high-pressure engine, 85.
Stearns, Peter, 39–40.
Structure–Behavior–Performance model of industrial organization, 118.
Supervision, 14–15: animate, 14; lower-level, 14, 159; upper-level, 14, 47.
Sweezy, Paul, 118.

Technical Association of the Pulp and Paper Industry (TAPPI), 160.
Technocracy, 127–128, 175, 178, 181.
Technocrats, *see* Technocracy.
Thermodynamics, 4; methodology of, 80, *see also* Second-law efficiency.
Tool, 9; basic, 12; composite, 12; primitive, 12; simple, 12; taxonomy, 12, *see also* Productivity.
Trevithick, Richard, 45.
Troske, Kenneth, 172.
Truman, Harry, 133.
Tugwell, Rexford G., 93, 108, 112–113, 126, 178–179.
Tylecote, Mabel, 16.
Tyron, F. G., 110, 114.

Underconsumption, *see* Underincome.
Underexpenditure, *see* Underincome.

Underincome, 22, 26, 49, 50, 52, 64, 66, 78, 119, 121, 132, 134, 152, 168; and underexpenditure, 66; and underconsumption, 66, 132.
United Kingdom, 93.
U.S. Department of Commerce, 138.
U.S. Department of Defense, 145.

Value added, 9.
Value theory, 181–183; energy, 182; modern, 188.
Vanhoudt, Patrick, 149.
Varian, Hal, 4.
Veblen, Thornstein, 124–125, 127, 130, 178–179.
von Helmholtz, Hermann, 34, 81.
von Schulze-Gaevernitz, G., 88.

Wagner, Robert F., 108.
Wagner Act, 134.
Walras, Léon, 110.
Watson, Elizabeth, 99.
Watt, James, 11.
Watt-Boulton steam engine, 38, 40, 61, 63.
Weavers, 7, 47–48.
Wicksell, Knut, 22–23, 26–27, 121.
Wicksteed, Phillip, 82, 125.
Wood, David O., 150.
Woolf, Arthur, 45.
Work: economic definition, 9; physical definition, 9.
World War I, 131.
World War II, 133–135.

About the Author

BERNARD C. BEAUDREAU is Associate Professor of Economics at Université Laval in Quebec. He is the author of *Mass Production, the Stock Market Crash, and the Great Depression: The Macroeconomics of Electrification* (Greenwood, 1996) and *Energy and Organization: Growth and Distribution Reexamined* (Greenwood, 1998).